SHORT SUMMARY

A new social contract for education

Our humanity and planet Earth are under threat. The pandemic has only served to prove our fragility and our interconnectedness. Now urgent action, taken together, is needed to change course and reimagine our futures. This report by the International Commission on the Futures of Education acknowledges the power of education to bring about profound change. We face a dual challenge of making good on the unfulfilled promise to ensure the right to quality education for every child, youth and adult and fully realizing the transformational potential of education as a route for sustainable collective futures. To do this, we need a new social contract for education that can repair injustices while transforming the future.

This new social contract must be grounded in human rights and based on principles of non-discrimination, social justice, respect for life, human dignity and cultural diversity. It must encompass an ethic of care, reciprocity, and solidarity. It must strengthen education as a public endeavour and a common good.

This report, two years in the making and informed by a global consultation process engaging around one million people, invites governments, institutions, organizations and citizens around the world to forge a new social contract for education that will help us build peaceful, just, and sustainable futures for all.

The visions, principles, and proposals presented here are merely a starting point. Translating and contextualizing them is a collective effort. Many bright spots already exist. This report attempts to capture and build on them. It is neither a manual nor a blueprint but the opening up of a vital conversation.

we need a new social contract for education to **repair injustices while transforming the future**

unesco

"Since wars begin in the minds of men and women it is in the minds of men and women that the defences of peace must be constructed"

REIMAGINING
A new social
OUR FUTURES
contract for
TOGETHER
education

REPORT FROM THE INTERNATIONAL COMMISSION ON THE FUTURES OF EDUCATION

Foreword

Audrey Azoulay
Director-General of UNESCO

If anything has brought us together over the last year and a half, it is our feeling of vulnerability about the present and uncertainty about the future. We now know, more than ever, that urgent action is needed to change humanity's course and save the planet from further disruptions. But this action must be long-term, and combined with strategic thinking.

Education plays a vital role in addressing these daunting challenges. Yet, as the pandemic has shown, education is fragile: At the peak of the COVID-19 pandemic, 1.6 billion learners were affected by school closures across the globe.

Never do you appreciate something more than when faced with losing it. For that reason, UNESCO welcomes this new report, *Reimagining our futures together: A new social contract for education*, prepared by the International Commission on the Futures of Education under the leadership of Her Excellency Madame Sahle-Work Zewde, President of the Federal Democratic Republic of Ethiopia.

Since being founded 75 years ago, UNESCO has commissioned several global reports to rethink the role of education at key moments of societal transformation. These began with the Faure Commission's 1972 report *Learning to Be: The World of Education Today and Tomorrow*, and continued with the Delors Commission's report in 1996, *Learning: The Treasure Within*. Both of these reports were insightful and influential; however, the world has fundamentally changed in recent years.

Like the reports that preceded it, the Sahle-Work Commission report is broadening the conversation on philosophies and principles needed to guide education to improve the existence of all living beings on this planet. It was developed over a two-year period and builds on extensive consultations with more than one million people.

If the report teaches us one thing, it is this: We need to take urgent action to change course, because the future of people depends on the future of the planet, and both are at risk. The report proposes a new social contract for education – one that aims to rebuild our relationships with each other, with the planet, and with technology.

This new social contract is our chance to repair past injustices and transform the future. Above all, it is based on the right to quality education throughout life, embracing teaching and learning as shared societal endeavours, and therefore common goods.

Realizing this vision of education is not an impossible task. There is hope, especially among the younger generations. However, we will need the entire world's creativity and intelligence to ensure that inclusion, equity, human rights, and peace define our future. Ultimately, that is what this report invites us to do. For that reason alone, it has valuable lessons for each and every one of us.

Audrey Azoulay
Director-General of UNESCO

Foreword

HE Sahle-Work Zewde
Chair of the International Commission on the Futures of Education
President of the Federal Democratic Republic of Ethiopia

The future of our planet must be locally and democratically envisioned. It is only through collective and individual actions that harness our rich diversity of peoples and cultures that the futures we want can be realized.

Humanity has only one planet; however, we do not share its resources well or use them in a sustainable manner. Unacceptable inequalities exist between different regions of the world. We are far from achieving gender equality for women and girls. Despite the promise of the ability of technology to connect us, vast digital divides remain, particularly in Africa. There are extensive power asymmetries in people's ability to access and create knowledge.

Education is the key pathway to address these entrenched inequalities. Building on what we know, we need to transform education. Classrooms and schools are essential, but they will need to be constructed and experienced differently in the future. Education must build skills needed in 21st century workplaces, taking into account the changing nature of work and the different ways that economic security can be provisioned. Furthermore, global financing for education must be expanded to ensure that the universal right to education is protected.

Respect for human rights and concern for education as a common good must become the central threads that stitch together our shared world and interconnected future. As this report argues, these two universal principles must become foundational in education everywhere. The right to quality education everywhere and learning that builds the capabilities of individuals to work together for shared benefit provide the foundation for flourishing, diverse futures of education. With consistent commitment to human rights and the common good, we will be able to sustain and benefit from the rich tapestry of different ways of knowing and being in the world that humanity's cultures and societies bring to formal and informal learning, and to the knowledge we are able to share and assemble together.

This report is the result of the collective work of the International Commission on the Futures of Education, established by UNESCO in 2019. Recognizing the commitment and contributions that came from all members of our diverse and geographically distributed group, I would particularly like to thank António Nóvoa, the Ambassador of Portugal to UNESCO, who chaired the Commission's research and drafting committee. The proposals presented in *Reimagining Our Futures Together* arise out of a global engagement and co-construction process which showed that creativity, perseverance, and hope are abundant in a world of increasing uncertainty, complexity and precarity. In particular, the futures of the following critical thematic issues which need rethinking are examined: sustainability; knowledge; learning; teachers and teaching; work, skills, and competencies; citizenship; democracy and social inclusion; public education; and higher education, research, and innovation.

The Commission's work over the past two years was shaped by the global health pandemic, and members of the Commission were acutely aware of challenges faced by children, youth, and learners of all ages who faced extensive school closures. It is to the students and teachers whose lives were disrupted by COVID, and to their remarkable efforts to ensure wellbeing, growth, and the continuation of learning in trying circumstances, that we dedicate *Reimagining Our Futures Together*.

Our hope is that the proposals contained here, and the public dialogue and collective action called for, will serve as a catalyst to shape futures for humanity and the planet that are peaceful, just, and sustainable.

HE Sahle-Work Zewde
Chair of the International Commission for the Futures of Education
President of the Federal Democratic Republic of Ethiopia

International Commission on the Futures of Education

H.E. Sahle-Work Zewde, President, Federal Democratic Republic of Ethiopia, and Chair of the International Commission on the Futures of Education

António Nóvoa, Professor at the Institute of Education of the University of Lisbon, and Chair of the research-drafting committee of the International Commission on the Futures of Education

Masanori Aoyagi, Professor Emeritus, University of Tokyo

Arjun Appadurai, Emeritus Professor, Media, Culture and Communication at New York University and the Max Weber Global Professor at the Bard Graduate Center in New York.

Patrick Awuah, Founder and President, Ashesi University, Ghana

Abdel Basset Ben Hassen, President, Arab Institute for Human Rights, Tunisia

Cristovam Buarque, Emeritus Professor, University of Brasília

Elisa Guerra, Teacher and Founder, Colegio Valle de Filadelfia, Mexico

Badr Jafar, CEO, Crescent Enterprises, United Arab Emirates

Doh-Yeon Kim, Professor Emeritus of Seoul National University, Former Minister of Education, Science and Technology, Republic of Korea

Justin Yifu Lin, Dean, Professor, Institute of New Structural Economics, Peking University

Evgeny Morozov, Writer

Karen Mundy, Director UNESCO International Institute for Educational Planning (IIEP) & Professor (on leave), University of Toronto – Ontario Institute for Studies in Education

Fernando M. Reimers, Professor, Harvard Graduate School of Education, USA

Tarcila Rivera Zea, President, CHIRAPAQ Centre for Indigenous Cultures of Peru

Serigne Mbaye Thiam, Minister of Water and Sanitation, Senegal

Vaira Vike-Freiberga, Former President of Latvia, currently co-chair, Nizami Ganjavi International Center, Baku

Maha Yahya, Director, Carnegie Middle East Center, Lebanon

Acknowledgements

This report would not have been possible without the valuable contributions of numerous individuals, networks and organizations.

The Commission would like to thank all those who contributed independent reports, background papers, as well as the individuals, organizations and networks that took part in the global consultations on the futures of education (see appendices for lists of contributors and contributions).

Invaluable input was provided by the Advisory Board on the Futures of Education representing leading figures and key strategic partners in global education, research and innovation (see appendix for full list or individuals and organizations).

A special thank you to the following experts who worked closely with the Secretariat at UNESCO in the process of analysis and drafting and who reviewed early versions of the manuscript: Tracey Burns, Paul Comyn, Peter Ronald DeSouza, Inés Dussel, Keri Facer, Hugh McLean, Ebrima Sall, François Taddei, Malak Zaalouk, and Javier Roglá Puig.

Finally, the Commission would like to sincerely thank the UNESCO Secretariat, and in particular, Ms Stefania Giannini, Assistant Director-General for Education, for her leadership, as well as Sobhi Tawil, Director of the Future of Learning and Innovation Division, and Noah W. Sobe, Senior Project Officer for the Futures of Education initiative, for the tireless support provided to the work of the Commission.

Contents

PART II
RENEWING EDUCATION

46

PART III
CATALYZING A NEW SOCIAL CONTRACT FOR EDUCATION

117

EPILOGUE AND CONTINUATION
Building futures of education together

141

APPENDICES

157

Executive summary

Our world is at a turning point. We already know that knowledge and learning are the basis for renewal and transformation. But global disparities – and a pressing need to reimagine why, how, what, where, and when we learn – mean that education is not yet fulfilling its promise to help us shape peaceful, just, and sustainable futures.

In our quest for growth and development, we humans have overwhelmed our natural environment, threatening our own existence. Today, high living standards coexist with gaping inequalities. More and more people are engaged in public life, but the fabric of civil society and democracy is fraying in many places around the world. Rapid technological changes are transforming many aspects of our lives. Yet, these innovations are not adequately directed at equity, inclusion and democratic participation.

Everyone today has a heavy obligation to both current and future generations – to ensure that our world is one of abundance not scarcity, and that everyone enjoys the same human rights to the fullest. Despite the urgency of action, and in conditions of great uncertainty, **we have reason to be full of hope**. As a species, we are at the point in our collective history where we have the greatest access ever to knowledge and to tools that enable us to collaborate. The potential for engaging humanity in creating better futures together has never been greater.

This global Report from the International Commission on the Futures of Education asks what role education can play in shaping our common world and shared future as we look to 2050 and beyond. The proposals presented arise out of a two-year global engagement and co-construction process which showed that vast numbers of people – children, youth and adults – are keenly aware that **we are connected** on this shared planet and that it is imperative that **we work together**.

Many people are already engaged in bringing about these changes themselves. This report is infused with their contributions on everything from how to reimagine learning spaces to the decolonization of curricula and the importance of social and emotional learning, and taps into their real and growing fears about climate change, crises like COVID-19, fake news and the digital divide.

Education – the way we organize teaching and learning throughout life – has long played a foundational role in the transformation of human societies. It connects us with the world and to each other, exposes us to new possibilities, and strengthens our capacities for dialogue and action. **But to shape peaceful, just, and sustainable futures, education itself must be transformed**.

A new social contract for education

Education can be seen in terms of a social contract – an implicit agreement among members of a society to cooperate for shared benefit. A social contract is more than a transaction as it reflects norms, commitments and principles that are formally legislated as well as culturally embedded. **The starting point is a shared vision of the public purposes of education**. This contract consists of the foundational and organizational principles that structure education systems, as well as the distributed work done to build, maintain and refine them.

During the twentieth century, public education was essentially aimed at supporting national citizenship and development efforts through the form of compulsory schooling for children and youth. Today, however, as we face grave risks to the future of humanity and the living planet itself, we must urgently reinvent education to help us address common challenges. This act of **reimagining means working together to create futures that are shared and interdependent**. The new social contract for education must unite us around collective endeavours and provide the knowledge and innovation needed to shape sustainable and peaceful futures for all anchored in social, economic and environmental justice. It must, as this report does, champion the role played by teachers.

There are three essential questions to ask of education as we look to 2050: **What should we continue doing? What should we abandon? What needs to be creatively invented afresh?**

Foundational principles

Any new social contract must build on the broad principles that underpin human rights – inclusion and equity, cooperation, and solidarity, as well as collective responsibility and interconnectedness – and be governed by the following two foundational principles:

- **Assuring the right to quality education throughout life.** The right to education, as established in Article 26 of the Universal Declaration of Human Rights, must continue to be the foundation of the new social contract for education and must be expanded to include the right to quality education throughout life. It must also encompass the right to information, culture and science – as well as the right to access and contribute to the knowledge commons, the collective knowledge resources of humanity that have been accumulated over generations and are continuously transforming.

- **Strengthening education as a public endeavour and a common good.** As a shared societal endeavour, education builds common purposes and enables individuals and communities to flourish together. A new social contract for education must not only ensure public funding for education, but also include a society-wide commitment to include everyone in public discussions about education. This emphasis on participation is what strengthens education as a common good – a form of shared well-being that is chosen and achieved together.

These foundational principles build on what education has allowed humanity to accomplish to this point and help to ensure that, as we move to 2050 and beyond, education empowers future generations to reimagine their futures and renew their worlds.

Between past promises and uncertain futures

Widening social and economic inequality, climate change, biodiversity loss, resource use that exceeds planetary boundaries, democratic backsliding and disruptive technological automation are the hallmarks of our current historical juncture. These multiple overlapping crises and challenges constrain our individual and collective human rights and have resulted in damage to much of life on Earth. While the expansion of education systems has created opportunities for many, vast numbers have been left with low-quality learning.

Looking to the future it is all too easy to paint an even darker picture. It is possible to imagine an exhausted planet with fewer spaces for human habitation. Extreme future scenarios also include a world where quality education is a privilege of elites, and where vast groups of people live in misery because they lack access to essential goods and services. Will current educational inequalities only worsen with time until curricula become irrelevant? How will these possible changes impact on our basic humanity?

No trend is destiny. Multiple alternative futures are possible, and disruptive transformations can be discerned in several key areas:

● The planet is in peril but decarbonization and the greening of economies are underway. Here children and youth already lead the way, calling for meaningful action and delivering a harsh rebuke to those who refuse to face the urgency of the situation.

● Over the past decade the world has seen a backsliding in democratic governance and a rise in identity-driven populist sentiment. At the same time, there has been a flourishing of increasingly active citizen participation and activism that is challenging discrimination and injustice worldwide.

● There is tremendous transformative potential in digital technologies, but we have not yet figured out how to deliver on these many promises.

● The challenge of creating decent human-centred work is about to get much harder as Artificial Intelligence (AI), automation and structural transformations remake employment landscapes around the globe. At the same time, more people and communities are recognizing the value of care work and the multiple ways that economic security needs to be provisioned.

Each of these emerging disruptions has significant implications for education. In turn, what we do together in education will shape how it responds.

At present the ways we organize education across the world do not do enough to ensure just and peaceful societies, a healthy planet, and shared progress that benefits all. In fact, some of our difficulties stem from how we educate. **A new social contract for education needs to allow us to think differently** about learning and the relationships between students, teachers, knowledge, and the world.

Proposals for renewing education

Pedagogy should be organized around the principles of cooperation, collaboration, and solidarity. It should foster the intellectual, social, and moral capacities of students to work together and transform the world with empathy and compassion. There is unlearning to be done too, of bias, prejudice, and divisiveness. Assessment should reflect these pedagogical goals in ways that promote meaningful growth and learning for all students.

Curricula should emphasize ecological, intercultural and interdisciplinary learning that supports students to access and produce knowledge while also developing their capacity to critique and apply it. Curricula must embrace an ecological understanding of humanity that rebalances the way we relate to Earth as a living planet and our singular home. The spread of misinformation should be countered through scientific, digital and humanistic literacies that develop the ability to distinguish falsehoods from truth. In educational content, methods and policy we should promote active citizenship and democratic participation.

Teaching should be further professionalized as a collaborative endeavour where teachers are recognized for their work as knowledge producers and key figures in educational and social transformation. Collaboration and teamwork should characterize the work of teachers. Reflection, research and the creation of knowledge and new pedagogical practices should become integral to teaching. This means that their autonomy and freedom must be supported and that they must participate fully in public debate and dialogue on the futures of education.

Schools should be protected educational sites because of the inclusion, equity and individual and collective well-being they support – and also reimagined to better promote the transformation of the world towards more just, equitable and sustainable futures. Schools need to be places that bring diverse groups of people together and expose them to challenges and possibilities not available elsewhere. School architectures, spaces, times, timetables, and student groupings should be redesigned to encourage and enable individuals to work together. Digital technologies should aim to support – and not replace – schools. Schools should model the futures we aspire to by ensuring human rights and becoming exemplars of sustainability and carbon neutrality.

We should enjoy and expand the educational opportunities that take place throughout life and in different cultural and social spaces. At all times of life people should have meaningful, quality educational opportunities. We should connect natural, built, and virtual sites of learning, carefully leveraging the best potentials of each. Key responsibilities fall to governments whose capacity for the public financing and regulation of education should be strengthened. The right to education needs to be broadened to be lifelong and encompass the right to information, culture, science and connectivity.

Catalyzing a new social contract for education

Large-scale change and innovation are possible. We will build a new social contract for education through millions of individual and collective acts – acts of courage, leadership, resistance, creativity, and care. A new social contract needs to overcome discrimination, marginalization, and exclusion. We must dedicate ourselves to ensuring gender equality and the rights of all regardless of race, ethnicity, religion, disability, sexual orientation, age, or citizenship status. A massive commitment to social dialogue, to thinking and acting together, is needed.

A call for research and innovation. A new social contract requires a worldwide, collaborative research programme that focuses on the right to education throughout life. This programme must centre on the right to education and be inclusive of different kinds of evidence and ways of knowing including horizontal learning and the exchange of knowledge across borders. Contributions should be welcomed from everyone – from teachers to students, from academics and research centres to governments and civil society organizations.

A call for global solidarity and international cooperation. A new social contract for education requires renewed commitment to global collaboration in support of education as a common good, premised on more just and equitable cooperation among state and non-state actors. Beyond North-South flows of aid to education, the generation of knowledge and evidence through South-South and triangular cooperation must be strengthened. The international community has a key role to play in helping states and non-state actors to align around the shared purposes, norms and standards needed to realize a new social contract for education. In this, the principle of subsidiarity should be respected, and local, national and regional efforts should be encouraged. The educational needs of asylum seekers, refugees, stateless persons and migrants, in particular, need to be supported through international cooperation and the work of global institutions.

Universities and other higher education institutions must be active in every aspect of building a new social contract for education. From supporting research and the advancement of science to being a contributing partner to other educational institutions and programmes in their communities and across the globe, universities that are creative, innovative and committed to strengthening education as a common good have a key role to play in the futures of education.

It is essential that everyone be able to participate in building the futures of education – children, youth, parents, teachers, researchers, activists, employers, cultural and religious leaders. We have deep, rich, and diverse cultural traditions to build upon. Humans have great collective agency, intelligence, and creativity. And we now face a serious choice: continue on an unsustainable path or radically change course.

This Report proposes answers to the three essential questions of What should we continue doing? What should we abandon? and What needs to be creatively reimagined? But **the proposals here are merely a start**. This Report is more an invitation to think and imagine than a blueprint. These questions need to be taken up and answered in communities, in countries, in schools, in educational programmes and systems of all sorts – all over the world.

Forging a new social contract for education is a critical step towards reimagining our futures together.

Introduction

We face an existential choice: continue on an unsustainable path or radically change course. To continue on the current path is to accept unconscionable inequalities and exploitation, the spiralling of multiple forms of violence, the erosion of social cohesion and human freedoms, continued environmental destruction, and dangerous and perhaps catastrophic biodiversity loss. To continue on the current path is to fail to anticipate and address the risks that accompany the technological and digital transformations of our societies.

We urgently need to reimagine our futures together and take action to realize them. Knowledge and learning are the basis for renewal and transformation. But global disparities – and a pressing need to reimagine why, how, what, where, and when we learn – mean that education is not doing what it could to help us shape peaceful, just, and sustainable futures.

We all have an obligation to current and future generations – to ensure that our world is one of abundance not scarcity, and that everyone enjoys human rights to the fullest. Despite the urgency of action, and in conditions of great uncertainty, we have reason to be full of hope. As a species, we are at the point in our collective history where we have the greatest access ever to knowledge and to tools that enable us to collaborate. The potential for engaging humanity in creating futures together has never been greater.

Education – the ways we organize teaching and learning throughout life – has long played a foundational role in the transformation of human societies. Education is how we organize the intergenerational cycle of knowledge transmission and co-creation. It connects us with the world and to others, exposes us to new possibilities, and strengthens our capacities for dialogue and action. But to shape the futures we want, education itself must be transformed.

This global Report from the International Commission on the Futures of Education asks what role education can play in shaping our common world and shared future as we look to 2050 and beyond. The proposals it presents arise out of a two-year global engagement and co-construction process which showed that vast numbers of people – children, youth and adults – are keenly aware that we are interdependent on this shared planet. We are connected to one another in that the world's problems affect us all. There is an equally strong awareness shared by many across the globe that we must work together starting from an appreciation of diversity and difference.

Anticipating futures is something we do all the time as humans. Ideas about the future play an important role in educational thinking, policy, and practice. They shape everything from students' and families' everyday decision-making to the grand plans for educational change developed in ministries of education.

This Report recognizes that in relation to education there are multiple possible future scenarios, ranging from radical transformation to profound crisis. It posits that the main purpose of thinking about futures in education is to allow us to frame the present differently, to identify trajectories that might be emerging and attend to possibilities that might be opening or closing to us. All exploration of possible and alternative futures raises profound questions of ethics, equity, and justice – what futures are desirable and for whom? And since education is not merely impacted by external factors but plays a key role in unlocking potential futures in all corners of the globe, it is natural if not obligatory that reimagining our futures together involves a new social contract for education.

> All exploration of possible and alternative futures raises profound questions of ethics, equity, and justice – what futures are desirable and for whom?

The survival of humanity, human rights, and the living planet are at risk

The very idea that the dignity of each person is precious; the commitment that all people have basic rights; the health of the Earth, our singular home – all are at risk. To change course and imagine alternative futures, we urgently need to rebalance our relationships with each other, with the living planet, and with technology. We must relearn our interdependencies and our human place and agency in a more-than-human world.

We face multiple, overlapping crises. Widening social and economic inequality, climate change, biodiversity loss, resource use that exceeds planetary boundaries, democratic backsliding, disruptive technological automation, and violence are the hallmarks of our current historical juncture.

Paradoxical development trends are leading us on a path toward unsustainable futures. Global poverty levels have fallen, but inequalities between and within countries have grown. The highest living standards coexist with the most gaping inequalities in history. Climate change and environmental degradation threaten the survival of humanity and of other species on planet Earth. More and more people are actively engaged in public life, but civil society and democracy are fraying in many places around the world. Technology has connected us more closely than ever yet is also contributing to social fragmentation and tensions. A global pandemic has further highlighted our many fragilities. These crises and challenges constrain our individual and collective human rights. And they are largely the result of human choices and actions. They derive from social, political, and economic systems of our creation, where the short-term is prioritized over the long-term, and the interests of the few allowed to override the interests of the many.

Climate and environmental disasters are accelerated by economic models depending on unsustainable levels of resource use. Economic models that prioritize short-term profits and excessive consumerism are tightly linked with the acquisitive individualism, competitiveness, and lack of empathy that characterize too many of our societies around the globe. The world's wealth has become intensely concentrated, and extreme economic inequalities are undermining the cohesion of our societies.

The rise of authoritarianism, exclusionary populism, and political extremism are challenging democratic governance precisely at a time when we need strengthened cooperation and solidarity to address shared concerns that neither know nor respect political borders. Despite decades of work to support societies' efforts to advance peaceful forms of solving differences, the world today is marked by increasing social and political polarization. Hate speech, the irresponsible dissemination of fake news, religious fundamentalism, exclusionary nationalism – all magnified with new technologies – are, in the end, used strategically to favour narrow interests. A world order anchored on the common values expressed in the Universal Declaration of Human Rights is weakening. Our world faces a crisis of values evidenced by the rise in corruption, callousness, intolerance and bigotry, and the normalization of violence.

Accelerated globalization and growing human mobility, together with forced migration and displacement, too often exacerbate the dehumanizing effects of racism, bigotry, intolerance, and discrimination. These forms of violence against human dignity are expressions of structures of power that seek to dominate and control, rather than cooperate and liberate. The violence of armed conflict, occupation, and political repression not only destroys lives but also undermines the very concept of human dignity. Frequently, those who enjoy privileges and benefit from hegemonic systems discriminate on the basis of gender, race, ethnicity, language, religion, or sexuality, and oppress groups they consider to be a threat, whether they be indigenous peoples, women, refugees, migrants, feminists, human rights advocates, environmental activists, or political dissidents.

The digital transformation of our societies is impacting our lives in unprecedented ways. Computers are quickly changing the ways in which knowledge is created, accessed, disseminated, validated, and used. Much of this is making information more accessible and opening new and promising avenues for education. But the risks are many: learning can narrow as well as expand in digital spaces; technology provides new levers of power and control which can repress as well as emancipate; and, with facial recognition and AI, our human right to privacy can contract in ways that were unimaginable just a decade earlier. We need to be vigilant to ensure that ongoing technical transformations help us thrive and do not threaten the future of diverse ways of knowing or of intellectual and creative freedom.

Our ways of living have drifted out of balance with the planet, with the abundance of life it supports, threatening our current and future well-being and our continued existence. Our uncritical embrace of technology too often pushes us dangerously apart, truncates conversation and unravels mutual understanding, despite a potential to accomplish the opposite. And these planetary and technological imbalances contribute to a third and equally dangerous divergence: our imbalance with each other in the form of ballooning inequalities, the subversion of trust and goodwill, the demonization of the 'other', and reluctance to cooperate and confront this growing array of global challenges more meaningfully.

Looking to the future it is all too easy to paint an even darker picture. It is possible to imagine an exhausted planet with fewer spaces for human habitation. Extreme future scenarios also include a world where quality education is a privilege of elites, where vast groups of people live in misery because they lack access to essential goods and services. Will curricula become increasingly irrelevant and current educational inequalities only worsen with time? Will our humanity become further eroded?

The choices we collectively make today will determine our shared futures.

The choices we collectively make today will determine our shared futures. Whether we survive or perish, whether we live in peace or we allow violence to define our lives, whether we relate to the Earth in ways that are sustainable or not, are questions that will be profoundly shaped and decided by the choices we make today and by our capabilities to achieve our common goals. Together, we can change course.

The need for a new social contract for education

Education is the foundation for the renewal and transformation of our societies. It mobilizes knowledge to help us navigate a transforming and uncertain world. The power of education lies in its capacities to connect us with the world and others, to move us beyond the spaces we already inhabit, and to expose us to new possibilities. It helps to unite us around collective endeavours; it provides the science, knowledge and innovation we need to address common challenges. Education nurtures understandings and builds capabilities that can help to ensure that our futures are more socially inclusive, economically just, and environmentally sustainable.

Families, communities, and governments around the world know well that, despite shortcomings, schools and education systems can create opportunities and provide routes for individual and collective advancement. It is widely recognized by governments and civil society organizations that education is a key, albeit not the sole, factor for making progress towards desirable developmental outcomes, building skills and competencies for work, and supporting engaged and democratic citizenship. Education is, rightfully, a pillar of the 2030 Framework for Sustainable Development – an inclusive vision for humanity to advance well-being, justice, and peace for all, as well as sustainable relationships with the environment.

Yet education across the world continues to fall short of the aspirations we have for it. Despite the significant expansion of access worldwide, multiple exclusions continue to deny hundreds of millions of children, youth, and adults of their fundamental right to quality education. Discrimination persists, often systemically, along lines of gender, ethnicity, language, culture, and ways of knowing. Lack of access is compounded by a crisis of relevance: far too often, formal learning does not meet the needs and aspirations of children and youth and their communities. Poor quality instruction stifles creativity and curiosity. Patterns of student disengagement and drop/push out at all levels of education point to the inadequacies of the current schooling model to provide meaningful learning and a sense of agency and purpose for children and youth. Increasingly, those accessing education are neither prepared for the challenges of the present nor those of the future.

Furthermore, education systems often reproduce and perpetuate the very conditions that threaten our shared futures – whether discrimination and exclusion or unsustainable lifestyles – limiting education's potential to be truly transformative. These collective failures undergird the need for a new shared vision and renewed principles and commitments that can frame and guide our actions in education.

The starting point for any social contract for education is a shared vision of the public purposes of education. The social contract for education consists of the foundational and organizational principles that structure education systems, as well as the distributed work done to build, maintain and refine them.

During the twentieth century, public education was essentially aimed at supporting national citizenship and development efforts. It primarily took the form of compulsory schooling for children and youth. Today, however, given the grave risks we face, we must urgently reinvent education to help us address common challenges. The new social contract for education must help us unite around collective endeavours and provide the knowledge and innovation needed to shape sustainable and peaceful futures for all anchored in social, economic, and environmental justice.

Constructing a new social contract means exploring how established ways of thinking about education, knowledge and learning inhibit us from opening new paths and moving towards the futures we desire. Merely expanding the current educational development model is not a viable route forward. Our difficulties are not only the result of limited resources and means. Our challenges also stem from why and how we educate and the ways we organize learning.

Redefining the purposes of education

Education systems have wrongly instilled a belief that short-term prerogatives and comforts are more important than longer-term sustainability. They have emphasized values of individual success, national competition and economic development, to the detriment of solidarity, understanding our interdependencies, and caring for each other and the planet.

Education must aim to unite us around collective endeavours and provide the knowledge, science, and innovation needed to shape sustainable futures for all anchored in social, economic, and environmental justice. It must redress past injustices while preparing us for environmental, technological, and social changes on the horizon.

A new social contract for education must be anchored in two foundational principles: (1) the right to education and (2) a commitment to education as a public societal endeavour and a common good.

Assuring the right to quality education throughout life

The dialogue and action needed to build a new social contract for education must remain firmly rooted in a commitment to human rights. The Universal Declaration of Human Rights written in 1948 sets out inalienable rights for the members of our human family and provides the best compass for imagining new futures of education. The right to education – critical for the realization of all other social, economic and cultural rights – must continue to serve as the guiding light and basis for the new social contract. This human rights lens requires that education be for all, regardless of income, gender, race or ethnicity, religion, language, culture, sexuality, political affiliation, disability, or any other characteristic that could be used to discriminate and exclude.

> A new social contract for education must remain firmly rooted in a commitment to human rights.

The right to education must be expanded to include the right to quality education throughout life. Long interpreted as the right to schooling for children and youth, going forward, the right to education must assure education at all ages and in all areas of life. From this broader perspective, the right to education is closely connected to the right to information, to culture, and to science. It requires a deep commitment to building human capabilities. It is also closely linked to the right to access and contribute to the knowledge commons, humanity's shared and expanding resources of information, knowledge and wisdom.

The ongoing cycle of knowledge creation that occurs through contest, dialogue and debate is what helps to coordinate action, produce scientific truths, and foment innovation. It is one of humanity's most valuable, inexhaustible resources, and a key aspect of education. The more people that have access to the knowledge commons, the more abundant it becomes. The development of language, numeracy and systems of writing has facilitated the spread of knowledge across time and space. This, in turn, has allowed human societies to attain extraordinary heights of collective flourishing and civilization-building. The possibilities of the knowledge commons are theoretically infinite. The diversity and innovation unleashed by the knowledge commons comes from borrowings and lendings, from experimentation that crosses disciplinary boundaries, as well as from reinterpretation of the old and generation of the new.

Unfortunately, barriers prevent equity in accessing and contributing to the knowledge commons. There are significant gaps and distortions in humanity's accumulated knowledge that need to be addressed and corrected. Indigenous perspectives, languages, and knowledges have long been marginalized. Women and girls, minorities and low-income groups are also severely underrepresented. Enclosures occur as a result of commercialization and overly restrictive intellectual property laws – and from the absence of adequate regulation and support for the communities and systems that manage the knowledge commons. We must protect the right to the intellectual and artistic property of artists, writers, scientists and inventors. And at the same time, we need to commit to supporting open, equitable opportunities to apply and create knowledge. A rights-based approach that includes recognition of collective intellectual property rights should be applied to the knowledge commons to protect indigenous peoples and other marginalized groups from illicit and unconsented appropriation and use of their knowledge.

An expanded right to education throughout life requires commitment to breaking down barriers and ensuring that the knowledge commons is an open and lasting resource that reflects the diverse ways of knowing and being in the world.

Strengthening education as a public endeavour and a common good

As a shared societal endeavour, education builds common purposes and enables individuals and communities to flourish together. A new social contract for education must not only ensure adequate and sustained public funding for education, but also include a society-wide commitment to including everyone in public discussions about education. This emphasis on participation is what strengthens education as a common good – a form of shared well-being that is chosen and achieved together.

Two essential features characterize education as a common good. First, education is experienced in common putting people in contact with others and with the world. In educational institutions, teachers, educators, and learners come together in shared activity that is both individual and collective. Education enables people to use and add to the knowledge heritage of humanity. As a collective act of co creation, education affirms the dignity and capacity of individuals and communities, builds shared purposes, develops capabilities for collective action, and strengthens our common humanity. It is therefore essential that education institutions include a diversity of students, to the greatest possible extent, so they can learn from each other, across lines of difference.

Second, education is governed in common. As a social project, education involves many different actors in its governance and stewardship. Diverse voices and perspectives need to be integrated in policies and decision-making processes. The current trend towards greater and more diversified non-state involvement in education policy, provision and monitoring is an expression of an increasing demand for voice, transparency, and accountability in education as a public matter. The involvement of teachers, youth movements, community-based groups, trusts, non-governmental organizations, enterprises, professional associations, philanthropists, religious institutions, and social movements can strengthen equity, quality and relevance of education. Non-state actors play important roles in ensuring the right to education when safeguarding the principles of non-discrimination, equality of opportunity, and social justice.

The public character of education goes well beyond its provision, financing, and management by public authorities. Public education is education that (1) occurs in a public space, (2) promotes public interests, and (3) is accountable to all. All schools, regardless of who organizes them, should educate to advance human rights, value diversity, and counter discrimination. We must not forget that public education educates publics. It reinforces our common belonging to the same humanity and the same planet, while valuing our differences and diversity.

A commitment to education as a public societal endeavour and a common good means that modes of educational governance at local, national, and global levels must be inclusive and participatory. Governments increasingly need to focus on regulation and protecting education from commercialization. Markets should not be permitted to further impede on the achievement of education as a human right. Rather, education must serve the public interests of all.

The new social contract must be framed by the right to education throughout life and a commitment to education as a public and a common good if it is to help us build pathways to socially, economically, and environmentally just and sustainable futures. These foundational principles will help guide dialogue and action for renewing key dimensions of education, from pedagogy and curriculum to research and international cooperation.

Organization of the report

This Report is organized across three parts comprised of several chapters, each of which advances proposals for building a new social contract for education and a number of guiding principles for dialogue and action. It concludes with an epilogue proposing ways the recommendations can be translated into action into different contexts. While the report refers to research evidence where appropriate, it does not reference these in the text. Background Papers, commissioned specifically as part of this initiative, are listed in the annex.

Part I of the Report, Between past promises and uncertain futures, presents the dual global challenge of equity and relevance in education that undergirds the need for a new social contract which can help redress educational exclusion and ensure sustainable futures. It consists of two chapters.

Chapter 1 chronicles the drama of the right to education as enshrined in Article 26 of the Universal Declaration of Human Rights through the promises it has fulfilled and fallen short of. Chapter 2 focuses on key disruptions and emerging transformations, considering four overlapping areas of widespread change: environmental change, technological acceleration, governance and social fragmentation, and new worlds of work. Looking to 2050, this chapter asks how education will be impacted by these disruptions and transformations, and how it can change to better address them.

Part II of the Report, Renewing education, argues for a reconceptualization and renewal of education along five key dimensions: pedagogy, curricula, teaching, schools, and the wide range of education opportunities across life and in different cultural and social spaces. Each of these five dimensions is discussed in a dedicated chapter that includes principles to guide dialogue and action.

Chapter 3 calls for pedagogies of cooperation and solidarity that foster empathy, respect for difference and compassion and build the capacities of individuals to work together to transform themselves and the world. Chapter 4 encourages ecological, intercultural and interdisciplinary curricula that support students to access and produce knowledge while also developing their capacity to critique and apply it. Chapter 5 stresses the importance of the transformative work of teachers and recommends that teaching be further professionalized as a collaborative endeavour. Chapter 6 explains the need to protect schools as social sites that support learning, inclusion, equity, and individual and collective well-being, while simultaneously changing them to better realize just and equitable futures. Chapter 7 discusses the importance of education across different times and spaces with recognition that it does not happen exclusively in formal institutions but is rather experienced in a multiplicity of social spaces and throughout life.

Part III of the Report, Catalyzing a new social contract for education, provides ideas for beginning to build a new social contract for education by issuing calls for research and for global solidarity and international cooperation.

Chapter 8 calls for a shared research agenda on the right to education throughout life, suggesting that everyone has a role to play in the generation, production, and negotiation of knowledge required to build a new social contract for education. Chapter 9 discusses the renewed urgent need to build and reinforce global solidarity and international cooperation, with tenacity, boldness, and coherence, and with a vision to 2050 and beyond.

The Report concludes with an epilogue and continuation, which argues that the ideas and proposals raised in the text need to be translated into programmes, resources, and activities in diverse ways in different settings. Such a transformation will result from processes of co-construction and conversation with others whose participation is essential to translate these ideas into planning and action. It is up to leaders at multiple levels of government, education administrators, together with teachers and students, families, communities and civil society organizations to define and implement the renewal of education.

The task before us is to strengthen a shared, ongoing global dialogue about what to take forward, what to leave behind and what to creatively reimagine in education and the world at large. We consider this the work of renewal: to awaken to the severities of the problems that confront us collectively, as human inhabitants of a more-than-human world, and find a path forward that resists mere replication. If we are honest, we know that more of the same, even if faster, bigger and more efficient, is propelling us towards a cliff: climate deterioration and faltering ecosystems being perhaps the most apparent and most momentous warning signs. Renewal implies sifting through hard won knowledge and experience to revitalize our education systems to excellence. It involves using and curating what is known to build anew and establish a more promising course.

> This Report is an invitation and a proposed agenda for dialogue and action to achieve that goal.

A new social contract for education has been in the making for some time. What is needed now is a broad-based, inclusive and democratic public dialogue and mobilization to realize it. This Report is an invitation and a proposed agenda for dialogue and action to achieve that goal.

Part I
Between past promises and uncertain futures

To launch a reflection on the futures of education, we must first examine where education stands and the probable futures that current challenges and emerging transformations point towards. In education, as in other areas of life, the past is very much with us. We need to take long-term historical trends into consideration. In examining yesterday's exclusions and shortcomings we can better understand how education has fallen short of the hopes we have for it.

This first part of this Report maps the state of education globally in relation to the normative commitments to equity, justice, and sustainability – and looks at ways we might expect these issues to develop in the future. It finds education situated in an acute tension between past promises and uncertain futures.

The first chapter of this part focuses on the progress achieved in education over the past 50 years. It explores factors like economic growth, poverty, and gender discrimination for how they intersect with (and are affected by) educational advancements. It argues that the past cannot be ignored but that what happens next will be determined by the choices we make and the actions we take today and over the next thirty years.

The next chapter in this part looks at emerging transformations in four key areas: the environment, technology, the political sphere, and the future of work. It is impossible to predict the future, but the million people who engaged with this initiative are in considerable agreement that the most dangerous and disruptive path would be to ignore these transformations-in-progress.

Chapter 1

Towards more equitable educational futures

> This is what our educational system has to encourage. It has to foster the social goals of living together, and working together, for the common good. It has to prepare our young people to play a dynamic and constructive part in the development of a society in which all members share fairly in the good or bad fortune of the group, and in which progress is measured in terms of human well-being, not prestige buildings, cars, or other such things, whether privately or publicly owned. Our education must therefore inculcate a sense of commitment to the total community, and help the pupils to accept the values appropriate to our kind of future.

Julius Nyerere, *Education for Self-Reliance*, 1967.

How far have we come in education in the past thirty to fifty years? Where does education stand at present? Where must it change course quickest as we look to a longer-term future?

This chapter reflects on the past half-century in education from two perspectives. First, it details trends that can be observed in education indicators over time, going beyond averages, where possible, to understand their disaggregation by region, income group, gender, age group, and other factors. Second, it presents a more qualitative discussion of these and other trends in education, with a focus on equity, quality, and the responsiveness of education to some of its more significant disruptions, such as conflict and migration.

Long-term statistical trends tell only partial stories, shaped by what can be measured and what cannot. Yet, when considered holistically, they show probable future directions and possible paths of change. Access to educational opportunity, the inclusion of marginalized populations, literacy, and the creation of lifelong learning systems, share some commonalities but also considerable differences between and within countries, regions, and income groups of the world. Trends analyses also highlight which areas have received the most attention, and those that require new and urgent responses. Looking at probable educational futures from the perspective of historical and current challenges helps us in thinking about other futures that might emerge.

Today's gaps in access, participation and outcomes are based on yesterday's exclusions and oppressions.

The past fifty years of progress have been vastly uneven and today's gaps in access, participation and outcomes are based on yesterday's exclusions and oppressions. Tomorrow's progress is dependent not only on their correction, but on a questioning of the assumptions and arrangements that resulted in these inequalities and asymmetries. Gender equality, for example, should not only be seen as a goal in its own right, but as a prerequisite for ensuring sustainable futures of education.

Incomplete and inequitable expansion of education

By many measures, the expansion of access to education globally, since education was adopted as a human right, has been spectacular. When the Universal Declaration of Human Rights was adopted in 1948, the world population stood at 2.4 billion, with only 45% of those people having set foot in a school. Today, with a global population at 8 billion, over 95% have attended school. Enrolment in 2020 surpassed 90% in primary, 85% in lower secondary and 65% in upper-secondary education. As a result, there has been a clear decline in the share of out-of-school children and adolescents across the world over the past fifty years. That this expansion in access has happened at a time of remarkable population growth is even more impressive. While more than one in four children were out of primary school in 1970, the share in 2020 dropped to less than 10%. Improvements have been most evident for girls, who comprised almost two thirds of children out of school in 1990. With near gender parity achieved globally in primary education, girls are no longer disproportionately represented in the out-of-school population, except in the lowest-income countries and in sub-Saharan Africa.

There has also been a significant increase in participation in pre-primary education around the world, across all regions and country income groups, especially since 2000. Global participation rates went from just over 15% in 1970, to 35% in 2000, reaching over 60% in 2019. In higher and middle-income countries, participation rates are converging, with near universal pre-primary participation expected by 2050. Globally, gender disparities have narrowed over time and gender parity or near parity have been reached in pre-primary school participation. This bodes well for primary gender parity in the coming years, as pre-primary cohorts age into primary, better prepared to succeed in schooling.

Expansion of participation in education has led to a steady increase in youth and adult literacy rates between 1990 and 2020 across all countries regardless of development status. Youth literacy rates in lower middle income and middle income countries have now converged with those observed in upper middle income countries at 90+%. There has also been significant improvement in female youth literacy rates across all countries over the past thirty years which has narrowed the gender gap. Gender parity in youth literacy rates is now observed across upper income and middle income countries and gender gaps are narrowing towards parity elsewhere. Equally, this bodes well for a future of universal adult literacy, as youth move into adulthood.

Participation in higher education has also increased significantly over the past fifty years. Global participation rose from 10% of youth and adults worldwide in 1970 to 40% today. Growth in enrolment has also come with a feminization of higher education participation over the past fifty years. While participation in higher education was predominantly male in the 1970s and 1980s, gender parity was reached around 1990 and female participation has continued to grow faster than that of men since then. This is the case for countries across all income groups, except for low income countries, and across all regions except sub-Saharan Africa where 7% of female students and 10% of male students participate. Projections based on trends since 1970 indicate that high income countries could reach 100% participation rates as early as 2034, while middle income countries will be reaching between 60% and 80% participation rates in 2050. On the other hand, higher education participation rates in lower middle income counties will only reach some 35% by 2050, and less than 15% low income countries.

Despite this remarkable progress in expanding educational opportunity over the past decades, however, access to high quality education remains incomplete and inequitable. Exclusion from educational opportunity remains stark. One in four youth in lower income countries is still non-literate today. Even in middle income and upper income countries, the OECD Programme for International Student Assessment has shown that sizable shares of the populations of 15-year-olds in school are unable to understand what they read beyond the most basic levels, in a world in which demands for civic and economic participation become ever more complex. And yet, even by conventional definitions, adult literacy rates are less than 75% in lower middle income countries, and just over 55% in lower income countries. While gender gaps in adult literacy have also narrowed since 1990, they remain significant, especially for the poor. In low income countries, more than 2 out of 5 women are not literate. One in five children in low income countries and one in ten across the world, or some 250 million children, are still out of primary school today. Beyond gaps in the basic literacies of reading, math and science, similar gaps have been observed in cross national studies conducted by the International Association for the Evaluation of Educational Achievement and by the OECD in civic literacy, global competency and socio-emotional competencies, all of which are increasingly important to participate civically and economically.

The situation is even more dramatic at the secondary level. Three out of five adolescents and youth in low income countries are currently out of secondary school, and this despite 2030 commitments to ensure universal completion of free, equitable and quality primary and secondary education. The disparities are clearly defined. While lower secondary enrolment is almost universal (98%) in high income countries, more than a third of adolescents (40% of girls and 34% of boys) are not enrolled in lower secondary education in low income countries. Disparities in participation in upper secondary education are even more pronounced, with fewer than 35% of girls and 45% of boys enrolled in low income countries, compared to over 90% of boys and girls in high income countries.

Beyond access and enrolment, trends in completion point to challenges in quality and relevance of educational provision. Worldwide, more than one in four lower secondary level students and more than one in two in upper secondary do not complete the cycle of study. Close to 60% of high school students in lower middle income countries and almost 90% in low income countries leave school before completing the secondary cycle. Such a dramatic loss of youth potential and talent is unacceptable. The massive scale of early school leaving may be explained by a range of factors, including weak relevance of learning content, lack of attention to the specific social needs of girls and the economic circumstances of the poor, lack of cultural sensitivity and relevance, and inadequate pedagogical methods and processes relevant to the realities of youth. This is a largely overlooked dimension of what many have called a global 'learning crisis'.

Insufficient quality in instruction is one of the key 'push' factors that can cause students to leave school before completion. Teachers are the most significant factor in educational quality provided they have sufficient recognition, preparation, support, resources, autonomy, and opportunities for continued development. With proper support, teachers can ensure effective, culturally relevant, and equitable learning opportunities for their students. The professionalization of teaching is essential to supporting students in developing the full breadth of capabilities necessary to participate civically and economically. This requires creating a continuum to support the profession that includes selecting talented candidates, providing them with high quality and relevant initial preparation, supporting them effectively in the first years of teaching and with continuous professional development, structuring teacher jobs in ways that foster collaborative professionalism, making schools into learning organizations, creating teacher career ladders that recognize and reward increasing expertise either in teaching or in administration, and including the voices of teachers in shaping the future of the profession and of education. The creation of such a continuum requires collective leadership so that these various components act in concert with one another. Many cultural norms undermine the professionalization of teaching such as the use of teacher appointments to serve interests other than those of the students – such as political patronage –, the use of teacher education programmes as 'cash cows' of the institutions that run them, career structures that do not recognize teachers' impact on student learning, lack of standards of practice or of standards for teacher preparation institutions, material conditions of the profession that are considerably below those of other occupations that require similar levels of preparation and work, pressures on teachers to perform work that diminishes their standing as professionals, such as demanding that they participate in political campaigns, or extracting mandatory financial contributions for causes not of their own free choosing or violations to their freedom, identities and human rights, including sexual harassment in the workplace, or coercion into religious or political allegiance.

Yet, as access to schooling has grown and the demand for teachers has expanded, there is a worrying regression worldwide in the share of qualified primary school teachers. This is the case in several regions of the world and in particular in sub-Saharan Africa where the share of primary school teachers with minimum qualifications declined from 85% in 2000 to some 65% in 2020. Declines are also seen in regions that previously had high shares of qualified primary teachers, such as in the Arab region when the rate dropped from 98% in 2004 to 85% in 2020. The declining share of qualified teachers in sub-Saharan Africa is even more significant at the secondary level. Only half of all secondary school teachers in sub-Saharan Africa possessed minimum qualifications in 2015, down from nearly 80% ten years earlier.

> There is a worrying regression worldwide in the share of qualified primary school teachers.

Participation in technical and vocational education and training (TVET) for young adults also remains low in many parts of the world. Some progress can be observed in vocational educational enrolment between 2000 and 2020 in Central Asia, Central and Eastern Europe, as well as in East Asia and the Pacific with up to 15% of 15-24 years enrolled in TVET programmes. In the lowest income countries, however, and in regions such as sub-Saharan Africa and South Asia, enrolment in TVET has remained low and stagnant at only around 1% of the age group. It is important to recall that vocational skills development is not restricted to formal education and training and that youth in the significant informal economies of many countries may have access to traditional apprenticeships or informal skills development. Yet, data from the International Labour Organization indicate that more than one in five youth (16-24) worldwide are not in education, training, or employment, two thirds of whom are young women.

These figures clearly reflect our collective failure to ensure the universal right to education for all children, youth, and adults despite repeated global commitments since at least 1990. This is particularly true for girls and women, children, and youth with disabilities, those from poorer households, rural communities, indigenous peoples, and minority groups, as well as for those who suffer the consequences of violent conflict and political instability. Marginalized communities continue to be excluded by a combination of social, economic, cultural, and political factors.

If education is to help transform the future, it must first become more inclusive by addressing. past injustices. Factors that shape these inequalities and exclusions must be clearly identified if policies and strategies are to support marginalized students, especially those who experience compounded disadvantages.

Persistent poverty and rising inequality

Poverty remains a key determinant of access to educational opportunity. It is a compounding factor that intensifies disparities for female students, those with disabilities, those experiencing situations of instability and conflict, and those who are marginalized due to ethnicity, language, or remote location.

The global economy has grown two and half times in size between 1990 and 2020, driven essentially by the rapid economic growth in countries of East Asia and the Pacific, and particularly China, and the consistent enlargement of the economies of high and upper middle income countries. Lower middle and low income countries, on the other hand, only accounted for one tenth of the global output, despite the fact that they were home to half of the world's population in 2020. This is the result of the widely divergent pace of growth across regions over the past thirty years. The economies of China and sub-Saharan Africa had similar sizes in 1990, representing some 2% and 1.5% of the global economy respectively. Thirty years later, China accounts for 16% of the world GDP, while sub-Saharan Africa represents a mere 2%.

Global economic growth has led to the improvement of individual incomes and living conditions and a reduction of global poverty rates. World Bank data shows that global annual per capita income increased by 75% between 1990 and 2020. While more than a third of the world population was considered poor in 1990, the global poverty rate today is under 10%. However, the reduced pace of economic growth in low income countries hinders progress in poverty reduction and hopes for income inequality reductions. The challenge of eradicating global poverty persists. Indeed, despite the global decline in poverty over the past thirty years, close to 690 million people across the world still live in poverty, on less than two US dollars a day. According to the World Bank, a quarter of the world population, or some 1.8 billion people, live on 3.20 US dollars or less a day. Extreme poverty is largely concentrated in sub-Saharan Africa, is predominantly rural, and disproportionately affects women. Two thirds of those who are poor are children and youth under 25 years of age.

Since the 1980s, rapid economic growth in emerging and middle income economies has led to a converging reduction of inequality between countries. At the same time, however, inequality *within* countries has increased, albeit at different speeds. Since the 1980s, income inequality has surged in China, India, North America, and the Russian Federation, with more moderate increases observed in Europe. Meanwhile, in countries of the Arab world, as well as of sub-Saharan Africa, and much like in Brazil, inequality has traditionally been high and has remained so. According to the 2018 World Inequality Report, more than half of all income in sub-Saharan Africa and in the Arab world, or in countries such as Brazil and India, is captured by the top 10% of income earners. In nearly all countries, capital has shifted from public to private ownership. While economies have expanded, governments have become poorer, limiting the opportunities for income redistribution and reduction of inequalities.

The significance of wealth inequality to education is manifold. Inequality translates into social exclusion for the poor, undermining the social cohesion necessary for societies to thrive and to have good governance. Inequality also translates into children born in different circumstances with very different levels of support for education, making it more challenging for schools to level the playing field. That schools provide equal educational opportunities to all children, regardless of their circumstances, is a precondition for more just and equitable futures.

This becomes more challenging in more unequal societies. Indeed, extreme inequality can also breed conditions for corruption in education, where unchecked fervour to get ahead can translate to illicit shortcuts, and where capacity for effective oversight is lacking. Transparency International's 2013 Global Corruption Report outlined how corruption in education can take many forms, including the diversion of resources intended for procurement and supplies, bribery for grades and admissions, nepotism in hiring and scholarships, academic plagiarism, and undue political and corporate influence on research. Weakened societal and institutional trust can dampen confidence in education's value and integrity, and more significantly, can breed acceptance of corruption as a social norm from one's earliest years.

A web of exclusions

Poverty and income inequality intersect with other factors of discrimination that lead to educational exclusion. Gender discrimination, for instance, compounds significantly with other intersecting factors such as poverty, indigenous identity, and disability to further marginalize girls from their educational rights. While most income groups and regions are showing convergence towards gender parity in school enrolment, this is not the case in the lowest income countries or in sub-Saharan Africa. UNESCO Institute for Statistics (UIS) data shows that for every 100 boys of primary school age out of school in sub-Saharan Africa, there are 123 girls also excluded from education. Exclusion of girls is even more pronounced in lower and upper secondary education. In 9 of the lowest income countries, the poorest girls spend on average 2 years fewer in school than boys. This gendered drop-off, particularly in secondary education, indicates how much more needs to be done to retain girls along the full lifespan of their education. Initial access is insufficient. Ensuring that girls complete a full cycle of secondary education is a responsibility that goes well beyond schools. It relates to the social and economic challenges that girls continue to face around the world, particularly at the age of puberty, around issues such as early marriage or early and unintended pregnancy, domestic work, and menstrual health and stigma.

Disability affects access to education across all regions and income groups when education systems do not have inclusive policies in place. The barriers to education experienced by those with disabilities is significantly compounded by poverty. The majority of children living with a disability are in poorer countries. At all ages, levels of both moderate and severe disability are higher in low and middle income countries than in rich countries. Poverty is both a cause and a consequence of disability, and education systems have an obligation to support the right to education for students with disabilities, and, to the greatest possible extent, include them in the least restrictive educational environment.

Conflict also accounts for half of the world's chronically out-of-school population. Violent conflict makes it unsafe to operate or attend schools and can displace entire populations. Educational institutions, personnel and students may be targeted and can be victims of kidnapping, rape, and armed recruitment.

Indigenous and ethnic minority children and youth face several barriers that limit their access to quality education at all levels. Beyond economic, linguistic and geographical barriers, factors such as racism, discrimination and lack of cultural relevance factor into high attrition rates among indigenous children and youth. In general, formal education fails to recognize indigenous knowledge and learning systems and does not respond to the realities and aspirations of indigenous peoples both in rural and urban settings.

Historically, education has also been used to violate the cultural and religious rights of children, for example, as a vehicle for assimilation of indigenous peoples and ethnic minorities into mainstream societies or as a vehicle of religious indoctrination or of obliteration of the religious or cultural identity of minority children in violation of their fundamental rights. The legacies of education's weaponization against indigenous children and families continue to be experienced through systemic discrimination and neglect. Children from remote indigenous and minority communities, for example, are often forced to leave their communities to continue their education, living at hostels or boarding schools that deprive them of their families and community and cultural support.

Economic globalization increasingly influences what and how students learn. It has reshaped expectations about what children and youth need to know to secure employment in the twenty-first century. Preparation for employment is an important educational goal. However, there are pitfalls in defining goals of education too narrowly, particularly in ways that do not align with the realities of students' and families' lives and opportunities. A broader approach to ways of knowing recognizes that a there is a wider diversity in the ways that knowledge can be applied, generated, and diffused across diverse contexts, cultures, and circumstances. These draw not only on basic skills in literacy and numeracy, but on the rich heritage of knowledge across cultures that recognizes the global, local, ancestral, embodied, cultural, scientific, and spiritual.

This is particularly true when it comes to indigenous, minority language, and ethnically diverse students who may be counted among those out of school. Equity in education must embrace humanity's many forms of knowledge and expression. Large-scale learning assessments often fail to account for mother-tongue competencies, which can further marginalize and push minority and indigenous students to leave school early. The Programme for International Reading Literacy Survey (PIRLS) results, for instance, showed that Grade 4 students who did not speak the language of the test at home were less likely than other students to reach the lowest level of proficiency in reading. We must embrace a world that contains many lived realities rather than impose a singular vision of social and economic development. Guaranteeing the full exercise of individual and collective rights, requires a true valuing of diverse human potentials.

> Equity in education must embrace humanity's many forms of knowledge and expression.

If human rights is to guide the new social contract for education, students' sense of identity – cultural, spiritual, social, and linguistic – must be recognized and affirmed, particularly among indigenous, religious, cultural and gender minorities and systemically marginalized populations. Appropriate recognition of identity in curriculum, pedagogy, and institutional approaches can directly impact student retention, mental health, self-esteem, and community well-being.

Different means and measures are required to reach those for whom other solutions have been inadequate. But these efforts become yet more challenging in the face of real and present social and educational disruptions resulting from climate change, global pandemics, and insecurity. In 2020, the COVID-19 pandemic alone left 1.6 billion children and young people around the world affected by closures of educational institutions. Even as schools reopened, millions of students will not return, particularly those from poorer and more marginalized communities. Inequality in educational opportunity has been further exacerbated.

Forging a new social contract for education is all the more urgent given emerging societal transformations underway and radical disruptions on the horizon. It must address the existing web of inequalities that perpetuate educational and social exclusions, while helping to shape environmentally sustainable, and socially just and inclusive shared futures.

Chapter 2

Disruptions and emerging transformations

> Here I would like to stress that one of the great lessons of my life is to stop believing in the permanence of the present, the continuity of becoming, and the predictability of the future. Relentlessly, the short, sudden eruptions of the unforeseen, come to shake up or transform, sometimes happily, sometimes unhappily, our individual life, our life as a citizen, the life of our nation, the life of humanity.

Edgar Morin, *Leçons d'un siècle de vie*, 2021.

As we move towards the mid-century milestone of 2050, the type of education we will need hinges, significantly, on what we can expect the world to look like, taking into account the likelihood of enormous variations across families, communities, countries and regions.

This chapter will look to this future, zooming in on disruptions that are expected to have a profound impact in four often overlapping areas: the environment, how we live and interact with technology, our governance systems, and the world of work.

Despite the uncertainty of foresight work, anticipating transformative shifts provides a foundation on which to plan and build alternative scenarios about how to better align education with humanity's needs in the coming decades and beyond.

A planet in peril

A scientific consensus has emerged that the decades leading to 2050, and the 2020s in particular, will be pivotal for the future of humans and all other life forms on Earth. The steps we take – or do not take – to reduce carbon emissions will determine what futures are possible in the 2030s and 2040s and will have ripple effects for hundreds of thousands, or even millions, of years. The scale and speed of the changes we are making to the Earth have no historical precedent and very few geological precedents. The chemical composition of the atmosphere is estimated to be changing ten times faster than even during the most extreme shifts seen during the entire span of the age of mammals. The Earth is now hotter than it has been at any time since the start of the last Ice Age which began 125,000 years ago. And because the effects of climate change which have already taken place are baked into our systems, they will shape life on the planet for the next thirty or so years. We need to adapt to, mitigate and revert climate change, and education about and for climate change needs to align with these three goals.

The signing of the 2015 Paris Climate Accords marked a historic global commitment to work to stabilize and reduce the global output of greenhouse gases such as CO_2 and methane which has been expanding since the dawn of the industrial era. Governments of the world pledged to help ensure the planet does not warm more than 2 °C above pre-industrial levels (and preferably not more than 1.5 °C). Yet despite commitments to scale back the burning of fossil fuels, emissions continue to increase. The 2021 report of the Intergovernmental Panel for Climate Change demonstrates that the speed of global warming is greater than anticipated even a few years ago. At the global level we have proven unable to steady the output of greenhouse gases, let alone reduce it dramatically. The impact of this inaction is all around us, and much of it is devastating with debilitating heat, more frequent and prolonged droughts, floods, fires, and accelerating extinction becoming the norm. And, despite constant warnings, far too many people still fail to understand the consequences of human activity such as mining and burning carbon to power the modern world. Human activities have precipitated climate shifts that have also caused up to half of the tropical coral reefs on the planet to die, 10 trillion tons of ice to melt, and the ocean to grow dramatically more acidic. Whereas it once seemed that net-zero carbon emissions could wait until 2050 to prevent some of the worst effects of climate change, recent scientific research suggests the deadline will come much sooner. What happens in the next several years – a mere nano-second in the expansive history of the Earth – may set us on a nightmarish course of living with an increasingly volatile and dangerous climate; or with a climate that will change, but with less severity and remain relatively hospitable to humans.

The urgency of the situation is increasingly recognized in homes, businesses, places of worship, and schools around the globe. Children and youth have, understandably, led some of the most forceful calls for action and delivered harsh rebukes to those who refuse to acknowledge the precarity of our moment and take meaningful corrective action. In the consultations that informed this report, consistent across the focus groups conducted with and by youth, and in youth surveys, a high level of concern is evident about climate change and environmental devastation.

Exceeding planetary boundaries

The warming of Earth's atmosphere and oceans goes hand-in-hand with the exploitation of resources pushing the planet to the brink. The human world population tripled between 1950 and 2020, growing from 2.5 billion persons to almost 8 billion, a result of increasing birth rates and rapidly increasing lifespans. The average person on Earth lived twice as long in 2020 than in 1920 – a remarkable achievement that reflects countless social and scientific accomplishments. Predictably, this population explosion has been matched by concurrent increases in resource needs. And populations continue to expand, albeit at a slower pace than in recent centuries. Current projections suggest population growth will reach 9.7 billion in 2050 and then likely plateau at around 11 billion in 2100.

This growth, coupled with a rapid acceleration of consumption and industrial activity, has placed huge demands on resources and often results in environmental stress. Since 1950, human water use has doubled, food production and consumption have increased 2.5 times and wood consumption has tripled. It is estimated that by 2050, demand for food will rise by another 35%, demand for water by 20-30%, and demand for energy by 50%.

Today we far surpass planetary boundaries in terms of material production, consumption and waste. By some estimates, the current ecological footprint of human beings requires 1.6 planet Earths to support us and absorb our waste. This means, that as our use of resources continues to grow, it now takes the planet one year and eight months to regenerate what we use in a single year. Without course correction, in 2050 we will be using resources at four times the rate it takes for them to replenish and will hand future generations a gravely depleted planet.

> Today we far surpass planetary boundaries in terms of material production, consumption and waste.

Pollution, a by-product of our consumption and resource exploitation, has quickly become the largest environmental cause of disease and death; it is estimated to be responsible for 9 million premature deaths per year, far more than AIDS, malaria, TB and warfare combined. Not only is it often referred to as the biggest public health crisis on the planet, it has been linked to learning difficulties and disabilities. Just getting to and from school can be hazardous to human health in many contexts, due to dangerous levels of air pollution, and, once there, many educational institutions lack functional air filters, appropriate sewage treatment, and clean water. Other learning facilities are located in areas with dangerous levels of chemical waste and other forms of toxic pollution.

Even if zero-emissions were achieved tomorrow and we had 100% clean energy systems, we would still face the damaging ecological consequences of unsustainable activity such as deforestation, overfishing, industrial agriculture, mining, and waste – all on top of the effects of climate change already built into our system. The cascading consequences are only coming into view. The Earth's biosphere is an integrated system – one that includes humans and that can withstand significant pressures – but the more we strain the ecosystems upon which we depend, the closer we come to tipping points that may result in irreversible breakdown.

Human beings are responsible for this – but not all humans equally. Privileged groups and wealthier areas of the planet use dramatically more resources and burn more carbon than others. As we work together to change direction, social justice must encompass ecological justice and vice-versa. We must ensure that those least responsible for causing these strains to the planet do not continue to disproportionately pay the price for them.

The effects of climate change on education

Currently climate change and ecosystem destabilization affect education in direct and indirect ways. The intensification of extreme weather events and associated natural disasters inhibit, and can even deny access to, education. Children, youth and adult learners may be displaced to locations distant from adequate educational facilities. School buildings might be destroyed or repurposed to provide shelter or other services. Even where schools and universities remain operational, teacher shortages due to displacement are a common consequence of natural disasters rooted in climate change.

Rising temperatures present special risks to education. Considerable research has shown that heat adversely impacts learning and cognition, and most of the world's schools and homes do not currently have appropriate materials, architecture and technologies to meaningfully reduce temperatures and ensure climate control. This is true in countries with extreme heat and in countries, many of them rich, that only periodically experience dramatic temperature spikes. Recent projections have suggested, without a dramatic shift in the output of greenhouse gases, up to one-third of the world's population is likely to live in areas that are considered unsuitably hot for humans by 2070. Already students around the world are becoming accustomed to directives to skip school and stay at home due to dangerous levels of heat and other extreme weather events that are likely to only increase in scale, degree and frequency.

Beyond the direct impacts of climate change and pollution on students, teachers, and school communities, there are indirect impacts on livelihoods and well-being. The increased likelihood of food insecurity, the spread of disease, and exacerbated economic precarity all introduce new challenges to ensuring the right to education. In these situations too, we know that effects are uneven.

Evidence shows that climate change increases gender inequality, especially among the most poor and marginalized, and those dependent on subsistence agriculture. Where resources are scarce, they tend to be distributed unequally. When women and girls are displaced by the effects of climate change, the potential for them to fall into a poverty trap is much higher. Their prospects for returning to and restoring their lives, including through education, is lower than their male counterparts. Climate change can also increase the out-migration of men, increasing the burden of family survival on women. In some contexts, arranging girls' early marriages is among the few options for families to sustain themselves, ending their future educational prospects. At the same time, women play important roles as agents of change for climate justice – as mothers, teachers, workers, decision-makers and members and leaders of the community – and are often at the forefront of adaptation and mitigation practices.

Indigenous women own knowledge that contributes to the mitigation and adaptation to climate change, such as sustainable forest management, sowing and harvesting of water, biodiversity, crop resistance, and seed conservation and selection, but their contributions are often ignored.

Too often those most affected by climate change are underrepresented in public debates – globally and within their countries and localities. Beyond this, the largest constituencies in education, encompassing students, teachers, and families, are often noticeably absent from discussions on climate change and its effects on education. It is vital that they play a leading role in shaping how education will respond. The need for participatory approaches extends beyond education policy and planning and applies also to research and knowledge production about human-caused transformations of the planet and education.

Currently, education attainment and completion correlate with unsustainable practices. The world's most educated countries and people are the ones most accelerating climate change. While we expect education to provide pathways to peace, justice and human rights, we are only now beginning to expect and indeed demand that it opens pathways and builds capacities for sustainability. This work needs to intensify. If being educated means living unsustainably, we need to recalibrate our notions of what education should do and what it means to be educated.

Cause for hope

For too long, education itself has been based on an economic growth-focused modernization development paradigm. But there are early signs that we are moving towards a new ecologically-oriented education rooted in understandings that can rebalance our ways of living on Earth and recognize its interdependent systems and their limits. The annual observance of Earth Day each April has become one of the largest secular celebrations in human history. The climate movement has spurred on children to become active participants to ensure that their visions of their own futures are heard and implemented. Their actions are rehearsals for a different kind of future.

Beyond this, sustainable development is increasingly elevated as both a guiding purpose for education and organizing principle for curricula.

We cannot discount the possible future of a 2050 where a radical transformation in human eco-consciousness, and our ways of living in balance with the living Earth, has already taken place.

While the importance of environmental education has been recognized for decades now, and endorsed in many government policy pronouncements, there is a large disconnect between policy and practice, and an even greater disconnect with results. Research on the effectiveness of climate change education finds that much of it focuses exclusively on scientific teaching, without cultivating the full breadth of competencies necessary to engage students in effective action. We need renewed and more effective approaches to help students develop the capabilities to adapt to and mitigate climate change. Our strategies should draw on existing knowledge about how to foster deeper learning and the development of civic competency, and on recent research on the development of skills for life and work.

> We need renewed and more effective approaches to help students develop the capabilities to adapt to and mitigate climate change.

The digital that connects and divides

Our historical moment is distinguished by an acceleration of the technological transformation of our societies, characterized by an ongoing digital revolution and advances in biotechnologies and neuroscience. Technological innovations have reshaped the ways we live and learn and are certain to continue doing so.

Digital technologies, tools and platforms can be bent in the direction of supporting human rights, enhancing human capabilities, and facilitating collective action in the directions of peace, justice, and sustainability. To state the obvious, digital literacy and access are a basic right in the twenty-first century; without them it is increasingly difficult to participate civically and economically. One of the painful realizations of the global pandemic is that those with connectivity and access to digital skills were able to continue to learn remotely while schools closed down (and to benefit from other vital information in real time), whereas those without such access and skills missed out on learning and the other benefits physical learning institutions bring. As a result of this digital divide, gaps in educational opportunity and outcomes between and within nations augmented. The first order of business is to close this divide and to consider digital literacy, for students and teachers, one of the essential literacies of the twenty-first century.

Yet the use of technology to advance human capabilities to make the world more inclusive and sustainable needs to be intentional and incentivized. Technology has a long history of subverting our rights and limiting or even diminishing our capabilities. The rushed adoption of new developments as 'magic bullet' solutions has rarely succeeded. What have yielded better results are developments that seek to make incremental improvements and a culture that encourages technological experimentation with recognition of risks and an understanding that there are no simple, universal solutions.

The digital – all that has been converted into numerical sequences for computer-enabled transmission, storage, and analysis – saturates vast areas of human activity. As a form of infrastructure (a linking element), the digital does much to 'connect' us. Yet, 'digital divides' persist both in terms of internet access and the skills and competencies needed to leverage technology for collective and personal aims.

There are inherent contradictions in digitalization and digital technologies. Digital technologies have multiple logics, some with great emancipatory potential, others with great impacts and risks. In this respect the 'digital revolution' is no different from the other great technological moments of change like the agricultural and industrial revolutions. Major collective gains come with worrisome increases in inequality and exclusion. The challenge is to navigate these mixed effects by engineering technological developments to ensure human rights and equal opportunities.

Technology is not neutral – it can frame actions and decision-making in ways that divide and reshape the world as well as human understanding and action.

Specific characteristics of digital technology can pose significant threats to knowledge diversity, cultural inclusion, transparency, and intellectual freedom, just as other characteristics can facilitate the sharing of knowledge and information. Currently, algorithmic pathways, platform imperialism, and patterns of governance of digital infrastructures, present acute challenges to sustaining education as a common good. The issues they raise have become central to contemporary debates on education, in particular, on the digitalization of education and the possible emergence of new hybrid or virtual-only models of schooling.

For several decades the worlds of education have been caught up in a set of varied, provisional, and emergent relationships with digital technologies. Computers are used in many classrooms and homes around the globe; mobile phones are increasingly used in diverse educational settings and play an especially important role in poorer settings and, in particular, sub-Saharan Africa where personal computers are less readily available. The internet, email, mobile data, video and audio streaming, and a host of sophisticated collaboration and learning tools, have generated vast and exciting educational opportunities and possibilities.

These ongoing transformations have significant implications for the right to education as well as for cultural rights related to language, heritage, and aspiration. Rights to information, data and knowledge and the right to democratic participation are also greatly impacted. Core principles of human dignity, including the right to privacy and the right to pursue one's own purposes, come into play when we look at the disruptive transformations digitalization has brought.

Advances in information communication technology continue to transform what learning is valued, the ways in which learning occurs and how education systems are organized. Digital technologies have greatly reduced the costs of collecting information and acting on the basis of it. They have also made it easier for more people to participate in these processes. Citizen and open science projects are excellent examples of how digital technology can help expand the volume of information collected and analyzed, and the numbers and diversity of people involved in this work. The generation, circulation and use of data and the knowledge that data can emerge through digital processes, has changed the ways that science advances and specialized expertise develops – as well as the ways that information and knowledge are and are not available to publics across the globe. Concurrently, the ease of computer-facilitated data collection and analysis has quickly eclipsed alternative forms of reasoning and meaning- making, with consequences such as the privileging of numerical datasets over other types of data, including personal experience and other types of information that, while relevant, can be difficult to quantify.

As we acclimate to a world where more textual and graphic information is instantly available on a pocket-sized mobile phone than in the sum of our greatest physical libraries across millennia, education needs to move beyond spreading and transmitting knowledge and instead ensure that knowledge empowers learners and that they use that knowledge responsibly. A primary educational challenge is to equip people with tools for making sense of the oceans of information that are just a few swipes or keystrokes away.

Digital knowledge and its exclusions

Digital technologies have come to reflect a specific and dominant strain of knowledge, unique to the post-Renaissance West, that has pushed much indigenous knowledge into the margins. The climate and navigation knowledge of fishers, sailors and adventurers has been marginalized by astronomers, climatologists, and meteorologists equipped with technology and data derived from it. Likewise, the knowledge of farmers, hunters, gatherers, and pastoralists, often passed down over centuries, has been marginalized by the technical expertise and technology employed by agronomists, forestry experts, professional conservators, pharmaceutical companies, and nutritionists. This side-lining of non-technology ways of knowing has deprived humanity of a vast and diverse archive of knowledge about being human, about nature, about environment and about cosmology. Educators can do much to recognize, reclaim and restore these knowledges which constitute the DNA of cultural diversity for humanity. In turn, the science of pedagogy has itself become an expert competence which has often rejected or treated with suspicion informal, indigenous, and not easily accessible knowledges.

One of the most precious forms of knowledge threatened by the triumph of digitality is that of the social itself. In spite of its boasts about sharing, connectivity and relationships, most profit-driven digital knowledge relies on the isolation of the individual – user, buyer or watcher – and can too easily promote loneliness, selfishness, and narcissism. And precisely because digital literacy, devices, platforms and bandwidth are very unequally distributed both between and within countries, there is a disregard for those who value and rely on indigenous, low-tech, ephemeral and non-commoditized forms of knowledge.

In part, the 'digital divide' exists because, by definition, it ignores those outside its sphere and all that evades its techniques of measurement, storage and analysis. In these respects, it could just as appropriately be called 'platform imperialism'. The solution is not a simplistic inclusive digitalization.

It is a more complex, public engagement with ways the digital can be marshalled to support the common good - coupled with a new appreciation of what remains outside its sphere.

Collectively we must all support and nurture the capacity to resist the negative aspects of digitality which could become increasingly widespread in 2050 – particularly with the focus on quantitative, algorithmic and 'solutionist' definitions of knowledge. But to resist these tendencies does not mean resisting digitalization itself.

In the era of COVID-19 we have seen that digital technologies are essential for public health and public education: an indispensable tool for distance education, for contact and vaccine tracing, for reliable information about the virus and more. Nonetheless, numbers without narratives, connectivity without cultural inclusion, information without empowerment, and digital technology in education without clear purposes, are not desirable measures of, or aids to, human development.

Despite the celebratory tone that accompanies a lot of commentary on the digital revolution, it can also be interpreted as a failure to capitalize on the profoundly transformative opportunities presented by such technologies. As used now, digital platforms mostly conform to purposes that advance broader business objectives. Their design communities also routinely exclude underprivileged groups, including women and linguistic, ethnic and racial minorities as well as the disabled, perpetuating bias and misleading information that fails to represent humanity as a whole. This, however, should not be the destiny of the powerful digital technologies currently at disposal. They can do so much more to empower and connect people than the usually commercial moulds we have established for them, and now expect.

> Numbers without narratives, connectivity without cultural inclusion, information without empowerment, and digital technology in education without clear purposes, are not desirable.

Creating a more supple digital environment will require some uncoupling of its underlying infrastructures from the business models and authoritarian regulatory impulses that currently constrain positive development and the potential common good that can be created.

Hacking human learners

Developments in biotechnology and neuroscience have the potential to unleash the engineering of human beings in ways that were previously inconceivable. Proper ethical governance and deliberation in the public sphere will become increasingly urgent to ensure that technological developments that affect human genetic make-up and neurochemistry support sustainable, just and peaceful futures.

New instruments of neuroscience already allow researchers to directly examine how human brains function, as opposed to inferring brain function from behaviour. However, most contemporary brain recording methods rely on highly controlled environments far removed from real life educational contexts and interactions. One research activity popular today is the identification of brain areas that are selectively activated during different learning activities (such as language comprehension or mathematical reasoning). However, so far, this reveals very little about how to design instruction and will require additional translational research.

Nonetheless, valuable insights are accumulating from research that takes the brain as a biological organ that can be in conditions less and more optimal for learning. The importance of brain health as a component of the body's physical health reinforces the interdependencies between learning and overall human welfare – and further concretizes the links between the right to education and other rights, such as the right to health.

There is increasing evidence that points to the neuroplasticity of the human brain – meaning that the brain physically changes over the human lifespan. While the early years remain a crucial formative period, we now understand that our brains are capable of considerable learning and 'rewiring' at all ages and that certain chemicals may play a role in facilitating the rewiring of the human brain, for example in enabling patients to overcome trauma. These insights have potential implications for adult education and learning.

> While the early years remain a crucial formative period, we now understand that our brains are capable of considerable learning and 'rewiring' at all ages.

Neuroplasticity also has important implications for human adaptation to environmental and technical change. As this Report argues, people of all ages, not just children, will be increasingly forced to learn to live with a damaged planet. Neuroplasticity also comes into play as more and more people around the globe engage with digital, screen-based reading. A set of important concerns have arisen about the ease of distraction, the difficulty of prolonged attentiveness, and the rise of tabular, 'skimming' modes of reading. Our current understanding of the ways that the brain reworks itself to improve its abilities to undertake the tasks it is presented with is a useful reminder that the linear reading associated with print is a tremendously complex neurological task in its own right. The cultural and biological significance of this for humanity has been pointed out by the many scholars who describe the transition in multiple human cultures from the oral to the written. In one sense, we humans have been 'hacking' ourselves for quite some time. Many rightly propose that in time we will adjust to the new reading technologies now in front of us. For the futures of education the choice should not be presented as one of digital or print reading – but rather as one where, in an effort to produce multiple literacies, teachers should ensure that students encounter both linear and tabular reading. Print and digital should be seen as complementary formats for text and as both essential.

Properly steering these emerging developments in neuroscience and biotechnology will depend on open data, open science and an expanded understanding of the right to education to include rights to connectivity, to data, to information and to the protection of privacy.

Democratic backsliding and growing polarization

Critical thinking, innovation, and the realization of individual and shared purposes thrive in participatory democratic settings where human rights are respected. Yet, over the past decade, the world has witnessed a significant backsliding in democratic governance and a rise in identity-driven exclusionary populist sentiment. Such sentiment thrives on the discontent of those left behind by a globalized world order – an order that saw walls brought down, borders disappear, and the movement of people, goods and ideas expand in ways unprecedented in contemporary history. It has been further fuelled by population migration and displacement resulting from conflict, economic hardship, and climate change pressures.

Organizations that research and monitor the state of democracy across the globe have described the effects of these changes in various ways. The *Economist* news magazine refers to a shift from *full* to *flawed* democracies. Freedom House sees movement from *free* to *partly free* political systems while V.Dem describes transitions from *electoral democracy* to *electoral autocracy*. Nomenclature aside, what is common is that, for many, democracy seems more fragile today than it was in the recent past.

Factors involved range from the rise of populist leaders and the growth of nativism manifesting as nationalism, to the power of social media with its capacity in real-time to disseminate intentionally misleading 'fake news' and the manipulation of data and micro-targeting of messages to influence social behaviour. The hubris of elites and a more general rising anxiety about one's place in the world and about futures which are increasingly uncertain, also plays in.

The world appears increasingly divided and polarized with many democratic institutions under siege. They are challenged by those who feel that democracy has not delivered on its promises, and by those who feel that it has already gone too far. Supremacist ideals and chauvinisms gain force, to the detriment of plural identities and of dialogue and understanding. Rights – civic, social, human, environmental – are being displaced or curtailed by authoritarian governments that rule by mobilizing fears, prejudices and discrimination.

The breakdowns in civic discourse and growing infringements on the freedom of expression all have great consequences for an education rooted in human rights, citizenship, and civic participation at local, national, and global levels.

> The breakdowns in civic discourse and growing infringements on the freedom of expression all have great consequences for education.

At the same time, there is increasingly active citizenship mobilization and activism in many areas. These counter movements point to resiliency and new futures for participatory democratic politics. They range from ecological movements, often youth-led, to citizen struggles against regimes that deprive minorities of basic human rights. They include demands across the world to restore democratic rights and respect the rule of law. This mobilization includes anti-racism movements such as Black Lives Matter, the '#metoo' movement challenging gender-based harassment and violence, as well as calls to decolonize curricula and educational institutions.

The concerns of these movements need to filter through to future curricula. Education has a role to play in encouraging and assuring robust democratic citizenship, deliberative spaces, participatory processes, collaborative practices, relationships of care, and shared futures.

The global health crisis sparked by the COVID-19 pandemic has given impetus and urgency to much of this civic participation and activism with an awakening of solidarity seen in numerous examples of communities coming together. Many governments have realized that public health and other emergencies cannot be faced without the help of society at large, through self-responsibility and mutual caring. The social has been rediscovered.

Concurrently, the pandemic has aggravated democratic backsliding. We have seen the expansion of executive powers, increased use of surveillance technology, restrictions on public gatherings and freedom of movement, the deployment of militaries in civilian areas, and disruptions in electoral calendars, among other effects. Whatever the rationales to ensure public health, it is worth recalling that what happens in conditions of public emergency is a defining expression of governance.

The unknown trajectories of these political transformations will be with us at least for several decades with many implications for education, both because the disruptions will shape educational agendas and because what occurs in regard to educational access, curricula and pedagogy will, in turn, shape political transformations around the globe.

The world is at a turning point in how political publics form with patience in short supply, diminished in part by the rhythms of social media. When we are unable to listen to each other, public life is severely curtailed. Care and respect for others need practice and reinforcement – something that education can well support – while building students' capacities for active citizenship and democratic participation.

The uncertain future of work

How will education in the future best support individuals, communities and societies for meaningful work and economic well-being?

The 2019 recommendations of the ILO's Global Commission on the Future of Work around ensuring a human-centred future of work are a valuable starting point. This agenda places people and the work they do at the centre of economic and social policy and business practice.

Today unemployment remains unacceptably high. Billions of people work in precarious informal employment. Over 300 million workers with paid employment still live in extreme poverty. Millions of men, women and children are trapped in conditions of modern slavery. Progress is still to be made on workplace safety and harassment. In most parts of the world there are still large gender gaps in terms of workforce participation and compensation for men and women.

Labour force participation rates have been declining slowly in nearly all world regions and income brackets since 1990. This is particularly true for youth participation (15-24), which shrunk from 50% in 1990 to under 33% today. While this can be partly attributed to improved levels of educational attainment at secondary and tertiary levels over the past thirty years, one in five youth today is not in employment, education, or training. And one in four youth is underemployed.

Significant discrepancies in labour market participation and opportunities persist based on gender. For the past several decades female labour market participation has consistently increased – narrowing the gender gap over time, but from such a low starting point that disparities remain troublingly wide. In 2019, labour force participation was under 50% for women, while it was close to 75% for men. Female participation rates are affected by greater enrolment in education. Better living standards may lead women to voluntarily leave the job market. However, considerable evidence points to a lower quality of jobs available to women. Unpaid and family labour are persistent obstacles to increasing female participation rates in salaried labour markets.

One of the indicators of the vast gender disparities that still exist is the perpetuation of occupational segregation between men and women. Overall, what is formally considered 'work' and what is measured as 'productivity' makes a great deal of essential labour invisible. This includes work that is vital to society but that has often been feminized and typically takes place in the home. Examples include caregiving, child-rearing, caring for the sick, cleaning, cooking and providing physical and emotional support to others. When this work is formalized, these professions are often lower-paid and have lower status.

Improving the quality of work, and expanding choice and freedom for individuals to pursue economic security in ways they desire for themselves, is likely to remain a global challenge for some time to come, particular in the short term due to the disruptions and setbacks caused by the COVID-19 pandemic. This global crisis disrupted the world of work in ways that are still coming into focus and are expected by many to have adverse long-term consequences. Workplace closures and working-hour losses have affected millions worldwide. Current ILO estimates are that as many as 150 million jobs might have disappeared.

Closing the gender gap and reversing damages wreaked by global inequality have been dealt a major setback by COVID-19. Despite initial optimism that the shift to working from home might be advantageous to women professionals, the exact opposite has occurred. Across all regions and across most countries regardless of income level, women have been affected by employment loss to a much greater extent than men.

> Closing the gender gap and reversing damages wreaked by global inequality have been dealt a major setback by COVID-19.

A challenging picture emerges looking towards the future of work. Technological advances, such as AI, automation and robotics, will create new jobs, but will also displace many, and those who lose their jobs in this process may be the least prepared to seize new opportunities.

The greening of our economies will create millions of jobs as we adopt sustainable practices and clean technologies, but other jobs will disappear as countries scale back their carbon- and resource-intensive industries. The platform economy could recreate nineteenth century working practices and future generations of 'digital day labourers'. Skills developed today are unlikely to align with those demanded by the jobs of tomorrow and many will become obsolete. These shifts will place additional demands on education and training systems to increase the support available to those directly experiencing labour market transitions.

Education, skills development, and the school-to-work transitions

These recurring challenges and recent setbacks all have implications for the worlds of education and training. Schools and other educational institutions have an important role to play in preparing and supporting individuals to pursue economic well-being in conditions of freedom and dignity. Whether this leads to success and fulfillment in the formal economy, in the informal economy, or, for example, in domestic work, care work, and other forms of labour, we rightly expect education to play a role in enabling equal economic opportunity and allowing people to pursue meaningful vocations and occupations.

At the same time, education cannot make up for inadequacies in other policy domains that have caused – and continue to cause – declining job quality as well as widespread unemployment. Education is one part of the mix, but macroeconomic, industrial and employment policy are usually more effective levers for creating quality jobs, especially in the near term. Educational attainment and youth unemployment sometimes rise in tandem. Underemployment, the inability to find work that matches one's aspirations, skillset and capabilities, is a persistent and growing global problem, even among university graduates in many of the world's wealthiest countries. This mismatch is combustible: social scientists have shown that a highly educated population unable to apply its skills and competencies in decent work, leads to discontent, agitation and sometime sparks political and civil strife.

In the school-to-work transition, skills mismatches cannot be discounted. Learning must be relevant to the world of work. Young people need strong support upon educational completion to be integrated into labour markets and contribute to their communities and societies according to their potential. Industry and community leaders must be better brought into secondary and higher education to ensure that students are exposed to the world of work and a range of occupations. Educational institutions should not only provide career counselling but must offer support to educators through lifelong learning opportunities to ensure they are kept apace with changes in their profession and the world of work. The provision of TVET, whether through secondary or tertiary education, should integrate opportunities for work-based learning. This not only provides learners with real-world experience but can also improve the quality and relevance of education and training. It is also important that learning pathways provide access to vocational subject options without closing future learning opportunities.

Education on its own does not produce labour demand. Nor can it solve problems of structural unemployment. The plethora of 'supply side' reforms which have affected TVET and skills development in recent years will not, in themselves, create jobs or employment growth.

But education can shape people to innovate, apply their knowledge, solve problems and perform complex tasks. Particularly at higher levels, schooling produces people with sophisticated knowledge and cognitive skills, as well as the expectation that they will have the opportunity to put their knowledge and skills to use. A singular focus on education for jobs or education to develop entrepreneurial skills is misplaced. Education should be geared to enable people to create long-term social and economic well-being for themselves, their families, and their communities.

> Education should be geared to enable people to create long-term social and economic well-being for themselves, their families, and their communities.

Learning to live well with technology is tremendously important for the future of work. One of the best strategies to prepare for green economies and a carbon-neutral future is to ensure qualifications, programmes and curricula deliver 'green skills', be they for newly emerging occupations and sectors or for those sectors undergoing transformation for the low-carbon economy. Another important step will be to fully green our learning environments. Empowering students to lead the way in creating carbon-neutral educational systems is one promising strategy to prepare them for meaningful work in green economies.

The changing future of credentials

Credentials are at the intersection of education and labour markets. A key role of schools, universities, and TVET programmes is to certify the mastery of skills, competencies, and knowledge. There is increasing awareness that individuals have a basic right to have their learning recognized and validated, even in non-formal and informal educational settings.

A sole focus on the qualification itself is insufficient. While it is important to think about outcomes, we should not lose sight of the social processes and interactions at the core of education. Qualifications are always only 'proxies' for what someone can do and work chiefly because of social trust, an evidence of the value of trust in educational purposes and activities.

As career and employment changes become more common and fluid, more research is needed on how we can better enable people to move between related occupations. Governments, educators, employers, and the general public will increasingly need to work together to identify the kinds of occupations and work that their societies will nurture and develop. Systems that monitor and analyse labour market shifts and the changing skill-needs of occupations and jobs are becoming more sophisticated, and education and training systems need to better use this information to adjust their programmes and offer relevant learning options for the world of work. Institutions need to be more outward looking and progressive in their approach to qualifications, curriculum, and programming.

Structural transformation of labour markets

Alongside technological and environmental change, a varied set of structural economic factors are reshaping labour markets. We are seeing the rise of 'gig,' freelance, and contractor economies and a future very likely to reinforce the significance of the informal economy for billions around the world. Such new employment models will add further pressure to the growing demand for reskilling and upskilling of existing workers. Education and training systems should continue to offer more flexible learning options, so institutions and programmes are accessible to a wider cohort of learners able to learn what, where and when they need.

Demographic change is also a key factor in the future of work and one likely to have considerable impact by 2050. A quickly expanding youth population in some regions is set to exacerbate youth unemployment and migratory pressures. Other regions will face ageing populations and additional strain on social security and other care systems.

At present, the international community uses 'dependency ratio' calculations that compare the total population to those in the 15-64 bracket who are assumed to be economically productive, and thus provide the means to support the young and the elderly. By 2050, dependency ratios are expected to increase sharply in Europe, North America, and more moderately in Asia, Latin America and the Caribbean – meaning that smaller groups of workers will be providing for larger groups of non-workers (primarily retirees). Meanwhile, the total dependency ratio for Africa is projected to decrease as half the region's population will be under 25.

These demographic shifts, where there is growth in the proportion of younger people and growth in the proportion of the elderly, have notable implications for the world of work and for education and training systems. Tied into this are tendencies to expand opportunities for TVET and adult education and to reinvigorate lifelong learning. Human longevity may also increase and perhaps with it, at least for some, the extension of the work period of life. If older people can remain active and engaged, they will enrich society and the economy through their skills and experience. Empowering young people to reach their full potential and access emerging opportunities will make them tomorrow's agents of change. This means investing in people's capabilities, enabling them to acquire skills, reskill and upskill and supporting them through the various transitions they will face over their life course.

As these transformations unfold there will be changing demands for education, some that can be modelled (like the need to expand primary school classrooms and hire more teachers in some regions) but others that cannot, given the complexity of the interconnected factors and unknown trajectories of possible transformations. Because of this, education and training institutions need to tighten links with their local communities and establish themselves as anchor institutions. Working closely with other local institutions will enable schools and institutes to better understand and provide for the learning needs of their communities.

What work will be valued in the future?

As we move towards 2050, a possible scenario arises that would represent an unprecedented break with human history: the world could, regardless of the depth of worker skills, simply run out of jobs in the formal economy because of breakthrough technological advances. How would education function in a society where only a small minority of people have formal employment? What new education would people need to live without formal work?

> What new education would people need to live without formal work?

Human societies have evolved to value individual work. The dream of a golden age of freedom from toil dates back millennia. But today the problem seems less one of managing unprecedented leisure. The spectre of mass joblessness now looms as large over wealthy countries as it has for decades in poor countries. Much would need to be rethought. How would the productive and creative impulses of human beings best be channelled in other socially and personally useful directions?

Fortunately, some of the best proposals for such a contingency equally serve existing education efforts to create decent work. The multiple layers of uncertainty around the future of work and the planet suggest that we should prioritize learners' ability to create meaning.

In fact, we may need to profoundly rethink what it means to produce value in the first place. When thinking about the future of work and education we face a choice: persist with the widespread contradictory habit of thought that expects both too much and too little of education – or focus on what education can do well.

In future, how and what we value may change in ways that are very different from anything humanity has known in our subsistence, agricultural, industrial, and post-industrial economies.

Economic security does not come from attending to the formal economy alone. We must also consider the care work undertaken within households, the provisioning of common good resources, and the enabling infrastructures (both material and regulatory) provided by governments. Though many of our traditional compartmentalized approaches and entrenched interests mitigate against it, broader approaches to understanding what promotes economic security could become commonplace in 2050.

Education supports the creation of long-term economic well-being for individuals, their families, and their communities when it takes a broad view that looks at the world of formal, waged work and goes well beyond. Flexibility in the face of uncertain employment futures must be built into the new social contract for the futures of education.

Part II
Renewing education

In 1921, educators from all over the world gathered in Calais, France for the first congress of the New Education Fellowship, a group whose work grew over the next two decades and helped shape the establishment of UNESCO and its educational mandate. At their first meeting they announced the emergence of 'a new education for a new era'.

The goal of this Report is no less ambitious. However, it is not just another call to start again. We need new pedagogies, new approaches to curriculum, a recommitment to teachers, a new vision of school, and a new appreciation of the times and spaces of education. But this does not mean we get rid of what we already have. We must, instead, examine the best pedagogical and educational traditions, renew this heritage, and add promising new elements that will help us shape the interlinked futures of humanity and the living planet.

Over the past century and more, societies and families placed their hopes in compulsory schooling to deliver the promise of education to their children. And, worldwide, schools came to be organized in remarkably similar ways. Although these characteristics have different configurations in different regions and cultures, they have spread and prevailed around the globe, flattening the diversity of educational experiences that marked earlier eras. The social contract for education established in the nineteenth and twentieth centuries translated into the following principles for organizing learning: First, education was seen as a pedagogical project rooted in lessons given by teachers within the structure of classes and classrooms that, despite the shared learning setting, prioritized individual accomplishment. Second, education was imparted through a curriculum that was organized as a grid of subjects. Third, teaching was conceived as a solitary practice that relied on the professional competency of a single teacher to orchestrate effective learning, usually within a discipline. Fourth, schools were organized according to a model that had considerable architectural, organizational, and procedural similarities regardless of context.

And, fifth, education was organized to teach groups of students of similar age in specialized institutions that operated at a relative distance from their families and communities, and ended when children and young people were thought ready for their future lives as adults.

A new social contract for education must reinforce education as a public endeavour, shared social commitment, as one of the most important human rights, and as one of the most important responsibilities of states and citizens. In turn, one of the key roles of education is to educate citizens who advance human rights. This entails building the capabilities that make students autonomous and ethical thinkers and doers. It means equipping them to collaborate with others and developing their agency, responsibility, empathy, critical and creative thinking, alongside a full range of social and emotional skills. To align education with this ambitious vision it is necessary to establish new ways of organizing learning. Education can be considered as one of the central elements for helping humanity achieve peace with one another and with the Earth. Part II of this Report proposes ways to realize a new social contract that advances the right to education, and strengthens education as a common good and collective endeavour that augments our human capacity to care and cooperate.

The guiding principles for dialogue and action put forward across these five chapters grow out of the global consultation the Commission engaged in over the past two years, and which was particularly attentive to the contributions of young people. But these guiding principles also derive from a well-established scientific knowledge base in education that has been built through decades of research and reflection, both in academic and professional communities.

Turning these guiding principles into policy and practice lies in the hands of all those who read this Report. Every learner, citizen, educator and parent has the potential and possibility to work locally, and to connect with others near and far, to transform day-to-day educational practices, institutions and systems. These many large and small acts of collaboration and partnership are what will ultimately transform the future. The aim of the Commission in producing this Report is to broaden the discussion with ideas and principles for this transformation. The making of the report was a collaborative endeavour. The realization of its ideas will be another.

Chapter 3

Pedagogies of cooperation and solidarity

Genuine education must engage the purposes and energies of those being educated. To secure such engagement, teachers must build relationships of care and trust, and within such relationships, students and teachers construct educational objectives cooperatively.

Nel Noddings, *Philosophy of Education*.

In a new social contract for education, pedagogy should be rooted in cooperation and solidarity, building the capacities of students and teachers to work together in trust to transform the world.

Reimagining the future together calls for pedagogies that foster cooperation and solidarity. *How* we learn must be determined by *why* and *what* we learn. A foundational commitment to teaching and advancing human rights means that we must respect the rights of the learner. We must create occasions for people to learn from one another and value one another across all lines of difference whether of gender, religion, race, sexual identity, social class, disability, nationality, etc. Respecting the dignity of people means teaching them to think for themselves, not what or how to think. This means creating opportunities for students to discover their own sense of purpose and to determine what will be a flourishing life for them. At the same time, we collectively need to build a world where such lives can be realized and this means collaborating to build capacities to improve the world.

Pedagogies of cooperation and solidarity should be based on shared principles of non-discrimination, respect for diversity, and reparative justice, and framed by an ethic of care and of reciprocity. Of necessity, they require participatory, collaborative, problem-posing, and interdisciplinary, intergenerational, and intercultural learning. Such pedagogies are both nourished by, and contribute to, the knowledge commons and continue throughout life, recognizing the unique opportunities of each age and level of education.

Active learning recognizes the importance of developing conceptual as well as procedural knowledge. It acknowledges the need to engage cognitively and emotionally in order to cultivate knowledge, the ability to translate knowledge into action, and the disposition to act. Pedagogical practices are based on generations of experience, reflection, and study, all of which need to be continually recast in the light of the exigencies of the present and the future. Powerful motivators of learning are authenticity (understanding the relationship of what is learned to the world we inhabit) and relevancy (understanding the relationship of what we learn to our values). Project- and problem-based learning provide many opportunities for authentic, relevant learning and tap into our intrinsic interest in knowing and understanding.

The first half of this chapter highlights possible approaches to pedagogy based on cooperation and solidarity including pedagogy that is collaborative, interdisciplinary and problem-posing; that treasures and sustains diversity; that invites students to unlearn prejudices and divisions; that heals the wounds of injustice; and that uses meaningful assessment to pedagogical advantage. These approaches are relevant to education in all settings including in informal and nonformal settings like museums, libraries, summer camps, and community centres among others. The chapter then examines the application of these pedagogical priorities to the unique needs and opportunities of formal education at each stage of life: supporting early childhood foundations and collaboration throughout childhood, releasing the unique capacities of adolescents and youth, and renewing the mission of higher education. The chapter concludes with 2050 guiding principles for dialogue and action of interest, in particular, to educators and education systems managers and planners, which include: forming deeper connections with the wider world, fostering collaboration, building ethical foundations, developing empathy, and using assessment to support learning.

Reimagining pedagogical approaches

Pedagogy is relational. Both teachers and learners are transformed through the pedagogical encounter as they learn from each other. The productive tension between simultaneous individual and collective transformation defines pedagogical encounters. Our inner lives influence our environments, and at the same time are deeply affected by them.

Students, teachers, and knowledge form the classic pedagogical triangle. Teaching and learning are both nourished by, and contribute to, the knowledge commons. Through pedagogical encounters, education also connects us to humanity's common heritage of accumulated knowledge and provides opportunities to enrich it.

Today this triangle needs to be envisioned within the wider world. We need pedagogies that help us to learn *in* and *with* the world and improve it. Such pedagogies call for us to continue to learn about the dignity of every person and the great accomplishment that the right to conscience and freedom of thought represent – but to unlearn human exceptionalism and possessive individualism. They should be based on ethics of reciprocity and care and recognize interdependencies among individuals, groups and among species. They should encourage us to understand the importance of what we share in common and the systemic interdependencies that bind us to one another and the planet.

> Together, teachers and students need to form a community of knowledge-seekers and builders.

Together, teachers and students need to form a community of knowledge-seekers and builders nourished by and contributing to humanity's knowledge commons. This entails thinking about what exists and what can be built and acknowledging that everyone, teachers and students alike, has the right to see themselves as capable of generating knowledge with others.

Behind all pedagogical intentions lie questions of meaning and purpose. What are teachers proposing to students as actions and interactions and for what purpose? What meaning do students give to their own learning efforts? .

Transformational pedagogical encounters enable dialogue with classmates, peers and community members. The art, science, and craft of teaching is wielded effectively by teachers who give students opportunities to explore, create and interact with the known and the unknown, nurturing curiosity and interest. The following sections present promising strategies for translating a new social contract for education into pedagogical encounters.

Interdisciplinary problem-oriented collaborative learning

The future will present students with novel problems and opportunities. Awareness that the world will continue to change can be built into curricula and pedagogy by intentionally cultivating learners' capacities for problem-recognition and problem-solving. Problem-posing education engages students in projects, initiatives, and activities that require discovery and collaboration. Facing clear goals and objectives, students must transcend disciplinary boundaries to find viable and imaginative solutions. A focus on problems and projects in learning can ground students in their personal experience, help them see the world as changeable rather than fixed, build knowledge and discernment, and develop students' powers of literacy and meaningful expression.

The 2030 Agenda for Sustainable Development recognizes students' needs to consider a wide range of converging approaches to the problems that they face. SDG target 4.7, in particular, identifies students as global citizens who require the knowledge and competencies to build sustainable futures in an increasingly interdependent world. Looking to and beyond 2050, nurturing these capacities becomes even more important. The SDGs themselves, offer a framework around which to structure problem- and project-based interdisciplinary learning that helps students develop the capabilities to advance the full range of goals.

A focus on shared problems and projects means priority is given to study, inquiry and co-construction. Individuals' knowledge and capacity expand in connection to others, by highlighting how agency is shared as well as the diverse and networked dimensions of knowledge itself. Project- and problem-based approaches do not diminish the need for knowledge, but rather place knowledge within a living set of dynamics and applications.

Many of the most rewarding forms of education take place in environments enriched by a constant flux of ideas beyond typical subject boundaries. Pedagogies need to reflect interdisciplinarity, just as the problems and puzzles of the planet do not limit themselves to the confines of disciplinary boundaries. Yet, as there are many possible solutions to a given problem, pedagogical approaches must be selected that also cultivate the values and principles of interdependence and solidarity. Service learning and community engagement soften the walls between classroom and community, challenge students' assumptions, and connect them with broader systems, processes, and experiences beyond their own experiences. It is vital that students approach service with a spirit of humility, free of paternalism, especially in connection with those who may face different material challenges. Service learning must not be a pursuit limited to the most privileged; all learners can contribute to a dialogical process of advancing well-being within their communities. Service learning has the potential to enlist solidarity as a central principle to problem-solving pedagogies, rather than favouring the solutions which are simply the most expedient or self-interested.

Treasuring and sustaining diversity and pluralism

To reimagine the future together is to envision a society where diversity and pluralism are strengthened and enrich our common humanity. We need education that allows us to go beyond the space we already inhabit and that accompanies us into the unknown.

A pedagogy of solidarity must be grounded in an education that is inclusive and intercultural – one that accounts for all forms of discrimination and segregation in access, including children and youth with special educational needs, and those who face bigotry based on race, gender identity, class, disability, religion or nationality. The right to inclusion, based on each person's diverse realities, is among the most crucial of all human rights. Pedagogy should welcome students into the educational community and help them develop the skills to be inclusive and appreciative of the dignity of all others. Pedagogy without inclusion weakens education as a common good and undermines the possibility of a world in which the dignity and the human rights of all are upheld.

And learning itself must value diversity, difference, and pluralism as a starting point and enable students to directly confront bigotry and discrimination. No single people or perspective can possibly possess all the solutions to the complex, multifaceted challenges facing the planet. Pedagogies of solidarity must also recognize and redress the systematic exclusions and erasures imposed by racism, sexism, colonialism, and authoritarian regimes around the world. Without the valuing of different cultures and epistemologies, different ways of living and seeing the world – it is impossible to build a pedagogy of solidarity. A pedagogy of solidarity mobilizes these differences in real time.

> Pedagogies of solidarity must also recognize and redress the systematic exclusions and erasures imposed by racism, sexism, colonialism, and authoritarian regimes around the world.

The increasing mobility of human beings across the world, whether through choice or forced displacement, has created new pedagogical realities that bring the cultural and racial diversity of the world directly into classrooms and educational settings. Teachers are working in new environments with students who have diverse educational histories, languages and cultures. Pedagogies of respect, inclusion, belonging, peacebuilding, and conflict transformation go beyond merely acknowledging or tolerating difference. They must support students to sit side by side one another and work together. Education that allows young people to understand and link their pasts, presents and futures, analyze the inequalities that shape their experiences, stand up to exclusion and marginalization, is one of the best preparations for unknown futures.

The world is rich in multicultural and multi-ethnic societies and education should promote intercultural citizenship. Beyond learning about the value of diversity, education should promote the skills, values and conditions needed for horizontal, democratic dialogue with diverse groups, knowledge systems and practices. The basis for intercultural citizenship is the affirmation of one´s cultural identities. Knowing who you are is the starting point for respecting others. Intercultural education should not be used as a tool for the assimilation of cultural minorities, indigenous peoples, or other marginalized groups to the dominant society, but rather to promote more balanced and democratic power relations within our societies. We need pedagogies that generate mutually enriching exchanges of knowledge, practices, and solutions, based on complementarity, reciprocity and respect.

It is through our differences that we educate each other, and through our shared contexts that what we learn accrues meaning. It is important to distinguish 'pedagogical differentiation', which attends to differences within a common space, from the hyper-personalized learning defined by AI, that decontextualizes and removes learners from public and collective spaces and relationships. Our differences need to be synthesized into greater mutual understanding.

Pedagogy always takes place in a space-time that is emergent, intrinsically heterogenous, and always under construction. There can be two identical copies of the same book, but there are no two identical ways of reading it. There can be two identical lesson plans or curriculum units, but there are no two identical ways of teaching. This idea urges caution with regard to some of the ed tech trends that are ascendent in the 'global education industry'. We need a human complement and counterbalance to the growing ubiquity of automated systems that employ AI and promise to provide readymade paths for teaching, learning, or evaluation. Where utilized, the limitations of such techniques should remain clearly in view, as well as the risks of reinforcing existing power structures and problematic assumptions that tend to marginalize those who 'perform' learning differently than others. Our energies need to focus on the risk-taking practices of empathy, ethics, solidarity, co-construction and justice, which need to be patiently taught and learned, and for which there are no technological short-cuts. These are deeply human acts best facilitated by human beings.

Learning to unlearn divisiveness

Pedagogies of cooperation and solidarity require more than embracing and committing to sustaining diversity. They require unlearning of bias, prejudice, and divisiveness. Indeed, knowledge is not a 'finished product' packaged for transmission. Pedagogy can illuminate how knowledge has been historically constituted and dialogically constructed, rather than just promote its transmission.

Cultural resources are a key part of our relationships with knowledge. Educational policy has increasingly aimed to address inequities of gender, race, ethnicity, religion, residence, nationality, documentation status, disability, sexual identity or social class of origin. However, less attention is paid to the silencing and exclusion of collective memories, aspirations, cultural traditions, and indigenous knowledges in education and the knowledge commons. Learning to critically examine established dominant knowledge is central to a pedagogy of solidarity. We must learn to unlearn.

> Cultural resources are a key part of our relationships with knowledge.

Coming together, exploring the unknown realities of each other, and critically engaging with established knowledge can be difficult, even dangerous. All educational environments should be places of safety, even of refuge, where learners are encouraged to experiment, dare, fail, and create. Pedagogy should stimulate imagination and creative thinking, and promote intellectual freedom, which includes the right to make mistakes and learn from them. Environments that allow and enable this, sometimes messy, learning work are crucial to developing true understanding, empathy, ethical frameworks, and an appreciation of differences in understanding and points of view. Educators should work to create environments that allow students to be vulnerable and free from fear of judgment when they grapple with new ideas and difficult knowledge.

Learning to heal the wounds of injustice

Knowing is intimately connected with feeling. Human intelligence is directly connected with consciousness and affect. In recognizing this interconnection, an immense field of educational possibility opens up. We can counter any single, monocultural vision and value a set of other ways of knowing and feeling, different ways of living, different epistemologies. The decolonization of pedagogy can be achieved through constructive, horizontal relationships among epistemological assumptions and perspectives.

We also foresee the importance of education for reparative justice and solidarity. Solidarity has always been vital to cohesive society-building and has recently become an important pedagogical aim in both formal and less formal learning. Pedagogies of solidarity have helped to transcend oppressive regimes by building consciousness of the need for collective awareness and action. Educational work can focus on an expansive solidarity through sympathy, empathy, and compassion to create possibilities for healing. Empathy, as the ability to attend to another and feel with them, together with ethics, is integral to justice. Learning to heal past injustices needs to be a critical component of pedagogies of cooperation and solidarity.

Strengthening meaningful assessment

At its most fundamental level, assessment is a natural process of making systematic empirical observations about the progress and challenges students face in their learning. When encoded, standardized, and used to classify and stream students, assessment must proceed with caution. All assessment decisions are based on a set of assumptions, and these must be in harmony with the assumptions of the curriculum and pedagogy they follow.

When considered in light of pedagogies of cooperation and solidarity, educators must clearly identify pedagogical goals that lend themselves to measurement, and those that do not. Much important learning cannot be measured or counted. To say that something cannot be quantified, however, is not to say that meaningful progress can never be observed. A goal of cooperation, for example, can be empirically observed when a group of students navigate through processes of negotiation, conflict resolution, and experimentation, and throughout this process, increase their capacities to listen to different points of view, give and take constructive criticism, and provide ample opportunities for each other's contributions.

Theories of assessment abound, and they will continue to be debated in the coming decades. Educators and policy-makers must bear in mind that every test, assessment, and scale, leaves a pedagogical trace. Pressures to push high-stakes testing regimes to ever younger students must be resisted as they limit schools' and teachers' pedagogical choices, encourage competition, and reduce opportunities for cooperation and co-construction. It is true that some element of contest can encourage students to reach higher degrees of excellence both individually and collectively. However, teachers should have the latitude to determine when competitive activities can be drawn on to serve specific pedagogical goals, rather than responding to external pressures that relate to benchmarks that are often distant and unknown.

Measurement and assessment are important for understanding the effects of education, but indicators must be appropriate, meaningful, and carefully thought out. The global expansion of private tutoring, often referred to as 'shadow education', is a prime example of how a narrow focus on limited measures of educational achievement (often emphasizing short term recall and low order cognitive skills) diminishes the curriculum necessary to prepare students to achieve richer purposes individually and socially. Looking to the future, it is clear that there is a need to reverse the adverse impacts of growing competition in education, and the narrow focus on instruction which high-stakes tests have induced.

Pedagogical journeys at every age and stage

Participatory and cooperative pedagogies are relevant to all levels of education, as well as to all educational settings, both formal and informal. These pedagogies can occur at any stage of life, though the opportunities for collaboration and pedagogical co-construction vary according to different stages of human growth and development. Globally, educational levels are often classified as early childhood, primary, secondary, and higher education. While there are multiple human intelligences, and much diversity in human interests and ways of learning, and while humans do not develop linearly, there are developmentally appropriate ways to support learning, and sound ways to honour differences among learners and personalize learning. The common notion that education proceeds through different phases speaks to a journey, replete with purpose, that needs to become available to all. The remainder of this chapter takes a closer look at the pedagogical dilemmas and possibilities that emerge at each level and life-cycle stage, with a focus on how participatory and collaborative pedagogies can be employed.

Supporting the foundations of early childhood

Young children can possess an ability to bear witness to the world in ways that renew it. Few can see things afresh the way a child can. Children's attention to the experiences of others and the curiosity they exhibit towards a world that is unknown and pregnant with possibility provide an example to people of all ages. A commitment to the potential of this period of emergence into the new should characterize early childhood education and, indeed, all educational settings.

Quality early childhood education must be a priority for every society. The early years of human life are a time of considerable brain plasticity and development when an extraordinary amount of essential physical, cognitive, social, and emotional growth takes place. A strong body of educational research points to the importance of early childhood education as a key foundation of all future learning and flourishing.

A pedagogical orientation towards cooperation and interdependence is implicit in much early childhood education. At this stage close human connections, exploration and play should be emphasized. It is important to remember that developmental precursors are not necessarily identical to the abilities and dispositions later developed. Some of the best scientific inquiry can originate in a simple fascination, for example, with insects. Imaginative roleplay can be a powerful base for sophisticated literacy. As early childhood educators tell us, what looks like a frivolous game is often the intensely serious business of understanding oneself and the world.

The environmental and climate change challenges now facing the planet have important ramifications for early childhood education. While individual child-centred pedagogies predominate in many settings, these approaches need revision to reflect that, like all human beings, children are part of a more-than-human world. Early childhood education plays an important role in developing children's relationships to place and to other living beings. To best support children to live well in future worlds, we must support early childhood pedagogies oriented towards critique, challenge and the creation of new possibilities.

The connections between home and school are often strongest at this level. Families play a key role and need to be supported to help children thrive and enhance their physical, socio-emotional and cognitive development. We know that human learning occurs in continuous interaction with the environment. Optimal learning environments provide infants and young children with ample stimulation in their home language (or languages). Shared book reading and the use of rich vocabulary in everyday interactions helps to develop the literacy skills that are a fundamental component of education. Plugging children into televisions, tablets or other electronic devices is a poor substitute for the quality interactive social experiences they need. Governments and businesses need to strengthen parental leave policies. For parents and families a supported and early childhood education is considerably advanced, when daycare centres, libraries, museums, community centres, and parks are well-funded and treated as essential public services. The proverb 'it takes a village to raise a child' has been banalized through overuse but this is, in part, because the core idea resonates so well with so many: early childhood education is something we achieve together.

Unfortunately, in many societies early childhood education is not recognized as a public responsibility in the same way that primary education is. There are not enough or adequate early childhood centres. Educators at this level are often poorly compensated, as if the only dimension that matters is to provide physical care. As a result, some of the most significant inequalities develop in early childhood, as families with higher education levels and greater resources provide high quality educational experiences for their children of the type often unavailable to those who rely on inadequate public centres that are underfunded and have poorly paid and less well-prepared educators. Governments must ensure adequate and sustained public funding for quality early childhood education to ensure the learning, growth and development of all children from birth.

The ingrained inequalities and prejudices that divide our societies are learned early and more often through observation than from direct instruction. For instance, if men continue to only represent, on average, less than 2% of early childhood educators, boys learn implicitly that they need not aspire to care for the young and vulnerable. If home and ancestral languages are not immersive in the earliest years, children risk losing that precious link to family members, and the cultural ways of knowing and communicating that connect them with their heritage across space and time. In many societies, where schools have been used as a tool to assimilate and repress, there has been a much-needed reckoning to redress and shutter oppressive institutions. Measures must be taken to ensure that future early childhood education initiatives avoid perpetuating cultural alienation and prejudice. Early childhood pedagogies must affirm and strengthen individual and collective cultural identities and promote intercultural dialogue based on appreciation of diversity.

Collaborative education for all children

Despite the massive expansion of access to primary education across the world between 1990 and 2020, there remains much to be done to strengthen quality in every area of learning, making full use of participatory and collaborative pedagogies.

Unfortunately, in too many schools and societies, the natural curiosity and inquisitive tendencies of early childhood become less and less encouraged as children advance to higher grades and have fewer opportunities to play, explore, collaborate, and connect. The value of individual practice of newly acquired understandings and skills across the arts and sciences cannot be denied. But arguably, too much time dedicated to isolated individual work at the primary level limits key opportunities for co-construction, cooperation, and problem-solving.

Nonetheless, there are increasing examples of collaborative and cooperative pedagogical initiatives, both within and beyond schools and formal educational institutions. In some regions, community schools represent creative responses of local communities to envision new educational possibilities and respond to local exigencies while tapping into deep cultural reservoirs. In other contexts, educational programmes, sometimes recognized as 'non-formal', that partner with schools are bolstering opportunities for collaborative education and cultural understanding, by connecting with local elders, community leaders, and knowledge-keepers.

Propelling the potential of adolescents and youth

Youth face many different realities around the world today. These include the different risks in accessing their rights to education, to protection from violence, female genital mutilation, and early marriage, and the increasing burdens of contributing to family livelihood. Others face increasing social isolation, mental health challenges, and crises of identity and purpose. To varying degrees, education over the past few decades has helped to mitigate challenges at this stage of life by fostering healthy social interaction, peer relationships, and a sense of purpose in present and future endeavours. In other instances, however, education has exacerbated challenges through increasing academic pressures and social alienation.

The period of youth is comparable only to early childhood in the considerable neurological and physical changes experienced over the short period of a few years or months. Young people undergo significant leaps in intellectual powers, but cultural expectations and philosophies may differ as to whether and when they are ready to assume the full responsibilities of adulthood, or focus on preparing for the future. Education can provide the opportunity to do both simultaneously – challenging them, while providing sufficient opportunities to engage with the world in meaningful ways.

It is often at this stage of life when young people refine their interests, pursue their talents, and identify those vocations through which they may best seek their calling. To bridge the divide between theory and practice, between seemingly endless preparation and meaningful experience, and to instil a strong sense of purpose, are important pedagogical goals at this stage. Often characterized by a strong sense of justice, youth become keenly aware of the hypocrisy of adults. In this light, deficit narratives that label youth as inherently troublesome, rebellious, or dangerous to the social good are especially harmful and limit opportunities for intergenerational collaboration and support of this important, yet sometimes difficult, transition. When seen from a perspective of possibility, it is clear that precious few secondary educational models are sufficiently releasing the incredible potential of young people.

There is, however, promising reimagining of the future already underway. Increasingly, youth-led movements and organizations are approaching problems differently. Fridays For The Future, the Sunrise Movement, and thousands of similar efforts worldwide, are rehearsals for a different kind of future. In a number of countries in Latin America and South Asia, education systems and pedagogies that take marginalized rural youth as the starting point – rather than extending an urban-centric model – are reinstating a sense of pride in indigenous and ancestral practices in youth and adolescents. These, and many other examples, are a practical expression of education's capacity to support youth in creating a much wider range of prosperous and equitable futures.

> Increasingly, youth-led movements and organizations are approaching problems differently.

Renewing the mission of higher education

Along with the production of knowledge and outreach, education is part of the central mission of a university, yet in many places it has been neglected in recent decades as a result of the ways that higher education is organized, accredited, and financed. In some settings, professors are evaluated solely on their individual outputs, which is a symptom of valuing perceived productivity over the quality, relevance, and value of the contributions they make to teaching, mentoring, capacity-building, and fostering collaborative relationships with the communities they aim to benefit.

Pedagogy has moved to the background in many universities. It is possible that future universities will follow this path by delegating teaching tasks to other institutions or to special centres equipped with sophisticated AI-infused technologies. It is also possible to imagine a future of university renewal where the intergenerational educational mission is at the centre and is always posed in relation to knowledge and research. Technical and vocational institutions sometimes face the other side of this pendulum – teaching is often limited to training and technique, and deeper social, ethical, and conceptual questions are left beyond their purview. The development and application of productive capabilities so vital to our individual and collective futures, however, should be seen as a rich pedagogical field for the development of profound understanding, proficient skills, and reflexive attitudes.

To renew the educational mission of higher education it is necessary to have strong connections with primary and secondary education and to engage in pedagogical strategies beyond the traditional lecture and the transmission model it implies. Cooperative work between students, the development of research projects, problem-solving, individual study, seminar dialogue, field study, writing, action research, community projects – these and many other pedagogical forms need to infuse higher education. To move pedagogy back to the foreground, it is necessary to give greater value to the teaching work of professors and support their pedagogical learning and growth.

Values such as respect, empathy, equality, and solidarity must be core to the mission of universities, colleges, and technical institutes in the future. Higher education must foster ethics and support students to be better and more capable citizens with greater awareness of their civic and environmental responsibilities. Higher education must also be socio-culturally relevant. Appreciation of cultural diversity, a commitment to defend human rights, and intolerance for racism, sexism, classism, ethnocentrism and discrimination in all forms must be key educational objectives. Higher education that advances such values and principles goes beyond the confines of lecture halls and virtual spaces. It is ever-evolving in its content as it empowers individuals to become better versions of themselves, to take strong value systems forward, and to transform their environments.

Principles for dialogue and action

This chapter proposed that, in a new social contract for education, pedagogy should be organized around principles of cooperation and solidarity, building the capacities of students to work together to transform the world. As we look to 2050, there are four principles to guide the dialogue and action needed to take this recommendation forwards:

- **Interconnectedness and interdependencies should frame pedagogy.** The relationships that exist between teachers, students and knowledge are located in a wider world. All learners are connected to the world and all learning takes place *in* and *with* the world. Students need to learn how others' actions affect them and how their actions affect others and, for this reason, classrooms and schools should bring students in contact with others who are different from them.

- **Cooperation and collaboration must be taught and practiced in appropriate ways at different levels and ages.** Education builds the capacities of individuals to work together to transform themselves and the world when cooperation and collaboration are defining characteristics of learning communities. This can be as true for adult education and learning as it is for early childhood education.

- **Solidarity, compassion, ethics, and empathy should be ingrained in how we learn.** We should welcome the full diversity of humanity's cultural resources into education and extend from valuing diversity and pluralism to supporting and sustaining them. Teaching should focus on unlearning bias, prejudice and divisiveness. Empathy – the ability to attend to others and feel with them – is essential for building pedagogies of solidarity.

● **Assessment should be aligned to these aims and be meaningful for student growth and learning.** Exams, tests, and other assessment instruments should harmonize with educational purposes and intents. A great deal of important learning cannot be easily measured or counted. Teacher-driven formative assessments that promote student learning should be prioritized. We must reduce the importance of competitive, high-stakes standardized assessment.

At local, national, regional and global levels we all need to work together to make pedagogies of cooperation and solidarity common in 2050, available to everyone.

Chapter 4

Curricula and the evolving knowledge commons

> The real difficulty is that people have no idea of what education truly is. We assess the value of education in the same manner as we assess the value of land or of shares in the stock-exchange market. We want to provide only such education as would enable the student to earn more. We hardly give any thought to the improvement of the character of the educated. The girls, we say, do not have to earn; so why should they be educated? As long as such ideas persist there is no hope of our ever knowing the true value of education.

Mahatma Gandhi, 'True National Education', 1907.

In a new social contract for education, curricula should grow out of the wealth of common knowledge and embrace ecological, intercultural and interdisciplinary learning that helps students access and produce knowledge while building their capacity to critique and apply it.

A new relationship must be established between education and the knowledge, capabilities, and values that it cultivates. This starts with examination of the capabilities and knowledge that enable students to build a peaceful, just and sustainable world and maps backwards along the curricular pathways that help them develop those capacities. To make a new social contract for education together, we need to think about curricula as much more than a grid of school subjects. Curricular questions need to be framed in relation to building competencies and two vital processes that are always present in education: the acquisition of knowledge as part of the common heritage of humanity, and the collective creation of new knowledge and new worlds.

Trends and theories abound about what and how to teach and learn. Learning designs can be framed as child-centred or subject-centred, learner-centred or teacher-centred. Knowledge can be categorized as academic or applied, scientific or humanist, generalist or specialized. While each approach has something to offer, new paradigms and perspectives are needed to reflect the increased complexity of the interactions of knowledge with the world. Educators should approach the acquisition of knowledge by simultaneously asking: what should be learned, and what should be unlearned? This is a particularly important question at this critical juncture in which the mainstream development and economic growth paradigm needs to be rethought in the light of the ecological crisis.

What should be learned, and what should be unlearned?

This chapter examines these questions by starting with a brief discussion of the knowledge commons arguing that it must be reconceptualized as the inheritance of all humanity and broadened to include diverse ways of knowing and understanding. The emphasis placed here on knowledge does not mean content must dominate. Knowledge is always evolving in how it is generated, applied, and re-examined. This chapter issues an open call to intensify our collective efforts at building widespread capabilities for further knowledge generation and application to the complex questions and challenges facing humanity.

Education can smoothly embrace both *knowing that* and *knowing how*. Content mastery does not need to compete with application, skills, or the development of capabilities. Instead, foundational knowledge and skills can intertwine and complement one another. For some decades now, curricular debates have swayed between content knowledge and competences. The time is ripe to configure a new set of dynamics that supports a strong knowledge approach while not renouncing what has been gained by the project-based and problem-based approaches, for example, in terms of a close dialogue with contemporary problems and making curricular learning relevant for students.

The chapter looks at the interactions between the knowledge commons and curricula, arguing that it is necessary to understand the inherent interconnectedness of knowledge around such capabilities as literacy, numeracy, scientific inquiry, the arts and citizenship. It concludes with 2050 guiding principles for dialogue and action, of equal interest to teachers and educators as to curriculum developers, which include enhancing access to the knowledge commons and prioritizing climate change education, scientific enquiry and human rights.

Participation in the knowledge commons

Curricula should approach knowledge as a great human accomplishment that belongs to everyone. At the same time, curricula must account for the fact that the knowledge commons retains significant exclusions and appropriations that require correction in the light of justice. Knowledge is never complete and educators should invite and enable students to participate in its further co-creation. In too many forms of education, knowledge transmission has been more related to erecting barriers and reproducing inequalities than to enriching all of humanity and our shared, collective well-being. Education that prioritizes deliberate, thoughtful engagement with knowledge helps to build epistemic, cognitive and reparative justice.

We should resist knowledge hegemonies and foster possibilities for creativity, border-crossing and experimentation that can only come through the full inclusion of humanity's diverse epistemological perspectives. Inherited prejudices, arbitrary hierarchies and exploitative notions must be rejected. Education can enhance people's abilities to build on the knowledge commons with each generation contributing their own reinventions of the world. Curricula must develop and refine our capacities to interact and engage with knowledge. Literacy, numeracy, and scientific inquiry, for example, are crucial for enabling people to make sense of and contribute to their world and must be broadened and deepened everywhere.

One part of designing curricula that are open and common is to resist the pressures that construct disciplinary and subject boundaries as fixed or essential limits. Instead, energies are better spent thinking about the complexity of the world and the historical quality of knowledge systems. Bringing this perspective on multiplicity and transversality into educational curricula helps us build on sturdy knowledge foundations in new and productive directions.

In all these essential areas of work it must be remembered that a curriculum is never organized with 'completed knowledge' but rather informed by knowledge that connects different generations, passes on cultural heritage, and makes room for review and update. This awareness should lead us to teach all subjects from a historical framing and as part of an intergenerational conversation – one that students will contextualize and give new meaning to through their learning.

Curricular priorities for educational futures

We must move from a narrow view of education to a serious engagement with its greater purposes. Curricular approaches should link the cognitive domain with problem-solving skills, innovation and creativity, and also incorporate the development of social and emotional learning and learning about oneself. The types of engagement with educational curricula put forth here aim to unite and liberate. The curricular priorities below are intended to support inclusion, gender equality, the dismantling of injustices, and the broad struggle against inequalities needed to reimagine our futures together.

Curricula for a damaged planet

How do we live well together on a planet that is under increasing stress? Education needs to respond to climate change and environmental destruction by preparing students to adapt to, mitigate, and reverse climate change. We must rethink and reimagine curricula to instil a fundamentally new way of looking at the place of humans as part of the planet. In all areas students should encounter the urgency of environmental sustainability – living within planetary boundaries and not compromising future generations or the natural ecosystems of which we are all a part. The art of living respectfully and responsibly on a planet that has been damaged by human activity can permeate all subject areas. We can no longer promulgate human exceptionalism or position the world as 'out there' as an external object to be learned about. Instead, we must motivate agency and action that is relational and collectively distributed. This means recognizing that we live and learn *with* the natural world.

Changing how we discuss the living world in educational curricula is one important strategy for rebalancing our relationships with it. However, curricula that teach students only to be protectors of nature are not sufficient. These approaches still presuppose a division between human beings and their environment.

Special emphasis should be given to climate change education. Effective and relevant climate change education is gender responsive, takes an intersectional approach to social and economic factors across time and geography, and fosters critical thinking and active civic engagement. It acknowledges that current global levels of production and consumption are unsustainable and recognizes that wealthy countries play a disproportionate role in contributing to climate change, and it is largely poorer countries who bear the brunt of its effects. It also recognizes colonial and industrial legacies that have disrupted harmonious relationships between the human and more-than-human world in innumerable indigenous communities. Climate change education should empower students to consider just and sustainable alternatives and to take action in their local communities and, in solidarity, beyond.

> Curricula must enable re-learning how we are interconnected with a living, damaged planet.

Curricula must enable re-learning how we are interconnected with a living, damaged planet and unlearning the human arrogance that has resulted in massive biodiversity loss, the destruction of entire ecosystems, and irreversible climate change. We can consider 'rewilding' curricula by developing deep connectivity with the natural world and embracing the biosphere as an educational space. We can reimagine curricula to include intergenerational conversations around knowledge practices that are relevant for living with the planet, such as those taking place in numerous youth-led and community-led movements.

Feminist perspectives and indigenous voices have much to contribute in navigating this crucial moment. Indigenous knowledge systems raise students' consciousness that they are part of the natural community, and can draw from the values, practices, and spiritual consciousness that have enabled humanity to live in harmony with the planet for millennia. Every living being has a role in a sustainable ecosystem and the capacity to live in harmony – taking no more or less than is needed for mutual existence and well-being – can be learned through education. Feminist perspectives argue against the adversarial premises that underlie much of humanity's abusive and exploitative relationship with nature. Economic models premised on ever-expanding consumption and domination of the Earth perpetuate a reckless fiction. There are thresholds of economic performance that we need to learn to live within, to achieve the fine balance of social well-being and ecological sustainability.

> The capacity to live in harmony – taking no more or less than is needed for mutual existence and well-being – can be learned through education.

Social justice is inseparable from ecological justice. We cannot learn to care for the living planet without also learning to care for one another. Care is not only related to affections or attitudes but has a central cognitive component. The curriculum should include a profound knowledge of how scientific and technical approaches to the planetary are produced, how the Earth and the universe are documented, visualized and understood, and how knowledge practices are intertwined in the practices of living on this damaged planet. The discussion about the strengths and limitations of information tools and of individual and collective projects is important to foster relevant curricula that raise collective awareness and mobilization towards defending the possibility of complex life on the planet.

An ethic of care enables us to understand ourselves as interconnected persons who are simultaneously capable and vulnerable. It forces us to reflect on how we affect and are affected by others and the world. It is important that curricula nurture an ethic of care for everyone regardless of their gender expression in order to address the traditionally gendered imbalances of caregiving in domestic and public life. The reproductive knowledge of raising children, caring for the ill and elderly, maintaining a home, and responding to the physical and psychological needs of families so vital to society, also belongs to humanity's knowledge commons, and naturally extend to the ways in which we treat and care for our damaged and vulnerable planet. Caring-about, caring-for, care-giving and care-receiving must be included in curricula that enable us to reimagine our interdependent futures together.

Integrating knowing and feeling

Curricula need to treat students as complete human beings who, young and old, bring curiosity and thirst for learning into educational settings. They also bring emotions, fears, insecurities, confidence and passion. Curricula that teach people as whole human beings support their social and emotional interactions with the world and make them more capable of collaborating with others to improve it.

Neuroscience shows that knowing and feeling are part of the same cognitive processes which play out, not in individual isolation, but in direct, extended relationships with others. Tremendous educational work has been accomplished in the last decade in particular, to bring social and emotional learning into the mainstream of educational practice in some parts of the world. The best approaches to social and emotional learning in curricula encompass social, emotional, cognitive, and ethical domains of students' identities. They connect individuals' developmental trajectories to their implications for broader social cohesion. Learning to empathize, to cooperate, to address prejudice and bias and to navigate conflict are valuable in every society, particularly those grappling with longstanding divisions.

> Learning to empathize, to cooperate, to address prejudice and bias and to navigate conflict are valuable in every society.

Social and emotional learning practices are heterogenous and need appropriate contextualization. They require consciously designed learning experiences, bonding with teachers, positive peer experiences, intergenerational understanding and community involvement. Mindfulness, compassion, and critical inquiry all support powerful social and emotional learning. It must be recognized however that such learning places extra demands on teachers and that they must be supported to accomplish this work. As we look to 2050 we cannot afford to short-change investments in social and emotional learning – it is fundamental to human creativity, morality, judgment, and action to address future challenges.

Treating learners as complete human beings recognizes the needs and capacities of their bodies through all stages of life. Healthy futures require quality physical education that promotes fundamental movement skills inclusive of all ability types, genders and backgrounds. Quality physical education can boost assurance and self-confidence, coordination and control, team work, responsiveness to the demands of one's physical environment and improved verbal and non-verbal communication. Physical education must not be seen as the exclusive pursuit of the most physically competent, and an overreliance on competition and comparison can exclude broader participation. It should be premised on the value that every learner can enjoy a healthy and active lifestyle, and that developing empathetic and respectful relationships through shared activity, can contribute to learning to interact together throughout life.

Likewise, taking a holistic educational approach to human sexuality that is age appropriate and culturally attuned recognizes the importance of social and emotional literacy, promotes discussions of respect and consent, builds understanding of the physical and emotional processes during physical maturity, and promotes respectful relationships and equality. A future in which girls in many parts of the world continue to feel excluded through the possibility of physical or sexual harm – a reality faced especially by adolescent girls in many contexts, preventing their continuation into secondary schooling – is unfathomable. Maternal and child health, mortality, and well-being are also closely related to comprehensive sexuality education. Alongside broader forms of health and well-being, education premised on the values of equality, respect, and self-confidence translates into enhanced capacity for just and equitable human relationships throughout all societies.

Broadening literacies and creating plurilingual futures

Our capacity for, and relationship to, language has been central to human identity, knowledge, and being in the world, enabling us to communicate and build on what others have learned in order to reach new heights of understanding. Language is fundamental to the existence of the knowledge commons itself. Over the past decades, education has enabled each generation to be more capable of reading and writing than the one before. In order to broaden participation and inclusion, however, the future of literacy must go beyond reading and writing to reinforce the capacities of understanding and expression in all their forms – orally, textually, and through a widening diversity of media, including storytelling and the arts.

Certainly, writing and speech are not the only ways in which humans have recorded their experiences and passed them on to newer generations, and images and bodily knowledge should enter the curriculum in much more decisive ways. But oral and written knowledge have played an undeniable role in human history; in particular, writing as a technology of human knowledge enabled inscriptions to circulate and travel, expanding the possibilities of accumulation and codifying human experience in many different cultures. This knowledge should not be lost for future generations.

Literacy is directly connected to possibilities for future learning and social participation. It is not an 'on/off' switch, however, and our abilities to communicate and understand through language can strengthen continually throughout life. The future of literacy education can develop the abilities to read deeply, widely, and critically, to communicate clearly and effectively in speech and writing, and to listen with care, empathy, and discernment. For example, nurturing students' abilities and inclinations to read independently and seek out complex texts in all disciplines opens doors to a much wider range of possible futures through more equitable interactions with the knowledge commons. Literacy education can go beyond classrooms and schools to become a society-wide commitment. For example, recent efforts in some of India's media networks to make same-language subtitling a standard practice has been shown to strengthen reading skills more broadly, especially among those who may have learned basic reading and writing skills in school but require further practice and confidence.

Curricula are showing a shift from national monolingualism towards plurilingualism, via the teaching of foreign languages, indigenous languages and sign languages, among others. This is a shift that needs to be sustained and expanded. It is also important that child, youth, and adult learners have access to educational options of the highest quality in their home and ancestral languages. This is intuitive for the efficacy of teaching and learning, but it is also important in terms of basic respect and orienting education systems around the world towards respecting and sustaining diversity. In many settings, bilingual and plurilingual educational policies are necessary to support learners' cultural identities and to allow full participation in society. This entails support for minority indigenous languages as well as creating a foundation for students to acquire dominant or majority language proficiency.

Plurilingual education creates further opportunity for participation in global conversations, work, and cultures. In a world that is increasingly interdependent, there is an obvious value to learning different languages, and their individual and collective benefits are not restricted to communication. Plurilingualism obliges us all to become active translators between different signifying systems and develop more autonomy and criticality towards established patterns of meaning. Language is more than a means of communication; languages carry perspectives on the world and unique ways of understanding. Linguistic diversity is a key feature of humanity's shared knowledge commons; education has a key role to play in sustaining it.

> Linguistic diversity is a key feature of humanity's shared knowledge commons.

Enriching numeracy

Numeracy is no less vital to futures of education, as people are increasingly called upon to apply their mathematical knowledge and skills to a wide range of situations. Numeracy is a fruit of human capacities to observe patterns, to classify and organize sets, to count and to measure, to compare quantities, and to identify relationships between them. Numerical systems such as the decimal system and the binary system are foundational to modern communications, transactions, computing, and calculations. In addition to mastery of the basic operations of addition, subtraction, multiplication, and division, numeracy requires their application to a diverse range of contexts and problems. Examples are limitless, including securing one's financial health and planning, health risks and incidences of disease, agricultural yields and inputs, thresholds for pollution and environmental quality, local enterprises and community banking, and so on. When understood in context, numeracy powerfully unlocks our human capacities to understand changes over time, to make projections and plans for the future, to understand relationships, and to put trends in meaningful perspective.

Numeracy belongs to all peoples and culturally responsive numeracy curricula can build meaningful social and emotional bridges to formal education. For example, the traditional braiding procedure of the original inhabitants of Arctic Norway has been used with students to transition from understanding discrete integer patterns to more complex operations, such as multiplication and algebraic variables. Similarly, school boards in Canada have drawn on indigenous artists and educators to teach link artforms such as beading, basket-making and moccasin-making with mathematical concepts including algebraic, proportional and spatial reasoning. Connecting mathematical knowledge with students' cultural knowledge helps to engage the socio-emotional dimensions needed to overcome disconnects between home milieu and school environment. It also challenges the false notion that mathematics is 'Western', and reminds us of the wide and longstanding existence of ethnomathematical systems such as Inuit mathematics, Māori mathematics, and so on.

Drawing on the humanities

Knowledge and study of human society and culture are essential to helping students to learn a wide range of approaches to the problems that face them. The humanistic tradition, in its various guises, has contributed much of value to the world's collective knowledge commons on vital aspects of our collective world building. At the same time, we must recognize that what we know is partial and skewed. Reframing what it means to be human requires rebalancing our relationships with each other, with the living planet and with technology. The humanities need to adjust, and, as a systematic field of study, can help us adjust in turn.

History, for example, when taught effectively, can develop an invaluable perspective on social change and social systems, including discrimination and privilege. Understanding historical contingency, that things could be other than they are, is valuable for projecting future possibility. However, to unleash this potential, history must move well beyond a fascination with chronologies and go headfirst into discussions of what constitutes evidence and how we are to understand human and non-human experiences in the first place.

Finding new ways to connect and reconnect education to the humanities is also tremendously important for the future of democracy. Philosophy, history, literature, and the arts can connect us with purpose, an appreciation of critical inquiry, empathy, ethics, and imagination. All of these humanist approaches are also vital to strengthening students' 'futures literacy' – their ability to understand the role that the future plays in what they see and do. Becoming 'futures literate' is to become empowered to use the future more effectively and efficiently and be better able to prepare, recover, and invent as changes occur. This will be supported by also strengthening the humanities in public spaces both within and beyond formal education. Collectively reconnecting education to the humanities from the perspective of our common humanity, shared planet and collective aspiration towards justice is a crucial task.

Scientific inquiry and understanding

The desire to understand the physical universe is reflective of our human capacity to inquire and learn. The nature of scientific inquiry – to observe, to question, to predict, to test, to theorize, challenge and refine understanding – is an emanation of the human spirit. The roots of modern science trace back to the earliest stages of recorded history in every culture and society. Its fruits are enjoyed in every part of our physical and material lives, from medicine to technology. Within a broad curriculum that has strong humanistic values and embraces the whole person, particular emphasis should be given to scientific literacy and investigation.

In human history, science has been a significant knowledge practice that has implied a fundamental gain: the notion that truth is the result of procedures and agreements produced through a collective endeavour. Yet, it grew to become a specialized field that was at times seemingly positioned above ethical questions, for example, on the effects of scientific discoveries or experiments. This produced debates and questionings that mined the trust science enjoyed for some centuries. Curricula should consider the methods, findings, and ethics of science as interconnected.

The expansion of extreme relativism and the wide circulation of mistruths in different media call for a strong and highly reflexive scientific literacy. The importance of scientific literacy has come sharply into focus with the spread of misinformation and fake news, accentuated at times of major crises such as the coronavirus pandemic and global warming. The denial of scientific knowledge and the misrepresentation of 'facts' has led to real-world consequences, stoking suspicion, distrust, fear and hate. Curricula must foster a commitment to upholding scientific truth and building the capacities for discernment and the sincere investigation of truth that is complex and nuanced.

> Curricula must foster capacities for discernment and the sincere investigation of truth that is complex and nuanced.

The global knowledge commons demands that all have a right to accurate knowledge that contributes to human well-being. This principle is especially important in curricula, where messages and concepts have great influence on developing minds. For example, in some regions or countries with large mining and oil industries, there is significant pressure on governments to downplay the environmental effects of resource extraction in official science curricula. It is essential to fight such misinformation by all educational means possible. Renewed efforts are needed to promote worldwide scientific literacy, especially in disenfranchised and marginalized populations. Unprecedented amounts of information circulate in today's world. Scientific literacy, method, rigour, empiricism and ethics are all curricular issues as important as they are urgent.

Skills for a digital world

Connected technologies underpin participation in ever-expanding areas of life, learning and work. Beyond supporting universal access to technology, education systems are justifiably striving to develop the digital skills and competencies that learners need to make meaningful use of technology. There is nothing 'native' or 'natural' about these abilities. They are constructed and refined over time through intentional educational interventions alongside various forms of informal and self-directed learning.

While digital education is commonly concerned with functional skills and technical know-how, it must also encompass 'critical digital literacy'– a set of understandings and dispositions towards the politics of the digital society and digital economy. This education foregrounds the ability of students to analyze the political features of digital technology and manipulate them to achieve particular outcomes. Learners need to recognize the motivations of actors in digital spaces and see the ways in which they, as individuals and as members of groups, are part of larger digital ecosystems. Today, connected technologies may exert profound influence even on people who never use or see them.

Education about technology also hinges, necessarily, on technology itself. The skillsets and critical outlooks required to understand technology and harness it for good will be in constant flux, changing at the pace of new technological development. This should not, however, imply a one-way street of education contorting to accommodate the latest technological advancements. Education must additionally play a role in steering technological innovation and the digital transformation of societies. Curricula should support teachers and students to act together on technology and help determine how it is used and towards what purposes.

> Curricula should support teachers and students to act together on technology and help determine how it is used and towards what purposes.

Building imagination, judgment and possibility through arts education

Education in the arts – music, drama, dance, design, visual arts, literature, poetry and more – can greatly expand students' capacities to master complex skills and can support social and emotional learning across the curriculum. It can enhance our human abilities to access the experience of others, whether through empathy or the reading of non-verbal clues.

The arts also make visible certain truths that are sometimes obscured and provide concrete ways to celebrate multiple perspectives and interpretations of the world. Many forms of artistic expression traffic in subtleties and grapple with life's ambiguities; students can learn that small difference can have large effects. Artistic experience often requires a willingness to surrender to the unknown; students can learn that everything changes with circumstance and opportunity. The arts also help us learn to say, show, and feel what needs to be said, shown, and felt, helping to advance the horizons of knowing, being, and communicating in and beyond the arts.

Curricula that invite creative expression through the arts have tremendous future-shaping potential. Artmaking provides new languages and means through which to make sense of the world, engage in cultural critique, and take political action. Curricula can also cultivate critical appreciation and engagement with cultural heritage and the powerful symbols, repertoires, and references of our collective identities.

Educating for human rights, active citizenship, and democratic participation

At its full potential, human rights education can be transformative, offering as it does a shared language and an entry point into a moral universe committed to the recognition and thriving of all. Human rights education can support learners' agency. Developing skills to analyze inequalities and nurture critical consciousness is a way to support participatory engagement and, in this respect, human rights education strongly supports education for citizenship.

Human rights education can also improve the overall effectiveness of national education systems, and in turn support sustainable and just economic, social, and political development. By educating about basic rights and for the dignity and freedom of all people, education itself must become a site for the promise of equality to be fulfilled. Human rights and citizenship education are deeply connected to peace education. In many contexts violence is the main way in which people relate to each other; entire populational groups, including women and children, are subject to discrimination, verbal and physical abuse, and see their possibilities to live and thrive severely curtailed. Together with protective laws and welfare agencies, human rights education can help build peaceful societies in which disagreements can be solved through negotiation and diplomacy.

Education builds capacity for sustained civic, social and political action by teaching people to reflect on and analyze their work together within a common framework. Relational and collective agency are strongly supported when curricula focus on building coalitions and making connections to larger histories and trajectories of activism and solidarity. Education supports strategic and transformational action when it is oriented around nurturing longer-term thinking, dialogue, and deliberation that takes place in a public space. Human rights education should also promote debates and dilemmas about what it means to be human and should explore ethical questions about the preservation of different forms of life on the planet.

It should also aim at providing skills and abilities needed for critical and creative political thinking and advocacy, monitoring injustice and human rights violations, as well as questioning, revealing, and confronting the power structures and relations that discriminate against groups due to gender, race, indigenous identity, language, religion, age, disability, sexual orientation or citizenship status. Thus, dialogue between education systems and social movements is fundamental.

Curricula also has an important role to play in addressing gender inequality. The pervasive effects of patriarchy – the ideological system by which men are afforded the majority of social rights and power – continues to inform messages and patterns of thought that are conveyed to children and young people in society and in schools. Oppressive gender roles and gender discrimination are harmful to everyone in society. The underlying principles of equality must be learned at an early age. Boys need to learn as early as possible to be proponents of gender equality, and not perpetuate unequal domestic or social systems that might give them subtle advantages over their sisters or female peers. Expectations that daughters and sisters carry out a larger share of domestic responsibilities and chores has negative impacts on school participation, as well as conveying implicit messages about their value and worth as subservient to others. The principles of gender equality must be consistent across the environments where children socialize and learn, in the home, the classroom, the schoolyard, and the community. Promoting equality is a collective endeavour that requires everyone's support.

In the same vein, curricula must address racism and aim at challenging the stereotypical and discriminatory representations and narratives about groups from diverse cultural and linguistic backgrounds that co-exist in our societies, such as indigenous peoples, Afro-descendant communities and ethnic minorities.

The enabling role of higher education

A new social contract for education will require reimagination of the ways that education not only draws from the knowledge commons but supports its further growth and greater inclusiveness. Nowhere is this more evident than in higher education, which has a key role to play in strengthening the knowledge commons. Higher education is presently experiencing one of the greatest periods of uncertainty in its long history. Universities house much of the world's potential for knowledge and research production. Open science and open access find a ready ally in higher education institutions dedicated to the advancement of research, innovation and inquiry alongside the education of future generations of researchers and professionals.

University research for open knowledge commons

Knowledges – in the plural – should be recognized as assets to be developed and used for the shared well-being of all. The current homogenization and unequal distribution of knowledges across regions must be challenged. Rather than create knowledges boxed in by the economic, political and social norms of our present, university research should prioritize new possibilities. This starts with the recognition that there are multiple forms of knowledge and by the greater use of different languages. In this way universities can make significant contributions to broadening the knowledge commons and ensuring its inclusiveness and diversity.

Inter-university cooperation and internationalization efforts are examples of openness that have great promise for furthering our shared global well-being. All projections point to a continuous growth in higher education enrolments in the coming decades. Many universities have a noble tradition of supporting the publicness of education in the way that they create public spaces for learning, are responsive and publicly accountable in their governance, and promote public interests. But universities are also places where many enclosures are produced, especially in recent decades, through cost barriers and intellectual property claims. Despite many efforts to the contrary, higher education systems remain places that exclude and marginalize. This must be urgently addressed.

> Higher education needs to be a fierce advocate for free and open access to knowledge and science.

Higher education needs to be a fierce advocate for free and open access to knowledge and science when it comes to academic scholarship, learning materials, software, and digital connectivity, among others. Importantly, the term 'open' does not only address availability and ease of access but also implies that individuals are able to modify and manipulate information and knowledge.

Technical and vocational higher education and knowledge commons

Post-secondary technical and vocational institutions, including community colleges and polytechnics, should also be seen not only as training institutions but as venues of applied research. They should give prominence to the importance of productive capabilities in our individual and collective lives, to the effective functioning of learning societies, to the numerous pathways for meaningful work, and to the potential for integration, partnerships, and cooperation between various sectors and communities. The local character of many vocational institutions closely connected to the community provides an opportunity to foster thriving local cultures of learning. Local communities have distinctive connections to the knowledge commons, and technical and vocational institutes can contribute to developing insights about their application in distinctive, contextually relevant ways.

Higher education to support diverse approaches to knowledge

The relationship between higher education and intercultural and epistemic diversity has often been ambiguous. On one hand, higher education has prided itself on introducing students to new world views and ideas. But at the same time higher education has developed distinctive ways of organizing, validating and legitimizing certain forms of knowledge production.

The methods of the natural sciences and social research concepts such as 'rigour', 'reliability' and 'validity' are not culturally neutral. The social processes, quality assurance and economics of scholarly publishing do not typically reward intercultural and epistemic diversity. Indigenous knowledges and modes of knowledge generation and sharing have generally been considered an object, rather than a form, of research.

As plurality in ways of knowing and doing becomes more widespread, knowledge ecosystems that draw from the wealth of cultures and experiences should become more valued. Partnerships between higher education institutions and communities in all parts of the world should become truly mutual. Appreciating plural ways of knowing and doing as a source of strength and sustainability will help to reduce some of the asymmetries within the higher education sector itself.

Diversity can also be supported by properly valuing institutional variety within the higher education landscape. If access to higher education continues to widen, as it should, we will need a range of different institutions. The openness of the knowledge commons also requires flexible higher education structures that enable access to as many people as possible.

Principles for dialogue and action

This chapter has proposed that, in a new social contract for education, curricula should emphasize ecological, intercultural and interdisciplinary learning that supports students to access and produce knowledge while developing their capacity to critique and apply it. As we look to 2050 there are four principles that can help to guide the dialogue and action needed to take this recommendation forward.

- **Curricula should enhance learners abilities to access and contribute to the knowledge commons.** The collective knowledge resources of humanity accumulated over generations should form the backbone of educational curricula. The knowledge commons should be widely accessible to draw from and add to. We should teach students (of all ages) to engage with knowledge creatively and critically, questioning its assumptions and interests. Education should empower people to correct omissions and exclusions in the knowledge commons and ensure that it is a lasting, open resource that reflects the diversity of ways of knowing and being in the world.

- **The ecological crisis requires curricula that fundamentally reorient the place of humans in the world**. Effective and relevant climate change education should be prioritized. Across the curriculum we must teach the art of living respectfully and responsibly on a planet that has been damaged by human activity.

- **The spread of misinformation must be countered through scientific, digital and humanistic literacies.** Curricula should emphasize scientific inquiry and the ability to distinguish between rigorous research and falsehoods. We should develop digital skills that empower learners to make meaningful use of technology. Curricula should ensure that students also gain an ability to 'act on' science and technology by taking a role in determining how they are used and for what purposes.

- **Human rights and democratic participation should be key building blocks for learning that transform people and the world.** We should prioritize human rights education that supports learners' agency and offers an entry point into a moral universe committed to the recognition and thriving of all. Gender equality should be addressed across all curricula and oppressive gender stereotypes removed. Students should also learn how to directly confront racism and discrimination of all forms.

These four guiding principles can serve to inspire the translation of a new social contract for education into educational practice.

Chapter 5

The transformative work of teachers

> The teacher does not necessarily have privileged access to the sagely truth. Like his students, he is in the process of becoming what he ought to be.

Wei-ming Tu, *Humanity and Self-Cultivation*, 1996.

In a new social contract for education, teachers must be at the centre and their profession revalued and reimagined as a collaborative endeavour which sparks new knowledge to bring about educational and social transformation.

Teachers have a unique role to play in building a new social contract for education. Teaching is a complex, intricate and challenging vocation that labours in the tensions between the public and the personal. Teachers work collaboratively to mobilize the knowledge commons in dialogue with younger generations who will inherit and co-construct the future. Teaching involves group work while simultaneously engaging each student's unique needs and capacities. These tensions and paradoxes characterize the irreplaceable work of teachers.

Teaching demands compassion, competence, knowledge, and ethical resolve. Wise and learned figures have been recognized in cultures around the world, and from this tradition the 'teacher' stands as a specialized actor in the context of a school. Teachers are key figures on whom possibilities for transformation rest. They, in turn, must recognize the agency of their students to participate, collaborate, and learn through their shared pedagogical encounters. To carry out this complex work, teachers need rich collaborative teaching communities, characterized by sufficient measures of freedom and support. Supporting teachers' autonomy, development, and collaboration is an important expression of public solidarity for the futures of education.

This chapter begins with recasting the future of teaching as a 'collaborative profession,' which thrives, evolves, and operates through team work and specialists who reinforce the multifaceted work of education for diverse learners. When teachers are recognized as reflexive practitioners and knowledge producers, they contribute to growing bodies of knowledge needed to transform educational environments, policies, research, and practice, within and beyond their own profession.

Next, the chapter considers the implications of the new social contract for education across the entire lifespan of teacher development – from recruit, to novice, to assured practitioner – as a journey undertaken individually and in the company of others in a rich continuum across different times and spaces.

The chapter calls on schools, communities, families, administrators, higher education, and political entities to rally in solidarity around teachers, to recognize the importance of their work and to create the conditions that enable their success. It concludes with 2050 guiding principles for dialogue and action, of particular interest to teachers, school leaders and governments, which include: supporting teacher collaboration; prioritizing knowledge generation; supporting teacher autonomy and participation in public debate on education.

Recasting teaching as a collaborative profession

Across different times and places, teachers have a range of social roles and functions. Ideas about teachers' roles vary culturally, for example they can be public servants and public intellectuals, professionals and artists, community leaders and change-makers, holders of moral authority and stewards of a future trust. Many of humanity's greatest historical figures are described as teachers; from spiritual leaders and scientists to ancient philosophers and mathematicians, all of whom have raised humanity's inherited knowledge to new heights while educating those around them.

Historically, teachers played a vital role in the construction of the social contract for education of the nineteenth and twentieth centuries. They were central to establishing mass, compulsory education, both in their relationship with society and in the organization of schooling. Early on, teachers often broke ground both as educators and initiators of the first public schools. The initial designation of 'normal schools' illustrates what was expected from them: the normalization of the standard school structure, curriculum, pedagogy, and routine work. Standardization and modelling were to establish norms and patterns that could serve as references for other schools. The work of the past century is visible in the worldwide consolidation of teacher education institutions from the United States of America to China, from Brazil to India.

As schooling has grown, individual teachers have become central agents in term of their work, roles, and merits. Likewise, the increased demand for education has seen the 'one room' model scaled to produce schools divided into age groups assigned to different classrooms. However, this expanded 'egg crate' model of schooling did not reimagine the role of teachers who remained individually responsible for their own lesson plans and materials, and rarely interacted. This model places increasingly unsustainable pressures on teachers.

> The individual talents and abilities of teachers need to be bolstered by collaboration and support.

The individual talents and abilities of teachers need to be bolstered by collaboration and support. Teachers have, and must continue to have, a central role in reconfiguring the social contract for education for our shared futures. Their abilities to do so are directly impacted by the degree to which cooperation and collaboration are woven into their modes of working.

Teachers in inclusive educational environments

To support students, teachers must work collaboratively with fellow teachers and other specialists in their schools to provide each student with the support they need to learn. The notion that education is the solo work of a teacher places demands that cannot be met by a single individual and can lead many to leave the profession. At the same time, students' physical, social, and emotional needs are integral to their ability to learn. Students need to be supported by a system that enhances the effectiveness of teachers with other essential supports. These can include support for health and nutrition, social services, mental health, and special learning needs. They include, especially, effective engagement from families in supporting the education of their children.

Promising initiatives are emerging for teachers to work in teams. For example, some schools create common planning teams with classroom teachers, literacy specialists and special education teachers, to ensure that everyone shares their insights, ideas, and observations about how to support a wide range of learners in the language arts. In such co-teaching partnerships, teachers work together to meet the specific needs of individual students, while simultaneously advancing the collective direction of the class. In other examples, public services and non-profit organizations work alongside schools in priority areas to connect to students and families outside the classroom in ways that support their overall learning, health and well-being. There are countless promising approaches to providing each student with the complete range of support they need, from mentors, counsellors, specialists and co-teachers.

In light of such collaborative possibilities, the convening role that teachers play in the construction of new educational landscapes with a multitude of sites and presences can be better understood. These new environments are not the result of chance, but of systematic and intentional work carried out in each locality. Local leaders, elders, authorities, communities and families all have crucial roles to play. Social workers, guidance counsellors, special education resources, librarians and literacy specialists can further bolster the unique dynamics that students bring to the learning environments that teachers assemble together.

Educational environments around schools should comprise a network of learning spaces. Divisions between classroom learning and extra-curricular activities within or beyond schools are better blurred or erased. Teachers are key to designing and building the connections that sustain these networks, but to effectively do this, there needs to be a shift in their ethos, identities and identifications. With this social and institutional role as convenors of new educational ecosystems and networks of learning spaces, teachers and their teams of colleagues emerge as critical agents in shaping the futures of education.

Teaching is not about an individual leading a student through activities or lessons behind a closed classroom door. Instead, we need to think of teaching as work that occurs throughout a school and together with other educators. The transition from a focus on classrooms to schools as learning organizations is not always easy. Indeed, the rigidity of schooling can make collaborative processes difficult within the teaching profession. The idea of collaboration does not reduce the obligations or importance of individuals. Instead, it introduces new responsibilities to act collectively throughout the school space and take on enhanced individual roles in the management and direction of schools. Attempts to force collaboration, however, are futile and counterproductive. Changes must be made in the organization of curriculum and pedagogy so as to naturally foster collaboration. If all education is organized with teachers lecturing in a classroom, then collaboration is useless. But if learning is organized in a diversity of spaces and times, based on problems and projects, collaboration becomes indispensable.

> Teaching is not about an individual leading a student through activities or lessons behind a closed classroom door.

Envisioning and enacting curriculum and pedagogy

Curricula is not only that which is designed and prescribed, but that which is enacted and implemented. Envisioning and enacting new forms of curricula, based on open and shared knowledge, depends greatly on the work of teachers. While digital technology offers a world of possibilities, innovations are most likely to be successful when they are designed to meet the particular needs and characteristics of students in specific contexts. Teachers have an important role to play in personalizing learning so it is authentic and relevant. They need latitude, adequate preparation, instructional resources and support to adapt, build, design and create the best learning opportunities for their students. The curricula of the future must provide teachers with a wide margin of autonomy that is complemented with strong supports, including what is offered by technology, and which comes through rich collaboration with peers and from partnerships with subject matter experts like university professors and scientists.

Pedagogies based in participatory and cooperative approaches unfold not only through cooperative learning that occurs within the classroom, but through cooperative learning between classrooms and collegial learning communities. Some of the complex challenges that teachers face cannot be solved on an individual basis but can be tackled by networks of schools, partnerships with universities, or professional communities supported by specialized education organizations. When it comes to designing high quality learning experiences, there are myriad ways that teachers can collaborate with others including study groups, teachers' councils, pedagogical teams, peer mentoring, coaching, observations and site visits.

Professional teaching knowledge is built on a dialogue between theory and practice and developed through individual and collective reflection on a growing repertoire of experiences. No two pedagogical situations are ever identical, which is part of what makes the relational work of teachers irreplaceable even by the most sophisticated machines. Pedagogy is what allows each student to be part of a human relationship with knowledge, to access a world with intelligibility, creativity and sensitivity. There can be no reimagination of curricula and pedagogy without the presence of teachers.

> There can be no reimagination of curricula and pedagogy without the presence of teachers.

Teachers and educational research

One of the most critical aspects for teachers to reflect upon is their relationship with knowledge. For some, of paramount importance is an excellent command of teaching subjects. For others, didactic and pedagogical knowledge come to the forefront. A third kind of knowledge is professional teaching knowledge. In any profession, the practitioners contribute to the generation and making public of expert knowledge, often as the result of systematic experimentation, evaluation of experience and practice.

Knowledge based on practice is vital to shaping a profession in which teachers identify as reflective practitioners. On a personal level, professional teaching knowledge has dimensions that are intuitive, practical, and relational. Collaborative teaching work naturally integrates a dimension of reflection and sharing among peers. Increasingly, this research can be translated into writing, with teachers assuming authorship. A profession not only needs to register its heritage, its experiences, and its practices; it also needs to identify new frontiers for inquiry and innovation, define research questions and pursue them. When teachers are recognized as reflexive practitioners and knowledge producers, they contribute to growing bodies of knowledge needed to transform educational environments, policies, research, and practice, within and beyond their own profession.

The life-entangled journey of teacher development

A wide range of systems and institutions currently exist in the world for preparing teachers to take up their roles. What must be acknowledged is that, regardless of certification or experiences, teachers are never 'finished' or 'complete' in their professional identities, capacities, or professional development. Teacher development is a rich and dynamic continuum of learning and experiences that are lifelong and life-entangled.

The personal and cultural dimensions of teachers must also be recognized and valued. Being a teacher requires broadening the repertoire of one's own experiences and engagement with the worlds of knowledge and ideas. Teachers who are not enthusiastic readers cannot promote reading among students. Similarly, it is impossible to effectively teach science without curiosity and interest in science. Students learn as much from teachers' lived example as they do from their words.

Each teacher's 'life library' is fundamental to their work. It is in this joy of learning and cultural enrichment that teachers are agents of an education entangled with life, and through this can contribute to new forms of conviviality and solidarity with others and the living planet.

Teacher recruitment

For some, the journey of becoming a teacher begins early in their own education. Others will see opportunities later in life, perhaps shifting from other career paths, for any number of reasons. The massive expansion of schooling over the past thirty years has pushed recruitment to a much wider section of candidates than may have previously been considered. This has had positive benefits, such as increasing the share of women in the profession in some places, and negative effects in some contexts, such as decreasing the share of professionally prepared teachers, lowering pay and social status, and stretching support systems beyond capacity.

In many places, demands on teachers have also grown, impacting the recruitment of talented candidates. Increasingly, the pressures, risks, and difficulties of teaching outweigh the interests and inclinations of those who wish to teach, resulting in a significant decline in those entering the profession. At the same time, demand continues to increase: close to 70 million new primary and secondary teachers will need to be recruited worldwide by 2030 to meet the targets of SDG4. The situation worsened during the COVID-19 pandemic, and many more will be needed to fill the gaps made by those leaving the profession. Without significant changes, it will be difficult to attract the large number of motivated teachers-to-be needed to respond to the shortage. This will be an urgent topic for public policies and for society at large.

This situation is especially unequal between countries and regions. The greatest teacher shortages are in sub-Saharan Africa, which is the region with the fastest growing school-age population. Urgent action will be needed to raise teaching capacity among new cadres of prospective teachers. While immense talent exists, supply-side barriers often limit who can access certification and qualifications in many areas, especially in those countries with limited opportunities for higher education. Creative approaches to teacher recruitment and development should be considered to strengthen local capacity where possible, drawing on the rich collaborative potential of local communities.

Shortages of qualified teachers can also be found at the subnational level, mostly because of inequality. Before the pandemic, well-trained and experienced teachers were already unequally distributed with stark differences between urban and rural settings and between schools serving children from different socioeconomic strata. Paradoxically, the environments that require the best and most experienced teachers are usually serviced by novice, voluntary or underqualified educators, with high turnover. Alongside policies to attract new generations to the profession, urgent measures are needed to retain the most qualified teachers.

Recruiting and affirming indigenous, local, and diasporic teachers in schools – in some cases, to better reflect the cultural heritages of their own students – can make important contributions to valuing diversity and enhancing student learning. Indeed, professionals from these groups have life experiences and maintain relations with communities that allow them to understand the needs, aspirations, and cultural patterns that are of enormous value in creating just and equitable futures of education.

> Urgent measures are needed to retain the most qualified teachers.

Teacher education

Teacher education needs to be rethought to align with educational priorities and orient better towards future challenges and prospects. The weak qualification of many teachers in various regions of the world, particularly in sub-Saharan Africa, calls for urgent measures. There is no one-size-fits-all model for this change. Collaboration of the various actors connected to teacher education – for example, public authorities, researchers, teachers' associations, community leaders, etc. – offer possibilities for creating new spaces for learning and innovation.

Teacher education cannot disregard the relevance of digital culture for how knowledge is produced and circulates, and for the changes it is bringing to human life and to the planet. Without using technology as a panacea, digital media need to be included not only as a means for blended and distant professional development but above all as a topic of study. In addition, research is needed on the affordances, pedagogical effects, epistemic and ethical possibilities as well as blind spots and shortcomings of digital media and platforms.

Effective teacher education must address the factors that contribute to teacher attrition. Supporting the profession requires more than attracting sufficient qualified candidates, it requires redesigning the role of teachers so that collaboration among teams, well supported with the necessary expertise, resources and infrastructure, enables professional success. For instance, throughout much of the world during the pandemic, teachers experienced stress and burnout as a result of inadequate technological platforms and professional development to support remote learning effectively, and subsequently some abandoned the profession.

Novice teachers

In any profession, there is nothing more important than how new generations are welcomed and socialized. Induction programmes should support novice teachers throughout their vital first years with collaborative structures to plan lessons and mentoring from more experienced colleagues. This transition phase between preparation and professional practice is the most decisive in the teaching professional life and yet it is often neglected, both by policies and by the profession itself, and as a result sees the highest rates of attrition.

The teaching profession, like others, is associated with a knowledge base. The professional knowledge of teaching requires integration and socialization processes that involve institutions of initial teacher preparation, schools, and experienced teachers. This connection is even more important if we consider the changing circumstances, contexts, learning environments as well as the diversity of learners in twenty-first century education. New challenges require collaboration across teaching generations. Nothing can help meet the challenges of the future more than this ability of teachers to support each other as a community of trusting peers.

Teachers lead the creation of knowledge when they engage with learners in action-research, problem-solving and project work, or in experimentation with new techniques. These processes should form the basis for induction programmes and for the integration of novice teachers into the profession alongside a collaborative community of colleagues.

Continuing professional development

Teachers need opportunities for professional development, education, and support to work with different population groups who are ethnically, culturally, and linguistically diverse, to include and adequately support students with special needs, and to personalize learning. They must ensure that learners from historically excluded and marginalized groups are adequately supported. This is becoming especially true for regions where the classroom makeup may be radically transformed by increased migration and internal displacement resulting from climate change, social and political violence, and armed conflict – conditions which are anticipated to grow in the coming years.

Professional development needs to be part of a continuum beginning with initial teacher education and supervised field experiences, followed by induction, mentoring and in-service professional development on a regular basis. Effective progression along a career path needs to be linked to meaningful continuing professional development that is focused and linked to the daily activities of teachers and is easy to integrate in professional practice.

Effective professional development programmes often focus clearly on what students should learn, and on what teachers can do to support such learning and assess their progress. The most effective programmes extend over relatively long periods of time, are at least in part school-based and embedded in experience, and provide repeated opportunities to apply what is learned and develop pedagogical and conceptual knowledge.

Public solidarity to transform teaching

For teachers to be able to contribute to a new social contract for education, important changes need to be made in policies that govern the selection, preparation and career trajectories of teachers and in the organization of the profession itself. Collaboration should not simply saddle teachers with greater responsibilities, but should be supported and financially resourced to allow them to engage with a wide set of educational stakeholders, particularly families and communities, higher education, and a variety of social institutions.

Teachers' working conditions

Despite studies demonstrating that quality teaching is the single most important in-school determinant of student achievement, teachers remain under-recognized, underappreciated, underpaid and inadequately supported. Issues related to teacher career structure, its management, teacher motivation, and job satisfaction have proved difficult to resolve worldwide without a requisite measure of public investment and public will. Overreliance on occasional or poorly qualified teachers can erode the profession and public education.

Poor working conditions and remuneration can drive away prospective teachers. The gendered nature of teachers' work should also remain visible in the analysis of these tensions and demands, as an increase of women teachers in some countries has provided an excuse to decrease pay or widen gaps in pay equity. It is necessary to improve the conditions for teachers' work, not only through monetary compensation but through reducing class sizes, improving school safety, strengthening professional recognition and legitimacy, increasing institutional support, and fostering cultures of collaboration.

Overall, teachers' careers need to be redesigned. Progress should be based on competence, professional development, and engagement with school programmes, and include mentoring for novice teachers, common planning with co-teachers, leading subject areas or cycles, organizing support services such as tutors or councillors, sabbaticals for research and further professional development, among others. Amid growing pressures, teachers are demanding a more balanced relationship between bureaucratic and pedagogical requirements, as well as accounting for the invisible work implied in teaching, for example, in settings where teachers are deeply engaged with their communities.

A thorough and gender-sensitive revision of teachers' labour statutes, norms, and workloads is needed to ensure they are aligned with new educational priorities. Moreover, it is important to acknowledge the appearance of new forms of control, through demands and accountability technologies that often reduce teachers' autonomy. The rise of large-scale testing, teacher evaluation, school inspection, teaching standards, are but a few examples of the heavy pressures imposed on teachers often without a commensurate degree of support.

Some education systems have welcomed AI technologies as a way to enhance internal governance, efficiency, and public accountability. While there are gains in terms of knowledge and the visibility of educational processes, the growth of machine learning technologies risks fragmenting educational processes into 'data sets' and accelerating trends towards managerialism, surveillance and the de-professionalization of teachers. In particular, the use of facial recognition software and AI for monitoring of students and teachers by states who could use such resources for political surveillance is antithetical to Article 26 of the UN Declaration of Human Rights which affirms the goal of education as advancing fundamental freedoms and human rights.

Teachers' work involves enormous responsibility and, as such, it must be accountable to society and, above all, to the future. For this they must feel safe to work within an environment of openness and trust and feel free to promote new ways of thinking and belonging to the world, something that is at odds with some recent forms of accountability based on excessive managerialism and corporatism which undermines rather than supports their work.

Universities' ongoing relationships with teachers

There is an intimate link between higher education and the teaching profession and new institutional configurations should embody this connection. The idea of reimagining our futures *together* should translate into a commitment to collaboration and cooperation between schools, teachers and universities in initial teacher education and ongoing professional development. Higher education is capable of challenging and shaping the mindsets and pedagogies of the next generation of educators. In turn, educators can help universities to transform themselves, renew their public mission and better understand the roles they play in broader educational ecosystems.

Among their more general connections, the concrete commitment of universities to teacher education must be elevated. Historically, this has been one of the main links between primary and secondary education and universities. However, in most places, there is need for fundamental changes in teacher education programmes and strategies.

The most important of these commitments is the need for a relationship-based approach when constructing and implementing teacher education programmes, particularly in initial teacher preparation. Neither universities nor schools are able to undertake initial teacher preparation on their own. Some programmes bridge this gap by focusing on building new spaces and settings where multiple actors in education, including public authorities, teachers' associations and non-governmental initiatives, can come together for dedicated joint work. Other programmes embed themselves deeply in schools, taking an inquiry-oriented approach to learning and action. These need not be limited to faculties of education but can connect primary and secondary learning to the full spectrum of the knowledge commons advanced and mobilized by universities. Just as universities in many places have started science and industry 'parks', we need similar education-focused spaces that bring together stakeholders of all sorts for shared learning design and teacher preparation work.

> Neither universities nor schools are able to undertake initial teacher preparation on their own.

A related commitment involves the strengthening of teacher professional induction programmes. The best of these prioritize mentorship and ensure the socialization of young teachers by providing an adequate transition between periods of professional development and professional practice – all of which requires strong collaboration on the part of universities and teachers' colleges. Ongoing contact between teachers and universities can contribute greatly to the improvement of schools and processes of educational transformation. Programmes and faculties need to stay engaged with teachers across their professional careers, encouraging a dialectical relationship in which educators bring insights from their work back into their colleges and universities.

Finally, the pedagogical development of teaching in higher education, the professoriate, also requires transformation. University and college instructors and professors have much to gain by committing to collaborative planning, teaching, and support of student learning. Pedagogies of solidarity and collaboration are no less crucial in higher education than they are for children and adolescents – in fact, they take on even greater relevance for the emerging generations of professionals, leaders, and researchers that universities aim to produce.

Teachers in educational decision-making and in the public sphere

Nowadays, the importance of a public sphere where educational issues are the object of discussion and deliberation is undeniable. It is not just a matter of discussing or consulting, but of building decision mechanisms with the participation of public authorities, parents, communities, public and private entities, associations and youth movements, as well as teachers and their organizations.

The teaching profession does not end within the professional space, it continues through the public space, through social life and the construction of the common good. In this sense, it is especially important that teachers participate in the definition of public policies. In several contexts this is not the case with teachers disempowered with little margin for action, and not welcomed in debates and deliberations on educational policies.

To be a teacher is to gain a position within the profession as well as take a position publicly on major educational issues and the construction of public policies. This participation is not primarily intended to defend their interests, but to project their voice and knowledge in a broader social and political sphere.

Looking to the future, it is important to point out that the work of teachers is not limited to the classroom space but should extend to the whole organization and action of the school. They play an essential role in enabling schools to become learning organizations, in which teachers shape and share a vision focused on learning for all students; and in which there are continuous learning opportunities for all staff. Teachers can pioneer efforts to collaborate and learn together in a culture of research, innovation and exploration, and foster integrated systems for the organization and sharing of learning.

Principles for dialogue and action

This chapter has proposed that in a new social contract for education teaching should be further professionalized as a collaborative endeavour, where teachers are recognized for their work as knowledge producers and key figures in educational and social transformation. As we look to 2050, there are four principles that can help to guide the dialogue and action needed to take this recommendation forwards:

- **Collaboration and teamwork should characterize the work of teachers.** We should support teachers to work in common as the master convenors of educational environments, relationships, spaces, and times. Quality teaching is produced by teams and enabling environments which ensure that students' physical, social, and emotional needs are provided for.

- **Producing knowledge, reflection and research should become integral to teaching.** Teachers should be supported and recognized as intellectually engaged learners themselves who identify new areas of inquiry and innovation, define research questions, and generate new pedagogical practices.

- **The autonomy and freedom of teachers should be supported.** A strong professional identity for teachers should be encouraged. This includes proper induction and ongoing professional development that ensures teachers are able to effectively use their judgment and expertise in designing and leading student learning.

- **Teachers should participate in public debate and dialogue on the futures of education.** We should ensure the presence of teachers in the social dialogues and participatory decision-making mechanisms needed to collectively reimagine education together.

In making a new social contract for education, we should take inspiration from these four guiding principles related to the transformative work of teachers. Shared dialogue on teaching and teachers is an essential part of the renewal of education.

Chapter 6

Safeguarding and transforming schools

> Home was the place where I was forced to conform to someone else's image of who and what I should be. School was the place where I could forget that self and, through ideas, reinvent myself... The classroom, with all its limitations, remains a location of possibility. In that field of possibility, we have the opportunity to labor for freedom, to demand of ourselves and our comrades, an openness of mind and heart that allows us to face reality even as we collectively imagine ways to move beyond boundaries, to transgress.

bell hooks, *Teaching to transgress: Education as the practice of freedom*, 1994.

Schools should be protected educational sites because of the inclusion, equity and individual and collective well-being they support – and also reimagined to better promote the transformation of the world towards more just, equitable and sustainable futures.

To enable pedagogies of cooperation and solidarity and strengthen relationships with the knowledge commons, it is crucial to have times and spaces dedicated to these purposes. Schools, with all their potential and promise, defects and limitations, remain among the most essential educational settings. Schools represent societies' commitment to education as a public human activity. Yet, how schools are designed is not neutral and reflects assumptions about learning, success, achievement, and relationships.

The built environment and regimes of time present in schools crystallize what is possible, what is prohibited, who is welcomed, and who is excluded. Teachers, as the master convenors of educational encounters, need to spend considerable time working with these organizational contours and the kinds of interactions and learning they enable. Will a school environment be conducive to collaboration, exploration, and experimentation? Will it be highly judgmental or encouraging of learning and reflection through trial and error? Will it facilitate a range of encounters, not only within a grade or age cohort, but across ages and stages of life? And what kinds of mentorships, friendships, and mindsets will these encounters build? Will a school environment centre on individual achievement above all else, or will it consider individual and peer development to be mutually supportive?

This chapter begins with a brief examination of the emergence of schools as vital social institutions that play important roles in virtually every culture and tradition. They not only represent unique times and spaces for primary and secondary education, but many have also become centres of society in their own right, bringing together a range of social goods and services that support the well-being of individuals, families, and communities. Nonetheless, schools have been limited in their accomplishments, in part due to narrow definitions of the spaces and time structures of learning. The chapter then discusses possible transformations. Expanding the purview of learning beyond the classroom; reconsidering lesson times and structures to facilitate deeper engagements; and reflecting on the potential of digital technology to support what occurs within schools are all elements to consider when translating the making of a new social contract for education into the transformation of the school.

Strong schools are vital if education is to help us build liveable collective futures that can adapt to crises, and the unknown and uncertain.

It concludes with 2050 guiding principles for dialogue and action, of interest to students, teachers and educators, governments and civil society partners, which include: protecting and redesigning schools as collaborative space; leveraging digital technologies positively; and modelling sustainability and human rights.

The irreplaceable role of schools

If the school did not exist, we would need to invent it. Schools are a central component of larger educational ecosystems. Their vitality is an expression of a society's commitment to education as a common good. Schools provide children and youth with unique environments to participate in the knowledge commons. They are places to take risks, be confronted with challenges and experiment with possibilities. Schools ensure that everyone has available to them the experiences, abilities, knowledge, ethics, and values that will sustain our shared futures. Looking to 2050, schools will need to nurture an ethic of solidarity and reciprocity through intergenerational, intercultural and pluralistic encounters.

Essential educational work takes place in many times and spaces, but the public time and space of school are unique. The space of the school fosters social relationships. Education and learning stimulate human interactions, dialogue and exchange, and schools should be purpose-built to nurture this. Schools are forms of collective living that bring people together to learn from and with others at different ages and life stages. Distance or remote learning provisions can support the work of schools but cannot fully replace their relational character.

> If the school did not exist, we would need to invent it.

Increasing disruptions – such as the global COVID-19 pandemic and Ebola epidemics in West Africa, violent conflicts, and climate emergences – have made the unique role of schools even more evident. These instances reminded us of the importance of schools for learning, but also as centres of social well-being. Schools are one of the few institutions intended to protect and provide opportunity for the poorest and most vulnerable. As centres of community life, schools can offer powerful support for self-reliance and for cultivating sustainable relationships within local communities and with the natural world. For example, in the face of sudden and unprecedented widescale school closures in 2020 and 2021, millions of children and adolescents around the world were deprived of access to their schools, classmates and teachers. This sustained lack of in-person education had profound impacts on the social, intellectual, and mental well-being of millions of children and adolescents which will be felt throughout their lifetimes.

Whatever the ages of their students, schools should foster curiosity and a desire for knowledge. Students should be exposed to ideas and experiences they would not ordinarily encounter at home or in their immediate communities. Intentional pedagogical encounters make schools irreplaceable. Unique among the multitude of other educational sites, schools are places of learning *and* teaching. Human beings learn and are also capable of teaching and being taught. This beautiful dynamic connects us to the knowledge commons across space and time, across generations and ways of knowing, and to each other. There are no schools without teachers. Teachers foster the pedagogical mission of making knowledge available to all, of building collective purposes and capacities, and of promoting emancipatory intellectual pursuits. Likewise, teachers depend on healthy functioning of the space and time of schools to reinforce and support their work.

Common historical commitments

Dedicated spaces and times for developing knowledge, skills, values, and understanding have been present in most cultures whose knowledge practices achieved a level of complexity that could not be learned merely through observation, imitation or storytelling. In many instances early schooling arose with the development of writing. Interestingly, the English word 'school' comes from the Greek *skholè*, meaning free or leisure time. And, though the Greek institution was a central model for the development of education in Europe, many cultures have developed institutions of schooling, for example the yeshiva, madrasah, and calmécac. As schools have developed and spread globally over the past two centuries, they have assumed a role as one of the central public infrastructures for organizing intergenerational conversations on how to live in the world, make worlds, and care for them. Schools enable us to become acquainted with cultural heritage as well as to re-create and expand it.

Schools have become one of the key space-times for the deliberate organization of encounters with the knowledge commons. Schools have had the power to promote epistemic practices by inducting students into the rich traditions of reasoning, study, research, and inquiry. School activities and exercises can serve to promote a particular ethos and relationship to knowledge. Historically more weight has been given to the transmission of established truth-claims (an assertion that the belief system holds true). However, important shifts in the past several decades have challenged the direct instruction methods found in many schools. Through more participatory schooling practices and schooling cultures, there has been an increased focus on nurturing understanding of the generation and consequences of truth-claims. The dilemmas and challenges we currently face can be productively addressed by ensuring that a range of epistemic practices flourish in schools and that we form constructive, wider alliances between epistemologies and ecologies of knowledge.

Throughout this shift from spaces of knowledge transmission towards greater participation and exploration in schools, school learning remains essential. Yet, to avoid rigidity and remain responsive to the challenges of the world, it requires an understanding of what multiple ways of knowing can be encoded into times and spaces of learning, in order to nurture rather than impoverish human experiences. Much more work remains to be done to create spaces and times of schooling that can facilitate the public activity of intergenerational learning.

The necessary transformation of schools

Schools need to become places where everyone is able to form and realize their aspirations for transformation, change, and well-being. Above all, schools must allow us, individually and collectively, to realize unforeseen possibilities. In many parts of the world, increased access to schooling has provided transformative opportunities for individuals and entire communities to raise consciousness, develop new skills and understanding, and envision new trajectories of learning and development. Too often, however, today's schools serve to entrench inequalities and widen disparities that need to be unlearned and corrected.

To bring about profound change, the future school's organizing principles should centre on inclusion and collaboration. Excellence, achievement, quality, measurement, and progress are also valuable commitments that can be realigned in ways that include rather than marginalize.

We can imagine these new school environments as a large library where some students study alone, connected to the internet or not, and others present their work to classmates and teachers. Others are outside the library in contact with people and worlds outside the school, possibly in far-flung places. The library supports an immense diversity of situations and space times. It is a new environment quite different from the usual structure of the school and the classroom. This library can be taken both as a metaphor and literally. It reminds us that school times and spaces need to serve as portals connecting learners with the knowledge commons.

> Schools must allow us, individually and collectively, to realize unforeseen possibilities.

Schools as platforms for cooperation, care and change

In becoming inclusive and collaborative learning environments, schools must also be safe spaces free from violence and bullying, that welcome learners in their difference and diversity. Learning collectively and collaboratively does not imply uniformity. Effective collaborative learning leverages the differences (of capacity, ability, cognition, interest, and aptitude) of students and teachers. From one vantage point, learning is an individual journey, which belongs to each one of us. Collaborative learning must be inclusive and equitable, without compromising the individuality of its learners. But from another vantage point, equally valid, learning is a collective journey, which takes shape in relationships with others.

Self-education is important as part of a much bigger picture, as the individual and collective functions of education mutually propel and reinforce one another. While we cannot learn *for* someone else, we can all learn more together. What we know depends reciprocally on what others know. It is in our relationships and interdependencies that education occurs. Effective collective learning is already occurring in many inspiring schools around the world. However, schools everywhere need to become better oriented around these relationships and interdependencies.

Schools and teachers do indispensable work supporting learners. Many people can point to a teacher or school experience that changed their lives positively. At the same time, schools too often exclude, marginalize, and reproduce inequality. About half of the world's students finish their secondary studies without reaching even minimum levels of proficiency in basic competencies – an unacceptable outcome, and a failure of schools to their students and their societies. Dynamic change of schools that is adaptive and transformative must be enabled and is entirely possible as countless examples from around the world show us.

The school has everything to gain from a closer articulation to other educational spaces. There is a clear consensus among the million people who have engaged with the Futures of Education initiative that the design of schools (in terms of built design, curricula, classroom organization and learning activities) needs to change. Artwork, inspired by visions of education in 2050, foresees a departure from rows of tables and lines of desks. Several panels with educational innovators addressed ways schools can transform once we properly recognize the ways that learning happens in multiple times and spaces, for example by softening the walls between classrooms and the outside world and reconceptualizing lessons as journeys. In sum, schools need to look and feel different to future generations by becoming more inclusive, more inviting, more engaging and relevant.

They need to become places where students learn to live sustainably and bring those messages to their homes and communities. There is tremendous potential to 'green' schools and bring education to carbon-neutrality. Students can lead the way in this work, developing knowledge and skills that will help them build the green economies our world desperately needs.

To achieve what we need them to achieve, schools must break with the rigid, uniform organizational models that have characterized a large part of their history over the past two centuries. Renewal is vital. The impressive nineteenth and twentieth century efforts that informed the conventional school models we know today are a source of insight for the future. Throughout the past hundred and fifty years, architects, public health experts, philosophers, civil servants, educators, communities, and families have built on educational insights from humanity's long history to expand possibilities for education. Over time, this has given shape in material form – for example, through school buildings and classrooms – to the extraordinary social institutions of mass public education. The same imagination, determination, and collaboration is needed today to give material form to new schools, oriented towards more just and equitable shared futures.

From classrooms to communities of learners

Around the world, classrooms have become the primary educational venues of teaching and learning in schools. In imagining new venues for inclusion and collaboration it may be the case that the 'room' can more often be left behind. But the value of being part of a dedicated and diverse community of fellow learners should not be abandoned.

> Students may no longer be limited to conventional classrooms in future schools, but they will continue to need sustained engagement with classmates.

Conventional school models have devoted great energy to classifying students according to age, achievement, ability, or gender. In contrast, teachers should be afforded flexibility to develop, experiment with, and adapt the groupings of students that occur within schools. At times these may best be smaller groups of learners, at other times larger. But the value of being part of a community of learners is a feature of the school to be reinforced. Students may no longer be limited to conventional classrooms in future schools, but they will continue to need sustained engagement with classmates, with all the joys and tears that shared learning brings.

Classroom expectations around learning also need rethinking. In too many places around the world, children and youth sit through the day, passively absorbing large amounts of information. This norm is embedded in school architecture, furniture design, and the objects and materials present in classrooms. A silent, obedient student has become synonymous with concentration and productivity. Too often, skilled teaching is equated with maintaining order and eliminating 'unnecessary' noise or movement. When immobility is seen as a requirement for learning, the school and its classrooms become tedious and unpleasant places. Deep, immersive, absorptive attentiveness can have tremendous educational value. But we need to ask whether our current classroom and school arrangements facilitate this in the right ways.

As much as we must protect the social space of the school, it does not need to be enclosed within four walls. It can be open and flexible, drawing on a wide set of social, cultural, and environmental resources. Constraining education to one-size-fits-all classrooms restricts learning and narrows the range of possibilities and opportunities schools should create.

Structures to support diversified pedagogies

Lessons and timetables need reformulation. The lesson plays the important function of focusing a set of students on a shared endeavour and is an important mechanism for structuring educational encounters and carrying an intergenerational conversation forward. However, conventional lesson designs also have considerable limitations, especially when defined exclusively as a fixed block of time repeated daily or weekly.

The lesson must give way to pedagogies that value a diversity of methods and modalities of study and learning. There are many other ways to bring people together in common endeavours using diverse modalities of study and learning that leverage intergenerational and intercultural exchange and capitalize on the high-level abilities and knowledge of teachers. For example, problem-based and project-based educational approaches can be more participatory and collaborative than conventional lessons offer. Inquiry-based and action-research pedagogies can engage students in acquiring, applying, and generating knowledge simultaneously. Community engaged pedagogies and service learning can imbue learning with a strong sense of purpose when undertaken in a humble posture of learning. A significant reworking of the organization of schooling is necessary to fully enable pedagogies like these to advance students' abilities to undertake joint work and expand our capacities for collective deliberation and action in a spirit of solidarity.

The digital in support of the school

When digital communication technologies allow students to connect with others with similar interests and questions, they support the work of teachers and schools. Digital connectivity greatly enhances possibilities for teachers and students to access information, texts, and artforms from across the world. The collections of the world's greatest libraries and museums can now be made available in all places at all times. Digital tools also enable students to produce videos, make mixed-media presentations, and code games and apps that take their creative ideas out into the world.

There is ground-breaking potential for digital devices to support innovative teaching and learning in schools. Digital tools have also become useful ways to promote effective communication between parents, teachers, and students, in turn assisting parents in supporting their children's school learning.

The pandemic has proved that the school cannot be entirely displaced into virtual spaces. Even in areas of high internet connectivity and relatively equitable access to devices, the total or partial closure of school buildings in times of disruption shed new light on the importance of shared physical and social presence in schools. Virtual classrooms accessed from home are limited substitutes for what physical school spaces can provide.

> The pandemic has proved that the school cannot be entirely displaced into virtual spaces.

The improvisations and experiments in times of challenge and disruption – from the COVID-19 pandemic to education in times of other emergencies – have shown the determination, commitment and resourcefulness of teachers and students. For example, as many school systems realized that personal needs and social welfare needed to be foremost, tests were postponed, the content-coverage requirements of curricula were suspended, and classroom interactions focused on authentic learning and well-being. During COVID, teachers' work became more publicly visible, particularly to parents. The high levels of expert knowledge and pedagogical engagement required of teachers became simultaneously valued and scrutinized by many. Some students felt comfortable with online and distance education, and their positive experiences remind us that future schools need to be student-centred in ways that support the social, emotional, cognitive, and moral development of the whole person.

Nurturing the social dimension of learning also implies sustaining citizenship education in an increasingly interconnected world to enable individuals to care about each other, embrace other perspectives and experiences, and engage in responsible practices towards the environment and our shared natural resources. Digital means alone cannot achieve these ends. Participatory and engaged learning in school sites and beyond them is necessary.

Schools should be places where students are more closely tied to the possibilities of their futures than to the limitations of their pasts. The principle of equal opportunity aims to enable students, regardless of their backgrounds, to emancipate themselves from being confined by the expectations of others so that social origin is not social destiny and the future can be better than the past, for individuals as well as societies.

The key problem of most machine learning is that it can only create futures by looking to the past. Research shows that the same stereotyping, gender bias and racism that is present in human decision-making is further entrenched in digital platforms for the simple reason that machines are 'trained' on datasets that contain the same biases found in society today. This is true of the algorithms that underlie most technology-based personalized learning programmes as well. The student following such a course of study is known and defined only in relation to past performance: how many problems were incorrect last time, the areas of weakness that have been exhibited. This leaves little room for reinvention, self-knowledge and the awareness of possibility that schools should foster.

Teachers can become designers of personalized learning based on a different set of assumptions, oriented not towards past personal failures but towards the possibilities of engagement and belonging. Digital means can support teaching and learning in many forms. However, it is our interpersonal encounters and strong relationships (between teachers and students, but also among students and among teachers) that enable the joint work that puts students in contact with the wealth and diversity of humanity's shared knowledge inheritance, supports intellectual emancipation, and enables co-creation of just and sustainable futures.

Schools are also places where we can teach students to see digital spaces and environments as malleable and fallible human creations. Coding and computational thinking have emerged as core subjects in many education systems; they are helpful for illuminating the ways our digital edifices are constructed and for providing toolkits both practical and theoretical for reconfiguring them. Merely consuming digital media, even educational media, rarely affords learners the critical distance to consider new possibilities for the digital. Different arrangements, incentives, directions, logics and functionalities are possible for technology and networks that connect us and inform so much of our thinking. For these reasons, education must treat digital interactions as a subject of inquiry and study themselves, and not only as a means for pursuing curricular objectives. Discussions about digital rights, surveillance, ownership, privacy, power, control and security need to be part of formal education. It is often said that we might one day live in virtual worlds, but to some extent and in some places, this is already true. In some countries it is not uncommon for an average person to spend more than ten hours a day online and immersed in digital technology. Schools need to help students learn to thrive in these environments and use them to create, tackle challenges and grow. Schools should promulgate an ethic of human control, collective as well as individual, over technology.

Building cultures of collaboration

Schools are fully capable of promoting collaboration, collective leadership, collective learning, and continuous growth toward more just and equitable futures. However, normalizing this as a central aim of schooling will require the development of new capacities among teachers, administrators and school staff. School accountability needs to evolve from a mode of compliance to a process of shared goal-setting and assessment. School management needs to foster professional collegiality, autonomy, and mutual assistance over command and control. Schools that promote collaboration among students must also promote the same among their teachers. This is supported by school cultures that promote continuous professional development for teachers, administrators and staff. Coaching, mentoring, individual and group study, action research and research collaborations with other schools and with universities all help to reinvent the school as a learning organization itself.

All over the world, hundreds of thousands of teachers and countless schools have already advanced in these directions. For example, in various indigenous settings, schools are being reimagined around learning and interaction interculturally and with the more-than-human world, drawing on intergenerational and ancestral knowledge, language, and research practices. In other instances, schools are organizing themselves along lines of inquiry involving constructive community participation and creative collective endeavours. Advances in TVET are also bridging the artificial divide between theory and practice through reimagined forms of apprenticeships, meaningful courses and effective training.

We need schools that identify with global solidarity, that commit to knowledge sharing with other schools and among nations, and dedicate to renewing and re-establishing themselves as public places and collaborative environments. Schools have an essential role to play in the overall strengthening of education as a common good.

Transitions from school to higher education

Historically, outside faculties of education, universities and colleges have paid little attention to primary and secondary education. However, recent decades have raised awareness that many of the problems of universities and colleges related to student achievement must be addressed prior to the start of higher education. From mathematics to the sciences, from literature to philosophy, a whole range of bridge and enrichment programmes have been developed to strengthen the links between higher education and schools, frequently with a mind to ensuring the participation of historically underrepresented groups. At the same time, university researchers have become more prominent in general debates on education.

Any considerations about the roles of higher education cannot miss the inescapable connections to primary and secondary education, as well as to adult learning and non-formal education. For learners to be able to flourish in and beyond higher education in 2050, the values and organization of all levels of education should be connected. Future policy agendas for higher education will need to embrace all levels of education and better account for non-traditional educational trajectories and pathways. Recognizing the interconnectedness of different levels and types of education, speaks to the need for a sector-wide, lifelong learning approach towards the future development of higher education.

> Future policy agendas for higher education will need to better account for non-traditional educational trajectories and pathways.

Partnerships between school systems and universities can contribute to reimagining and strengthening education. University libraries and research facilities can support primary and secondary-level students. The expertise of professors should be readily on-call for local schools. Such partnerships enhance the institutional capacity of education systems to devise solutions and to implement them. They are also an opportunity for universities to be more deliberate about integrating their three core functions of research, teaching and outreach in the service of public action on some of the most significant issues of our day.

Principles for dialogue and action

This chapter has proposed that in a new social contract for education schools should be protected educational sites because of the inclusion, equity and individual and collective well-being they support – and simultaneously reimagined to better promote the transformation of the world towards more just, equitable and sustainable futures. As we look to 2050 there are four principles that can guide the dialogue and action needed to take this recommendation forwards:

- **Schools should be protected as spaces where students encounter challenges and possibilities not available to them elsewhere.** If schools did not exist we would need to invent them. We should ensure that schools bring diverse groups of people together to learn from and with one another.

- **Building collective capacity should guide the redesign of schools.** School architectures, spaces, times/timetables, and student groupings should be designed to build the capacities of individuals to work together. Cultures of collaboration should pervade the administration and management of schools, as well as relations among schools.

- **Digital technologies should aim to support – and not replace – schools.** We should leverage digital tools to enhance student creativity and communication. When AI and digital algorithms are brought into schools we must ensure they do not simply reproduce existing stereotypes and systems of exclusion.

- **Schools should model the futures we aspire to by ensuring human rights and becoming exemplars of sustainability and carbon neutrality.** Students should be trusted and tasked with leading the way in greening the education sector. We should ensure that all education policies sustain and advance human rights.

In making a new social contract for education, everyone everywhere should be able to take inspiration from these four guiding principles related to safeguarding and transforming the school – one of humanity's most essential and powerful educational institutions.

Chapter 7

Education across different times and spaces

The City becomes educative through the necessity of educating, learning, teaching, knowing, creating, dreaming and imagining that all of us — men and women — who occupy its fields, mountains, valleys, rivers, streets, plazas, fountains, houses, buildings, leave on everything the stamp of a certain time and style, the taste of a certain epoch... The City is us and we are the City.

Paulo Freire, *Politics and education*, 1993.

In a new social contract for education, we should enjoy and expand enriching educational opportunities that take place throughout life and in different cultural and social spaces.

Many people today think of education as primarily aimed at children and young people with the aim of preparing them for their lives as adults. Much public discussion assumes 'education' is synonymous with those specialized institutions that operate at a relative distance from student's families and from society. Specialized settings have proven useful for safeguarding dedicated times and spaces for collective teaching and learning. Education in schools has become an important space-time of human experience with its own distinct characteristics. The prioritization of children and youth has been essential for advancing equality and access to opportunity.

However, a discussion about education limited to formal institutions alone does not encompass the rich educational possibilities that exist within and across society as a whole. A foundational principle of the social contract for education proposed in this Report is the right to education for all throughout life. This principle recognizes the fact that just as learning never ends, education must be further extended and enriched in all times and spaces. This principle has vast implications for all levels of society and our collective life – for our communities, cities, villages and towns, for our national ethos and cultural systems, and for our regional and international communities. Work, caretaking, leisure, artistic pursuits, cultural practices, sports, civic and community life, social action, infrastructure, digital and media engagement – these are all potentially educative, pedagogical, and meaningful learning opportunities for our shared futures, among countless others. A new social contract for education must see the need and value of dynamic cultures of learning in all times and spaces.

One of our major tasks is to broaden our thinking about where and when education takes place. This newly urgent challenge was raised 50 years ago in the Faure Commission report which set out a vision of the *Cité éducatif* in an effort to rethink educational systems. Translated in varying ways into other languages (for example into English as the 'learning society'), the 'city' here is metaphor for a space that encompasses all possibilities and potential, especially as they are interconnected. It is based on the idea that we need to think holistically about the richness and diversity of the spaces and social undertakings that support education, as well as who is involved.

Today's established patterns still generally conceive of education beginning at 5 or 6 years of age and reaching an endpoint about a decade later. This range has widened over the years and many efforts have been made to extend educational efforts to early childhood, with attention even turning to new-borns and infants, and to adults throughout life. In the first case, early childhood education is seen as an essential educational moment in its own right, although it is still often framed as 'pre-primary' preparation for schooling. In the second case, often from the perspective of 'second chances' or workplace re-skilling and TVET, adult education has become central in educational policies and strategies in most countries across the world, although it is still often framed as an extension of school.

What we mean is that education models based on the 'school format', often ended up prevailing in the way of educating younger children and adults, reducing the possibility of different and distinct forms of education. It is true that there is a long tradition of resistance to this extension of the 'school format' to groups with specific ages and characteristics, which, for this very reason, must have different educational processes and frameworks.

In the case of early childhood education, this tradition is well established, with the adoption of different educational strategies, strongly focused on valuing experimentation and well-being, as well as the affective, sensorial and relational dimensions. Many even believe that the transformation of the school, from the point of view of a new organization of spaces and times, should be inspired by the more open and flexible models of early childhood education.

In the case of adult education, this tradition is even more evident, with countless proposals over the decades to 'deschool' adult education, that is, to adopt forms and processes that respect the autonomy of adults, their experiences of life and work and learning done outside formal school frameworks. These are emancipatory educational proposals, which fight against systems of dehumanization, oppression or colonization and which seek to empower adults in their relationship with education.

But, despite these forms of resistance, it is impossible to deny that the 'school format' has extended to early childhood education and to adult education, namely with the hegemony of lifelong learning trends. In order to think about education towards 2050, we must understand the importance of all spaces, all times and all forms of education. However, this does not mean that we transform the world into an immense classroom. The fundamental shift in thinking that we must bring about is understanding that today's societies have countless educational opportunities, through culture, work, social media and digital, which need to be valued in their own terms and built as important educational opportunities. Over the next 30 years, one of the central aspects of the new social contract for will be an understanding of how education is intertwined with life is central. Thus, while we defend schools as a unique space-time for education, we must also extend our vision to all spaces and times of life.

> While we defend schools as a unique space-time for education, we must also extend our vision to all spaces and times of life.

This chapter begins with a discussion of the multitude of educational sites and opportunities that exist, arguing that we should direct our efforts at ensuring they support inclusion and responsiveness to new challenges. It then discusses the essential role that states play in ensuring the right to education is realized, as well as the need for governance of digital spaces to ensure that technology supports the reimagining of education in ways that will serve our shared futures. Earth's biosphere is also a vital educative space that must not be overlooked. The chapter concludes with a set of 2050 guiding principles for dialogue and action, of special interest to governments and civil society organizations alike, including: emphasizing the importance of inclusive adult education; imagining new learning spaces; strengthening funding; and broadening the right to education.

Steering educational opportunities towards inclusion and sustainability

To work best, the governance of education must acknowledge and appreciate the capillarity, porosity, and ubiquity of educational institutions, social institutions, and temporal relationships. Ensuring that such diverse actors are committed to inclusion and sustainability, however, requires collaboration and commitments that ensure that educational opportunities, whether formal or not, remain accessible for all.

An ethic of inclusion needs to guide our collective work to govern education, drawing from the principles of inclusive design. The starting point must be those who are typically among the most marginalized and the settings that are most fragile and precarious. Without clear and inclusive values, educational ecosystems can become unhealthy and pathological. Issues of power, privilege, exploitation, and oppression can work their way into any educational relationships. All too often educational designs and institutions produce failure and exclusions; ethnic groups, indigenous peoples and other marginalized groups can be pushed out more than they simply drop out of formal education. Refugees and those with disabilities can be particularly poorly served. A broader approach to education systems places clear emphasis on chain reactions and interlinking effects between institutions, actors and spaces, making these failures more difficult to overlook.

The role of governments and states

There is global consensus that education is a fundamental enabling human right and that states and societies have a particular responsibility to ensure that this right is realized for all children, youth and adults. Accordingly, governments and states have a critical role to play in educational ecosystems and significant responsibilities for which they must be held accountable.

Established in Article 26 of the Universal Declaration of Human Rights, the right to education has been further elaborated in several treaties that are legally binding upon states. These include the 1960 Convention against Discrimination in Education (CADE) and Article 13 of the 1966 International Covenant on Economic, Social and Cultural Rights (ICESCR). In this last, all states parties have agreed that education shall enable all persons to participate effectively in a free society and promote understanding, tolerance and friendship among all nations.

Under current international law, states parties have a responsibility to make primary education free and compulsory. Secondary education, in its different forms, should be generally available and accessible to all. Higher education is to be equally accessible to all on the basis of individual capacity. States have threefold obligations with regard to the right to education: to fulfil, respect, and protect. The state's obligation to *fulfil* includes a duty to facilitate and to provide, while the obligation to *respect* involves prevention against measures undermining the right to education. Last but not least, the state has an obligation to *protect* and prevent third parties from interfering with the right to education.

The right to education is tightly linked with other human rights. In this sense, as guarantors of rights, states have the responsibility to make intersectoral efforts to create the necessary conditions to enable and facilitate learning of all children and youth. This means ensuring access to fundamental rights such as the right to water and sanitation, to healthy food and nutrition, to social protection, to live in a stable and healthy family and community environment that promotes emotional and physical well-being, and to live free from all forms of violence.

Since the early 2000s, UN Special Rapporteurs on the Right to Education have referred to education as a public good that safeguards the collective interests of society. The United Nations Human Rights Council also recognizes education as a public good in its 2005 and 2015 resolutions on the right to education. In 2015, the *Education 2030: Incheon Declaration and Framework for Action* was adopted by representatives from over 160 countries at the World Education Forum. This document reaffirms that education is 'a fundamental human right and a basis for guaranteeing the realization of other rights'. It also reiterates that 'education is a public good, of which the state is the duty bearer' and sees the state as essential in setting and enforcing standards and norms.

Governments have a key role to play in ensuring that educational ecosystems uphold education as a public good. As argued earlier, we need an all-hands-on-deck approach. The charge to renew education as a common good applies to all educators, all schools, all educational programmes, everywhere. And, it should also be recalled, that, in many instances around the world, a host of state and non-state actors together ensure the publicness of public education.

> States have a key responsibility for ensuring educational systems are financed adequately and equitably.

States have a key responsibility for ensuring educational systems are financed adequately and equitably to meet the needs of their citizens and others living under their protection. They must raise adequate public finance through taxation policies that ensure that private wealth is not sequestered in offshore tax havens but appropriately contributes to the public good. Governments must spend these resources equitably and efficiently in order to realize the common right to education.

States also play a key role in regulating educational provision by ensuring that all providers within a given ecosystem respect human rights and provide learning experiences that are safe and of good quality.

Finally, states must ensure education is responsive to the needs of citizens and others living within their territorial borders, in particular the needs of those historically excluded or marginalized. Good governance of educational systems requires the engagement of citizens and other stakeholders in decision-making and dialogue, and implies a need for greater transparency and accountability at all levels

In the case of indigenous peoples, additional provisions apply. The UN Declaration on the Rights of Indigenous Peoples notes that, in addition to having the right to access all levels and forms of education ensured by the state, indigenous peoples have the 'right to establish and control their educational systems and institutions providing education in their own languages, in a manner appropriate to their cultural methods of teaching and learning.'

With forced migration increasing around the world – particularly the displacement of human populations due to climate change pressures – special attention needs to be paid to refugees who do not enjoy the protection of a state. International bodies and increased international cooperation are essential for ensuring the right to education in such situations, which can only be expected to become more common.

Governing digital learning spaces

Used well, technology can support publicness, inclusivity and common purposes in education. There are multiple logics underlying digital technologies, some with great emancipatory potential, others with great impacts and risks. In this respect the 'digital revolution' is no different from other great technological revolutions of the past, like the agricultural or industrial revolutions. Major collective gains have come with worrisome increases in inequality and exclusion. The challenge is to navigate these mixed effects and steer their future outcomes.

It is necessary to ensure that key decisions about digital technologies as they relate to education and knowledge are made in the public sphere and guided by the principle of education as a public and a common good. This implies addressing the private control of digital infrastructures and defending against the anti-democratic capture and enclosure of the digital knowledge commons that increasingly figure as part of education's ecosystems.

While digital platforms have made some contributions to knowledge, education, and research in the past few decades, the social benefits that have accrued have been mostly incidental to the tech industry's actual, advertising-heavy business models. Google/Alphabet, for example, has become one of the most important intermediaries to the digital public sphere as it strives to expand its reach into our public digital lives. Some of its most significant services to education therefore, such as Google Scholar and Google Classroom, do not actually generate any advertising revenue, and incur considerable cost for as long as Google deems them in its interest to support. This presents a highly precarious position for the digital infrastructures on which education is becoming increasingly dependent.

Given the extremely long list of other Google services which, finding themselves in a similar situation, eventually shut down, concern about the overall fragility of the current arrangement is quite justified. The COVID pandemic closures of many university facilities in 2020 and 2021 meant that even scholars in some of the richest and most well-off universities on the planet only had access to materials because of Google's internal decision-making about the benefits of a service like Google Scholar. In its many years of existence, Google Scholar has seen few changes and had no substantial new functions added, revealing the low priority that it occupies on the company's overall agenda. This should serve as a word of caution about the fragility of such privately-run learning infrastructures and make us ask if there are more durable models for reliable public digital infrastructure for our futures of public education.

The ability of digital platforms to remain free of cost to the public also relies largely on the massive and systematic extraction of personal user data as a commodity so lucrative that it has been likened to 'the new oil'. Initially, this data was gathered with the explicit intent of using it to sell advertising. Later, the platforms behind the digital services discovered that some of this massive and ever-expanding store of user data is useful not only in building and improving commercial services and products, but to engineer ideas, opinions, and preferences through AI and machine learning.

This inaugurated a race for dominance in AI between the world's largest companies, eager as they are to emerge victorious in the fight for market share. As a result, today's digital economy is guided by an extractivist imperative, sanctioning the proliferation of sensors, algorithms, and networks into domains and pockets of life previously off limits to both corporate and private eyes, ranging from e-book readers to internet browsers to smart watches. The feeling of many that we are living in times of ubiquitous and permanent surveillance has vast political consequences. It has chilling effects on freedom of expression and people's sense of intellectual autonomy. The anxieties associated with surveillance create invisible self-censoring obstacles to creative activity, prompting uneasy secondary questions about whether one's reading of an edgy or dangerous book might have serious implications for one's reputation, which, today, is often a direct consequence of our online actions.

Similar effects and anxieties can be produced when surveillance and extractivism extends into our education's ecosystems. The continued normalization of surveillance – especially if education systems habituate children to it from young ages – puts us on a trajectory towards a radical erosion of the concept of human dignity and a massive undermining of the human right to privacy and to free expression as laid out in the Universal Declaration of Human Rights.

Concern about the protection of student and teacher data needs to feature in any conversation about the place of digital platforms in education's ecosystems. The ease of data capture, storage and monitoring in digital spaces can help to improve teaching and learning. Proper rules and protocols are needed to protect students and teachers from overreach. An ethic of transparency should guide data policies, with the default setting always being to anonymize data so that individuals cannot be harmed.

> The best strategy for bending the digital disruption in the direction of supporting education as a common good is to ensure its democratization within a robust public sphere.

One reason why digital platforms with their algorithmic mode of knowledge curation have risen to the top in so many domains, including in educational ecosystems, has to do with the absence of a viable public answer to the challenge of systematically organizing and curating the rapidly growing volume of global knowledge. As a result, even experts now have to rely on the intermediary services of digital platforms, which make their qualified and informed opinions hostage to the whims of the curation algorithm of the platform where they publish. Finding long-term solutions to problems like 'fake news' and the crisis of faith in science and in public institutions that we presently witness in many places, requires our informed, collective engagement with truth and expertise, and the democratization of knowledge curation.

These many examples underscore the fragility of education's digital infrastructures. While better digital instruments can and must be engineered, the best strategy for bending the digital disruption in the direction of supporting education as a common good is to ensure its democratization within a robust public sphere. Many digital communities and early internet technologies were developed through open-source, collaborative efforts. The continued development of digital technologies in education in directions guided by sustainability, justice, and inclusion will require action from governments, support from civil society, and a broad public commitment to treating education not as an arena for profiteering, but as a space for public investment in sustainable, just, and peaceful futures.

Learning with the living planet

We must widen our conception of where learning happens beyond human-centred spaces and institutions to also include parks, city streets, rural paths, gardens, wilderness, farmlands, forests, deserts, lakes, wetlands, oceans and all others that are sites of more-than-human life.

Human beings are part of a living planet Earth. Many longstanding indigenous cultures take an appropriately expansive view on the formation of mutually beneficial relationships involving humans and non-humans. The biosphere is an important learning space. The fact that today indigenous-governed lands are home to approximately 80% of the world's biodiversity is itself enough to demonstrate that indigenous perspectives have much to teach everyone about education that cares for the planet.

Indigenous land- and water-based knowledge and teachings, as well as many African and Asian cosmologies, posit relationships in which non-humans are understood not only as beings with their own rights, but as educators and teachers with whom humans can learn in relationship. In some traditions, elements of the more-than-human world are understood as older, wiser and deserving of respect, and it is recognized that they have much to teach us.

In Western education traditions there is also a long history of addressing some of these questions. The fields of place-based, environmental, outdoor, and experiential education have attempted to create a presence for the natural world and the environment as co-participant in learning processes. Nonetheless, this work has often positioned the environment as being in service to student learning. The case is often made that students learn important things through these encounters that they would not otherwise. In many instances, then, the human-nature relationship is not envisaged as reciprocal and interdependent. Nor is it necessarily one in which non-human beings are understood as teachers with their own forms of agency. More recent forms of environmental and place-based education are departing from this position. The metaphor of 'rewilding' education, drawn from environmental conservation and restoration, is particularly promising in relation to the idea of building education in new ways.

Many of the pedagogic encounters that are emerging through dialogue between the world's many knowledge systems and cosmologies are similarly promising for reframing the relationship between education and the living planet as one of co-evolution and co-emergence with the world. Human beings need to understand themselves as ecological beings, not just social beings. Principles of environmental stewardship that position us a 'caretakers' and 'protectors' of nature still presuppose a division between human beings and their environment. Our ecological imaginations need to fully position ourselves within the living planet.

The ecological crises humans have caused require a rethinking of the learner who is at the core of an education oriented towards common purposes. Education cannot just aim for an idealized cosmopolitan learner who feels at ease and capable in an interconnected world – the so-called 'twenty-first century learner' envisioned in education that typically focuses only on human development. For education to support just and sustainable futures we must promote a consciousness of the planetary. The learner who assumes responsibility for worldmaking *with* other beings must be placed at the centre of education. This perspective has implications for educational practice in nearly all domains. Global citizenship education in particular must become keenly attuned to this consciousness of the planetary.

Rebalancing our relationships with the living planet requires that we relearn our interdependencies and reimagine our human place and agency. Many cultures have known for centuries or millennia that we cannot separate humanity from the rest of the planet. For example, the Quechua notion of 'Sumak Kawsay' accords rights to nature and describes a way of life that is ecologically balanced. The principles of relationality (I am because we are) of the Nguni Bantu philosophy of Ubuntu has much to offer as does the Buddhist ethic of Karuna (compassion), just two examples from the rich cultural resources humanity has to draw on.

Other societies are still, sometimes painfully, coming to grips with our shared human and planetary interdependencies. How will we live in 2050 as part of the Earth through principles of harmony, well-being and justice? Globally we do not yet have all the answers. An education rooted in the wholeness of life must be one of our key tools to work out solutions together.

Expanding 'when' education happens

As more and more people live longer and healthier lives, the ways that education is entangled with life will change. Educational needs, priorities and modalities change when there are shifts in the balance between youth and the elderly, in the proportion of people in the working-age population, as well as in the kinds of caregiving and care work (waged and unwaged) that is undertaken, by whom, and when. In fact, these issues shine a bright light on the basic assumptions our societies make on what it means to produce value.

Education and care across the lifespan

It is increasingly recognized that our well-being and economic security do not come from the formal economy alone. Paid work is one part, but the work done within households to provide care for people is certainly no less important. This includes the labour of caring for children and older adults, producing and preparing food, building shelter, and in many areas of ecological stress, gathering water. Women and girls carry the greatest load in terms of supporting families, communities, health, food security, even environmental and ecosystem health, and receive little recognition or support for their enormous and essential contributions.

Over the next 30 years, complex interactions will re-shape the balance between all these kinds of 'provisioning' activities in regionally and locally distinct ways. In some areas, improving health and/ or labour shortages may generate opportunities and demands for older adults to remain longer in the workforce. In other instances, the challenges of elder care may parallel the challenges of childcare that have characterized the last three decades as women were entering the workforce in increasing numbers. New household forms could emerge if co-operative living and extended family support become more significant to more parts of the world. All of this means that the capacity of people to build and form longstanding and robust caring relationships is also an educational issue for learners of all ages.

Learning to care, and making caring a feature of life-entangled education, is not simply a 'nice to have' feature. Looking to 2050 and beyond there is a hard-edged logic to this. Education that supports the day-to-day work of preparing and sometimes growing food, and education that supports the nurturing and sustaining of bodies and families, must be prioritized. This is the broader perspective on learning that a strong understanding of education as entangled with life and taking place in different spaces and times points us towards.

Adult learning and education as an emancipatory project

In recent decades, the principle of lifelong learning has become central in the formulation of educational policies worldwide. SDG4, for example, calls on us to 'ensure inclusive and equitable quality education and promote lifelong learning opportunities for all'.

There is a strong emancipatory tradition of adult learning and education, which is reflected in the potentials it unleashes for individuals and what it means for citizen participation broadly. However, this has been whittled down in recent years by an excessive focus on the vocational and skills dimensions of lifelong learning. In essence, what was one of the most important 'rights' of adults – especially those who had not had full access to education earlier in their lives – became for many an 'obligation' as people have become required to keep up-to-date and employable. The result is a permanent logic of skilling and reskilling.

> Adult education will need to extend far beyond lifelong learning for labour market purposes.

Adult learning and education must look very different a generation from now. As our economies and societies change, adult education will need to extend far beyond lifelong learning for labour market purposes. Opportunities for career change and reskilling need to connect to a broader reform of all education systems that emphasizes the creation of multiple, flexible pathways. Like education in all domains, rather than being reactive or adaptive (whether to change in labour markets, technology, or the environment), adult education needs to be reconceptualized around learning that is truly transformative.

Looking to the horizon of 2050 and beyond it is possible to anticipate a set of profound changes in adult education. Some forecast that quite soon human lifespans could regularly exceed 100 years. Leaving the radical expansion of human longevity aside, the fact that so many already live longer lives further builds the case for continuing to rethink when education is meant to occur. In some areas four generations will be co-living in the same space-time in a way never seen in history. Cultural notions of adulthood and maturity will be tested. Habitual ways of living, and our relationships to work and leisure will change. Already, it is commonly acknowledged that jobs and the nature of employment can change dramatically over the span of a single individual's working life. We need to recognize that civic and political life also change over a single lifespan and perhaps increasingly so in the future. The new eco-consciousnesses and the reframed humanism called for in this Report are examples of new educational concerns which need to be encountered by learners of all ages, regardless of age. As the twenty-first century progresses, educational policies will need to shift their focus to the whole of life and pay special attention to adults and the elderly.

A second dimension, which is part of the best tradition of lifelong learning, concerns the idea of the participation and inclusion of vulnerable groups who are so often excluded from educational opportunities. Participation and inclusion go hand-in-hand with emancipatory visions of adult education, which includes an appreciation of informal learning – the knowledge and capabilities acquired outside formal schooling settings. Adult education policy will need to recognize informal learning across the lifespan as part of prioritizing inclusion and participation.

Finally, those engaging with adult education need to grapple with the ways that participation is increasingly mediated and enabled through digital means. While younger generations have exposure to the digital world from early ages, older generations will also need these tools to continue developing and building knowledge. Adult education should promote broad access to digital media and should strongly support open access and open-source movement agendas. Strengthening scientific literacy and combating all forms of misinformation are central elements of any adult education strategy for the present and the future.

Adult learning and education plays multiple roles. It helps people find their way through a range of problems and increases competencies and agency. It enables people to take more responsibility for their future. Furthermore, it helps adults understand and critique changing paradigms and power relationships and take steps towards shaping a just and sustainable world. A futures orientation should define adult education, as much as education at all moments, as an education entangled with life. Adults are responsible for the world in which they live as well as the world of the future. Responsibility to the future cannot be simply passed on to the next generations. A shared ethic of intergenerational solidarity is needed.

Broadening the right to education

Given the intense challenges in front of us, it is increasingly urgent for educators, governments, and civil society to carry forward the proposals above for properly governing education across different times and spaces. What is proposed here is not a utopian model but rather a concrete survival strategy for the human species. Education must be called upon to reconnect us with the deep meaning and joy of living, of which learning is a fundamental part.

This Report affirms a need to think about education in the wholeness of life. However important it is, education in institutions like schools and universities should not be seen as the only form. Education at its best is a collective process that acknowledges the value of peer and intergenerational as well as intercultural learning. This social dimension emphasizes learning to care for each other, for our communities and for the planet. These collective processes and social dimensions need to exist within schools and universities, but not only.

At we look to 2050 it will become increasingly important that the right to education not be limited by conventional understandings of when and where education occurs. The right to education will need to apply more clearly to all people, and not only children and youth. It will need to more clearly address education that takes place across a multitude of sites, and not only classrooms and schools.

The deployment of radio and television to support the continuation of students' academic learning during COVID-19 school closures reminds us of the importance of these media for education, culture and general knowledge, especially for students who lack access to online materials and smart devices. The COVID-19 crisis has also revealed the massive importance of digital connectivity and online platforms – to the extent that we need to begin considering access to information, which is itself also a fundamental right, as connected to the right to education in ways that were not foreseen even a decade ago.

The right to education is supported by (and supports in turn) the right to information and the right to culture. Freedom of opinion and expression can only be properly maintained when people have the ability to seek, receive and impart information and ideas. In our media-saturated contemporary world, rife with fake and misleading news, education has an essential role to play in supporting people's quests for accurate information and enabling their desire to pass it along faithfully, free of manipulation. Education supports the right to participate in cultural life by providing access to cultural resources that shape identities and expand worldviews. In turn, education can support people's abilities to contribute to cultural resources. Open and horizontal dialogue among cultures is key to supporting cultural pluralism. Education should model dialogue as one of its many contributions to encouraging cultural pluralism.

> Education supports the right to participate in cultural life by providing access to cultural resources that shape identities and expand worldviews.

Broadening understanding of the right to education across different times and spaces reinforces education as a common endeavour, something made, governed and conducted by and through us. Education as a common good – a shared well-being that is achieved and chosen together – should be closely connected to our everyday lives. Children and adults should not experience education as clients or spectators, but as actors. We play different parts in education at different points in life and in different areas of life, and we become part of it. Everyone has the right to become part of an education that strengthens what they think, know, feel and do in their own lives, and strengthens what we all do together.

Principles for dialogue and action

This chapter has proposed that in a new social contract for education we should enjoy and expand the educational opportunities that take place across life and in different cultural and social spaces. As we look to 2050 there are four principles that can guide the dialogue and action needed to take this recommendation forward:

- **At all times of life people should have meaningful quality educational opportunities.** Learning should be lifelong, life-wide, with weight and recognition given to adult education. We should employ inclusive design principles and begin any planning with a focus on serving those most marginalized and those settings that are most fragile.

- **Healthy educational ecosystems connect natural, built and virtual sites of learning.** We should better appreciate the biosphere as a learning space. Digital learning spaces are now integral to educational ecosystems and should be developed to support the public, inclusive and common purposes of education. Open access and open-source platforms, with strong protections for student and teacher data, should be prioritized.

- **Government capacity for the public financing and regulation of education should be strengthened.** We should build the capacity of states to set and enforce standards and norms for educational provisions that are responsive, equitable and uphold human rights.

- **The right to education should be broadened.** We are no longer well served by framing the right to education simply around schooling. Everyone everywhere should have a right to lifelong learning. We should support the right to information and the right to culture as necessary enabling components of the right to education. A right to connectivity must be built in.

In making a new social contract for education, these four guiding principles should be taken forward. At local, national, regional and global levels we need to commit to dialogue and action around these principles and support the reimagining of our futures together.

Part III
Catalyzing a new social contract for education

Stepping up to the multiple overlapping crises that threaten the survival of humanity and the living planet necessitates a radical change of course. We must urgently build together a new social contract for education – inspired by principles of social, epistemic, economic, and environmental justice – that can help transform the future. A new social contract for education implies renewed approaches that strengthen education as a public societal endeavour and a common good and protect the knowledge commons. It recognizes that a range of governmental and non-state partners need to work together to meet unfulfilled commitments of the past and unlock the transformative potential of education for the future. Universities and other partners will have a key role to play in research and innovation to support the renewal of education as a common good and the co-construction of a new social contract for education. Similarly, it is important to recast the role of regional and international education development organizations in shaping the type of international cooperation and solidarity we will need as we look to 2050. Ultimately, however, beyond the international and regional levels key to governing education as a common good, catalyzing a new social contract for education will need to be continued through broad social dialogue across multiple constituencies across the world in specific contexts. This Report is an invitation to continue this dialogue.

Chapter 8

A call for research and innovation

> 'In all community approaches process – that is, methodology and method – is highly important. In many projects the process is far more important than the outcome. Processes are expected to be respectful, to enable people, to heal and to educate. They are expected to lead one small step further towards self-determination.'

Linda Tuhiwai Smith, *Decolonizing Methodologies*, 1999.

To catalyze a new social contract for education, the Commission calls for a worldwide, collaborative research agenda grounded in the right to education throughout life, and welcoming contributions from grassroots associations, educators, institutions, sectors, and a diversity of cultures.

Advancing the propositions described in the previous chapters will require efforts, experiments, inquiries, and innovations for education in a wider range of contexts and circumstances than ever before. The chapter raises a call for collaborative research and innovation about education for our reimagined futures. Like education itself, research and innovation are public goods and processes that have key roles to play in catalyzing a new social contract for education.

A research agenda on the Futures of Education begins where learners and teachers are. In many ways, elements of the futures of education are already among us, at least in some initial form. A starting point in any education system will be to look for those bright spots, those positive instances that already embody the principles articulated in this Report. Study and the analysis of their effects alongside the conditions which made them possible, can provide grounding to the ideas in this Report, as communities look for ways to translate their ideas into an operational strategy with details on what to do differently in practice. Education has a history of drawing on a wide range of research sources, methods, and paradigms. These instruments need to be reinforced and strengthened at all levels, from practitioner and community dialogues to universities and research partnerships, and to national and international fora, including those of UNESCO.

This chapter emphasizes, above all, ways that research and innovation enable us to systematically learn *together* – to reflect, to experiment and have an impact on society together and, in doing so, to reimagine our futures together. Seen in this light, research and innovation must strengthen our capacities for foresight and futures literacy by empowering the imagination and advancing our understanding of the role the future plays in what we see and do in education. An ethic of collaboration, humility, and foresight imbues all aspects of our research agenda for education.

> Research and innovation must strengthen our capacities for foresight and futures literacy.

This chapter calls for the contributions of all participants in education to advance knowledge and research on the propositions of this Report. In addition, special calls are made to universities, research institutions and international organizations to support and systematize learning and insights on these themes. To carry forward the precepts of a new social contract for education, we will need to equip ourselves at the international level with the instruments that allow for its implementation. It concludes with 2050 guiding principles for dialogue and action, of interest to all participants in education, and including: a call for an inclusive worldwide research agenda drawing on differing perspectives, content and places.

A new research agenda for education

This Report has put forward a set of observations, principles, and propositions that the Commission asserts should guide a new research agenda for the futures of education. This research agenda is wide-ranging and multifaceted as a future-oriented, planet-wide learning process on our futures together. It draws from diverse forms of knowledge and perspectives, and from a conceptual framework that sees insights from diverse sources as complementary rather than exclusionary and adversarial.

The priorities highlighted in this Report reinforce one another towards a coherent common research agenda. As highlighted in Chapter 1, this research agenda must concern itself centrally with the right to education, interrogating all barriers to quality, equitable education for all. Research must also trace how the vectors of change described in Chapter 2 will intersect with education – our changing climate and environment, accelerating technological transformations, deepening fractures of the body politic, and uncertain futures of work and livelihoods – in the crucial years to come. Research must also go beyond mere measurement and critique to explore the renewal of education along the operational principles described in Part II of this Report – pedagogies based on solidarity and cooperation, curricula's relationship with the knowledge commons, the empowerment of teachers, the reimagination of schools, and the entanglement of learning with all times and spaces of life. The learning, insights, and experiences generated from such a far-reaching research agenda will be catalytic to forging a new social contract for education together.

Research from within education

A long and important heritage of educational research exists from the beginning of the twentieth century and beyond, with a diversity of works, currents and perspectives, cultivating and crystallizing influential genealogies of thought and action. Educational research allows us to better understand the reality of what is occurring in schools, classrooms, and the many sites where education takes place. It also provides insights into the transformations taking place in individuals, in communities and in society at large.

Practitioner research, action research, historical archival research, case study research, ethnography, etc. are among the many methods that have proven fruitful for use by those within the field. In this way, education must be understood not merely as a field for the application of external experimentation and study, but as a field of inquiry and analysis itself.

The affirmation of schools as places where knowledge is produced and of teachers as knowers, depends deeply on how universities, organizations and researchers interact and collaborate with those embedded in education and draw on their rich insights, reflections and experiences. Universities play pivotal roles in promoting educational research, both for their expertise in advancing disciplinary knowledge and transcending different disciplines. Teachers will always be among the central authors of knowledge on their profession, as it results from shared reflection on that experience and, in this, they should be supported in publishing their research and reflections.

Students are also important sources of knowledge and understanding about their own educational experiences, aspirations, achievements, and reflections.

> Students are also important sources of knowledge and understanding about their own educational experiences, aspirations, achievements, and reflections.

Universities and researchers can extend support by being always in dialogue with schools, teachers and students. Participatory evaluation, collaborative research, youth-led research, and practitioner inquiry are among the many methodological traditions that can be drawn on to further systematize the learning between those researching within and externally to education. Educational research will be a key tool to project and monitor the transformations necessary to engage with a new social contract for education.

Mobilizing the learning sciences

One of the most unique scientific advances for education in recent decades has been through neurosciences and the study of the brain in relation to learning. These include greater understanding of neuroplasticity in all stages of human development; the anatomy, structure, and functions of the brain and human neurology; faculties of memory, information processing, language development and complex thinking; and the effects of both positive and negative stimuli on learning, such as sleep, physical activity, emotion, stress, and abuse. The cognitive processes of learning themselves are also richly important, giving insight on specialized skills such as speech, reading, writing, spatial awareness, and so on.

Even though scientists are still at the start of true understanding about this field and how it might be applied to education, it has vast implications for teaching and learning and insights should be made as accessible as possible to teachers, researchers, and learners themselves. For example, scientists are able to observe strong patterns and correlations between behaviours and brain activity in controlled laboratory settings, but it is not yet clear in what ways these patterns might translate into complex social learning environments, or how they may vary in diverse populations, peoples, times, and spaces.

Future learning sciences must involve researchers from a wide diversity of backgrounds – gender, culture, socioeconomic background, linguistic background, age, and so on – to ensure that a wider range of research questions, assumptions, hypotheses, and priorities are equitably represented. Neurodiversity, learning differences, disability studies, and special education can also benefit from significant advances in the learning sciences.

As powerful and vital as insights of the learning sciences are, they do not encompass the entirety of education. Cognition is not the only way that we learn; social knowledge, embodied knowledge, emotional intelligence and so on interact with what can be understood through neuroscience but are not defined by it alone.

As highlighted in earlier chapters on pedagogy and curricula, the complexity of education derives from the fact that it intersects inseparably with all aspects of the world, including its social, economic, environmental, material, and spiritual dimensions. There is considerable danger in divorcing mind from matter, leading to ideas about education irrelevant to many of those who learn. In order to advance the priorities described in this Report, neurosciences for learning will need to increasingly put their findings in context with these diverse and complex facets of education to yield the cognitive and social benefits offered by high quality education.

Transforming research partnerships for education

Research partnerships that are interdisciplinary, inter-sectoral and cross-cultural, that span academic, civil society and educational milieus, and that foster shared communication and mutual learning, offer tremendous potential to advance the priorities and proposals put forward in this Report.

Not all research partnerships are fair and equitable, and partners with greater resources or institutional power can exert undue influence on the course and outcomes of a partnership even if inadvertently. Epistemic humility is needed to challenge assumptions in and around education, many of which are deeply embedded in our conception of the nature of human beings, of society, and of the more-than-human world. Our operating paradigm will need to shift away from simplistic categorizations of knowledge relationships such as 'North/South' or 'Western/non-Western,' towards complex and relational ecologies of knowledge.

For a new social contract in education, these ecologies of education will need to be enriched by diverse experiences and ways of knowing, not depleted by exclusion, deficit thinking, and narrow epistemic assumptions. Education is a relational process – between students, teachers, families, and communities – and as such we should seek relational rather than hierarchical knowledge. This could be the empowering of national and local research capacities, and include the capacities of people who may produce and represent knowledge in ways specific to different contexts, cultures and languages.

In addition, the voices of grassroots communities and social movements are important sources of knowledge and insight that education will need to increasingly listen to, draw from, and contribute towards, as they are at the frontline of disruptions and changes shaping our futures. Movements that oppose the destruction of our planet and that reject all forms of prejudice and discrimination, are among the many examples of reimagining our futures together. Collaborations with such communities and movements may not always be formalized or institutionalized but will be no less vital to the collective work of learning about education's role and relationships with such movements.

Expanding knowledge, data, and evidence

Mobilizing a new research agenda for the futures of education will both draw from, and generate significant amounts of, knowledge, data, and evidence, in a wide range of forms: quantitative and qualitative, normative and descriptive, digitizable and ephemeral, theoretical and practical.

Knowledge needs to be channelled and expanded in order to understand present conditions and imagine new future possibilities for education. Historically, however, certain forms and sources of knowledge have been given prominence, while others have been excluded. Knowledge – both generally speaking, and knowledge in education – intersects closely with power. Dominating modes of power *over* people and the planet must be replaced with modes of power *to* and *with* people, in ways that allow us to find new forms of inclusion and participation in education. As a research agenda to advance the futures of education in the coming decades, it will need to continually reconsider the nature of knowledge, data, and evidence in education.

Strengthening complex ecologies of knowledge

To imagine a greater diversity of possible futures beyond the present, research and innovation cannot afford to exclude the many ways in which diverse human populations, cultures, and traditions read and understand the world. Indeed, the guidelines of this Report for pedagogy, knowledge, participation, collaboration and solidarity already have rich knowledge traditions in many cultural worldviews and perspectives. Decolonizing knowledge calls for greater recognition of the validity and applicability of diverse sources of knowledge to the exigencies of the present and future. It requires a shift away from seeing indigenous epistemologies as objects to be studied rather than viable approaches to understanding and knowing the world.

In many fields, from development, to economics, to education, certain types of knowledge are privileged over others. Often, knowledge from the Global North is transferred to developing contexts under the assumption that locally generated knowledge is non-existent or deficient. Yet, these imposed 'solutions' often fail to contribute to the sustainable development of these contexts, or benefit a few at the expense of the vulnerable, and of environmental well-being over the long term.

> Indigenous and pluralistic ways of knowing challenge assumptions to development models and practices.

To value and recognize multiple ways of knowing should not be construed as an embrace of extreme relativism, or an abandonment of a commitment to truth. Far from it. Indigenous and pluralistic ways of knowing challenge assumptions to development models and practices that have failed to adequately address their reality. For example, it has become customary in many Western traditions of thought including education to think in terms of dichotomies: theory and practice, individual and collective, arts and sciences, human and nature, progressive and conservative, knowing and feeling, intellectual and physical, spiritual and material, modern and traditional, etc. A necessary contribution of many non-Western perspectives has been to challenge the very premise of these polarities, shedding new light on their mutual relationships and generative tensions, as coherent parts of a complex, interrelated world.

At times of crisis, for example, local communities are often able to channel tremendous reservoirs of experience, knowledge and creativity towards mitigating and adapting education to emergencies. The long accumulated ancestral knowledge about sustainable agricultural processes, social reciprocity, and ways of living with the natural world, to name a few, are important sources of accumulated knowledge that humanity needs more than ever. Yet, entire swathes of such knowledge have been entirely unrecognized, uncanonized and omitted from formal education.

Research on the futures of education will require renewal and inclusion of diverse types and sources of knowledge on the key priorities identified in this Report. As mentioned in previous chapters, this depends on the dynamic participation in a knowledge commons based on just and equitable terms. Successful knowledge production for the futures of education will need to become consciously inclusive, socially and culturally diverse, inter-disciplinary and inter-professional, and able to foster communication, collaboration, ownership and mutual learning.

Statistical data, indicators, and analysis

Statistical data has the power to present a snapshot in time about a particular indicator, and, when put in relation to other data points, can offer invaluable insights about correlations, changes, and conditions across times and places. They can illustrate directions that certain indicators have taken over time and can forecast a range of possible outcomes according to varying scenarios, choices, events, or interventions.

UNESCO's Institute for Statistics (UIS) plays an important role in collecting and making public vital statistics on a range of indicators for education. UIS's approach has been one of capacity-building for the collection and corroboration of statistics at national, regional, and international levels. Increasing disaggregation by gender, location, income level, and other characteristics help to give Insight into issues of equity and equality. UIS's work to continually refine definitions, while at the same time ensuring statistical integrity for meaningful analysis, is vital to evolving and ensuring their quality and usefulness. Supporting their continued work will be essential for providing vital information on our most crucial educational indicators and ensuring that these data are available to everyone.

At the same time, approaches to statistical and quantitative data in the coming decades must stringently avoid reductionism. Categorization is useful for analysis but, at the same time, should not be seen as immutable and fixed. Categories are always more nuanced, complex, and blurred in reality than quantification can account for. The work of statistical data collection and corroboration, especially at large scales, can also be labour intensive and expensive. Where possible, data collection efforts need to strengthen and reinforce existing national data sources to avoid the high demands and costs of imposing parallel data sets.

Likewise, careful consideration will be needed to identify meaningful indicators in ways that correspond with local educational priorities as well as international goals. Such approaches need to recognize that not everything is worth being measured, and not everything that is worthwhile in education can be quantified. The humble approach of those who collect and use statistics, therefore, is key to seeing the resulting insights as a starting point for further inquiry and exploration in advancing educational objectives and priorities. Thoughtful work by UNESCO's departments, among other agencies and researchers, can bring educational statistics to life, making projections where possible but also telling stories that illuminate and challenge their explanatory power.

Big data and the changing nature of knowledge

Technological advancements have generated new assumptions about what knowledge is and how it should be generated. Our current technologies have contributed to expectations that information, and the knowledge and understandings it gives rise to, will be big (drawn from multiple data points, not singular experiences), searchable (retrievable and easy to find), storable (able to be archived), transmissible (seamlessly sharable), and individualizable (optimized for personal consumption). Each of these qualities merit careful examination because they frame and mould ideas about education, including its purposes and processes, opening some possibilities and closing others.

Greater access to digital tools has given researchers unprecedented power to organize, synthesize, and process wider educational data sets than ever before. The power of digital methods, instruments, data collection and storage, and algorithmic data processing has kindled great enthusiasm in terms of how they can be used to advance understanding, practice and effectiveness of educational methods and approaches. Statistical data processing and charting, geographic mapping, network mapping, pattern seeking, and keyword tracing are among the tools that researchers can deploy. There is also great opportunity for research on the increasingly digitized aspects of our educational lives.

Today the praises of 'big data' are sung in university lecture halls, government offices, and corporate headquarters. This habit has two effects. The first is to presuppose that without large numbers of data points, or a large aggregation of profiles, micro-behaviours, keystrokes, eyeballs or electronic signals, no pattern can be discerned. And, according to one logic of data analytics, without patterns there is no meaning. The second effect is the subtler tendency to see data, especially quantifiable data that plays well with digital technology, as the most important form of knowledge. We have now witnessed the birth of data science as a special field of technical expertise, and, as in many fields, data science has tremendous sway in shaping compelling narratives and explanations in education.

As with any tools, it is important for researchers to clarify what can and cannot be achieved through digital research instruments. Depending on the purpose of a given inquiry, more data is not necessarily better or more precise. Our position is for a purpose-centred, rather than instrument-centred, research agenda and culture. The insights that computers can arrive at are not the same as those available to human beings. Sometimes software can reveal surprising and illuminating findings because of their ability to process data at greater scales and paces than humans ever could through analogue methods. Other times, human minds can understand contexts, meaning, values, and implications in ways far too sophisticated for AI.

As researchers draw on the immense potential of big data and digital tools in education, we must resist being enamoured with digital analytic software for the presentation of presumed objectivity. In particular, we need to continually evaluate the biases and blind spots of our digital research methods from a lens of justice and equity, to account for what lies beyond the purview of its programming. If these trends continue, there is considerable danger that in 2050 much of our knowledge will have become reshaped into quantitative, algorithm-friendly, molecular, easily storable, rapidly shareable forms that are only accessible through the mediation of digital devices. We should be concerned that the exploding field of AI seeks to make these properties self-sustaining, autonomous and independent of human management. The ethical risks of such ambitions will need vigilant attention over the next thirty years.

Innovating educational futures

Innovation in education reflects the ability to experiment, share, extend, and inspire others. It is possible at every site and scale, from a teacher working with an individual student or class, to school-wide or country-wide approaches. Innovation is often the fruit of much collaboration and inspiration from the experiences and successes of other educators, policy-makers, researchers, and schools in diverse contexts.

Developing, borrowing, and adapting policy and programming

Extending educational experiences and innovations to new settings through sharing of practices and policies will be crucial. The impulse to learn comparatively has the power to 'make the familiar strange,' by broadening perspectives and examining taken-for-granted idiosyncrasies and assumptions. Adaptation and borrowing should be seen as learning and innovation processes in their own right. We can all celebrate and draw inspiration from experiences elsewhere, in the light of the normative principles identified in this Report, while accounting for contextual conditions, experiences and existing knowledge.

Actors within educational systems are also important sources of innovative approaches and insights. Innovations that are entirely imposed from 'outside' the field will necessarily be limited, or even distorted, in their insights and proposed solutions. Educational knowledge is produced and legitimated in a range of ways. Its central actors – teachers, students, principals, schools, etc. – are all participants in the production of research and innovation. Curriculum development and reform can be especially enriched through the contributions of those who use it, as they enter into deeper participation with the knowledge commons. Governments have an important role to play in this regard, providing adequate support for teachers and schools to participate in dialogue and revision of public education systems and processes.

The question of scale often arises in research and innovation. Promising experience can be useful and shared. Yet 'best practices' themselves are often more focused on the outcomes than on detailing the process or conditions that led to them. Increasing collaborative networks and learning communities – among teachers, schools, literacy specialists, policy-makers etc. – can help support the real-time research and application of curricular, programmatic and policy insights from different contexts. An ethic of humility can help guard against ahistorical and decontextualized assumptions, on which any educational innovation is dependent.

Universities, research institutions and their partners are called on to put a special focus on research and innovation to support the renewal of education as a common good and the co-construction of a new social contract for education. They can become most effective, however, when they position themselves in relationship and in dialogue with those already working, thinking, reflecting in education – with teachers, students, schools, families, communities. As mentioned in earlier chapters, this will require a renewal of the public mission of universities towards the generation of an open and accessible knowledge commons, and the education of new generations of researchers and professionals who are committed to the advancement of knowledge for the benefit of themselves and humanity.

> Universities, research institutions and their partners are called on to put a special focus on research and innovation to support the renewal of education as a common good.

International organizations also have a unique and powerful role to play in the advancement of research and innovation in education towards a new social contract in education. Following this Report, UNESCO is invited to develop a clearinghouse of experiences that can dialogue with each other and make real, each in its own way, the proposals put forward in this Report. The speed of the world changing and new knowledge emerging requires this report to be dynamic and to be able to be rewritten at every moment.

Evaluation, experimentation and ranking

Evaluation and reflection represent necessary processes in the lifecycle of educational programmes and policies. Evaluations can help ensure that the aims motivating a programme or policy design are those that are being realized in action. They can understand and describe the outcomes of a programme and design, and importantly, they must account for their intended and unintended outcomes. For example, if a programme or policy is yielding clear benefits for some at the cost of increasing overall equality, or if it incentivizes short-term performance at the expense of long-term endurance, the assumptions of such intervention must be quickly rethought.

In keeping with the collaborative ethic of this Report, evaluation should harness the reflective capacities of those within education systems – teachers, students, and schools – to not only identify the challenges, weaknesses, or strengths of an innovation, but also to propose meaningful possibilities for its changes, improvements, or rejection. Importantly, a clear analytic framework is needed that ensures coherence between the purposes of an innovation's design, evaluation and recommendations.

Testing, experimentation and randomized control trials can help to validate assumptions, adjust techniques, correct miscalculations, and understand the limits of generalizability. The ability to isolate variables in complex systems, however, requires careful thought and sophisticated design. Crucially, in advancing a collaborative ethos for establishing a new social contract for education, we should recall the ethical principle that we do not experiment *on* people. All people – students, teachers, and families – should be seen as full participants in learning about their own education and development. The use of 'natural' experiments to understand the effects of how broader interventions or changes that are already being felt within educational experiences can also yield insight in coming years, particularly in the light of significant changes and disruptions on the horizon. These kinds of analyses can lend greater foresight knowledge to our understanding of education's resilience and responsiveness to change.

Useful comparisons can also be made to offer other vantage points for reflection, improvement, or inspiration, or highlight priority areas for greater inquiry, attention or support. Too often, however, comparisons and rankings are used punitively, steering away financial support or family enrolment from those settings that need it most. Comparison does little when it flattens experience, homogenizes expectations, and ignores the diversity of context, resources and historical factors.

It will also be important to rethink the ways comparative rankings are made in higher education. It is difficult to make comparisons in good faith, ethically, and without imposing homogeneity. Comparisons become problematic when vastly different higher education institutions, operating in contrasting contexts, feel compelled to compete in international rankings regardless of their own distinctive circumstances. Elite models of well-resourced research-intensive universities disproportionately influence the ambitions of other higher education institutions, often at the expense of local relevance and meeting the needs of local students and their communities.

However, higher education institutions themselves are not solely to blame for rankings and competition-driven institutional homogeneity. Governments and the global policy community also need to focus less myopically on the research-intensive end of higher education systems. More attention will need to be paid to the majority of institutions that the global majority attends. How well institutions serve their students' learning, professional futures, and their communities; how well institutions support civil discourse and political deliberation; how well institutions advance environmental, economic and social justice – these are often overlooked but hugely valuable points of comparison from which all can learn. Evaluation in higher education needs to go beyond competitive rankings, and instead seek to improve teaching and research capacities among all higher education institutions to fulfil their public mission.

Principles for dialogue and action

As we look to 2050 there are four key priorities related to research and innovation for the futures of education:

- **The Commission calls for a generalized, worldwide, collective research agenda on the futures of education.** This research programme must centre on the right to education for all, it should explore future disruptions and changes, and must advance understanding and experience with the tenets put forward in Part 2 of this Report. In the spirit of this Report, this research programme needs to recast its priorities in the light of futures literacy and futures thinking.

- **Knowledge, data, and evidence for the futures of education must be inclusive of diverse sources and ways of knowing.** Insights from differing perspectives can offer different vantage points to a shared understanding of education, rather than exclude and supplant one another.

- **Educational innovation must reflect a much wider range of possibilities across diverse contexts and places.** Comparisons and experiences can inspire one another but must respond appropriately to the distinct social and historical realities of a given context.

- **Research for a new social contract for education must be recast with everyone invited to take it forward.** The seeds are already sown, particularly among teachers, students and schools. Special responsibilities rest with research institutions, governments and international organizations to participate and support a research agenda that catalyzes the co-construction of a new social contract for education.

Chapter 9

A call for global solidarity and international cooperation

> A New Social Contract within societies will enable young people to live in dignity; will ensure women have the same prospects and opportunities as men; and will protect the sick, the vulnerable, and minorities of all kinds... Within a generation, all children in low- and middle-income countries could have access to quality education at all levels. This is possible. We just have to decide to do it... To close those gaps, and to make the New Social Contract possible, we need a New Global Deal to ensure that power, wealth and opportunities are shared more broadly and fairly at the international level.

António Guterres, UN Secretary-General, Nelson Mandela Lecture, 18 July 2020.

To catalyze a new social contract for education, the Commission calls for renewed commitment to global collaboration in support of education as a common good, premised on more just and equitable cooperation among state and non-state actors at local, national, and international levels.

The principle of education as a common good is inextricably linked with global responsibility. In 2020 and 2021, we have seen an unprecedented mobilization of scientific communities around the world to develop vaccines for COVID-19, supported by governments, public and private entities and civil society. Yet this impressive example of what global scientific cooperation can do when the future of humanity is at stake, has been muted by the much more difficult challenge of ensuring international equity in the delivery of these same vaccines. Despite widespread recognition that no one is safe until all are safe, vaccine nationalism has highlighted serious gaps in our ability to work collectively for the global common good.

> Vaccine nationalism has highlighted serious gaps in our ability to work collectively.

Education cultivates human ingenuity and our potential for collective action, each essential for meeting the major challenges of our time. Thus today, more than at any other time in human history, building a prosperous, just, sustainable, and peaceful world requires that all human beings, regardless of their origins, cultures and conditions, participate in quality education across their lifespans. Access to formal education and learning will need to be complemented by equitable access to knowledge and information: everyone, everywhere, will need digital access. Just as the health of any is connected to the health of all, our future survival depends on meeting the educational needs of every child, youth, and adult worldwide, so that they can participate conscientiously and actively in shaping and managing our common futures.

This awareness of education as a common good must be the foundation for strengthening international cooperation in education and public financing of education, both domestic and international. Ensuring that all children and young people have access to quality education is an essential pillar of a more just and sustainable global order, as UN Secretary-General António Guterres has recently argued. The obligation to respect, protect and fulfil the right to education falls not only on each state, but also on the international community.

Responding to an increasingly precarious world order

International educational cooperation operates within an increasingly precarious world order with the notion of a world society anchored in common universal values profoundly eroded. Global fora, such as the United Nations, which are responsible for establishing common goals and organizing global collective action, face harsh critique and fiscal constraint.

Nonstate actors and civil society – the boundary spanners and norm entrepreneurs responsible for advancing both domestic and international human rights during the twentieth century – struggle to build lasting alliances and coalitions within an increasingly fragmented world order. Their room for manoeuvre will be affected by the economic realities of a post-pandemic world, as international financing for their work contracts. Meanwhile, illiberal nonstate actors are on the rise as norm entrepreneurs and educators in their own right, ever more capable of exploiting digital technologies and flows of information in ways that work against values inscribed in the United Nations Declaration of Human Rights and made explicit most recently in the SDGs.

Economic changes of the past half century have been at least as profound as these political shifts. Technological and scientific advances, along with economic globalization, have certainly contributed to improvements in prosperity, a decline in household poverty worldwide, and better access to education. But they are no longer celebrated for creating an increasingly 'flat', and more open world. Economic growth has created powerful enclaves for those with wealth. Technological development has occurred in tandem with new forms of economic and informational monopoly that threaten the very foundations of liberal democracy. Despite long-held faith in the reinforcing relationship between economic growth and democracy, capabilities for collective action and democratic governance, both within nation-states and across them, have been unexpectedly constrained during recent decades of economic progress.

As tragically illustrated by the slow progress made on climate action, and in other areas in critical need of international cooperation (migration, peace, information privacy), in recent decades there has been limited consensus (or capacity for consensus) about global common goods and the kinds of international cooperation needed to meet our present challenges which disproportionately affect the poor.

Current UN reforms attempt to innovate in response to this crisis of multilateralism. In this chapter, three new approaches are suggested: inclusion of diverse non-state actors in global governance through partnerships; a movement away from top-down towards multi-centric action; and new forms of regional cooperation, especially South-South and triangular cooperation.

From aid to partnerships

International cooperation in education not only operates within a precarious world order but must also respond to it. Realizing a new global deal for education requires renewed modalities of international cooperation. At the same time, educational institutions themselves can help lay the foundation for broad-based understanding of current challenges and the need for collective action, especially by young people.

History shows us that the international architecture for educational cooperation has been profoundly shaped by colonialism alongside the drive for national economic and geopolitical interests. This architecture has been defined around flows of finance and the transfer of ideas from North to South. Today, international educational development and foreign aid remain problematic. Not only does education receive a very small share of overall official development assistance

(ODA), but aid to education is disproportionately skewed towards middle-income countries. Aid to education is decreasing for sub-Saharan Africa – a continent that will be home to the world's largest share of youth in 2050, and which is projected to face some of the most direct environmental and economic challenges on earth.

Moreover, education ODA tends to favour higher education, including scholarships, especially among the largest economies of the Group of Seven (G7) donor countries. Too little support is provided to ensure the realization of universal access to early childhood education and good quality primary and secondary education. A convincing global strategy for collective action to eradicate childhood illiteracy – a goal first adopted by the United Nations in the mid-twentieth century – has not emerged. A stubborn number of children remain out of school, and large numbers of children and youth attend school but learn little. The educational needs of refugees and involuntary migrants are also underfunded.

> The educational needs of refugees and involuntary migrants are also underfunded.

Lack of coordination among education aid donors remains a challenge. This is especially true among bilateral organizations from the North, who dominate in volume of aid. Almost twenty years after the Paris Declaration on Aid Effectiveness, education donors still tend to offer development aid in siloed, projectized formats that do not align with country needs. Multilateral channels for educational development are underutilized; and opportunities for pooling and harmonizing resources in ways that support innovation, better use of evidence and strengthening of national capacities, are lost.

Yet there are also new and promising developments in educational cooperation that can be built upon. Civil society engagement in education at local, national and international scales has flourished over recent decades, and new partnerships among governments and nonstate actors have emerged. South-South and triangular forms of development cooperation are on the rise. Powerful recent advocacy efforts have helped to place education higher on the global political agenda. Education is increasingly present on the agenda of global and regional political bodies.

Moving forward, three kinds of global public goods will be particularly important for achieving common, more equitable, more relevant and more sustainable educational futures. First, the international community needs to work together to help governments and non-state actors to align around the new shared purposes, norms and standards needed to achieve a new social contract for education. Second, the international community must invest in and promote a commonly accessible store of knowledge, research, data and evidence on education, and ensure that educators at all levels can generate and utilize evidence to improve educational systems. Finally, international financing must expand and be used to support those populations whose realization of the universal right to education is under greatest threat.

Towards shared purposes, commitments, norms and standards

From the mid-twentieth century, which saw the creation of the United Nations and UNESCO, and the adoption of the Universal Declaration of Human Rights, international cooperation in education has played a significant role in consensus-building about education's purposes and goals. Today, the need for deliberation about shared educational goals is ever more crucial.

We have to reframe international cooperation away from the historical focus on replication of ideas and institutions from the industrialized world. We need to foster South-South and triangular forms of deliberation. There is a particularly strong need for improved dialogue and consensus-building across different types of educational actors: teacher unions, student movements, youth organizations, civil society, private sector suppliers and employers, philanthropies, governments, and citizens. Cooperation focused on longer-term futures cannot fail to centre on the voices of children and youth.

As we enter a period of fiscal constraint caused by the prolongation of the Covid-19 pandemic, there will be growing need to prioritize around shared goals more sharply; and to ensure that international and domestic finance follows commitments. Global actors must come together to support common advocacy and fundraising agendas for achieving these goals, coordinating rather than competing for bilateral and philanthropic funding.

In setting common goals and frameworks for action, the education sector can draw on pertinent lessons from the climate and health sectors. We can do more to ensure that all actors who come to the international cooperation table set their own specific, timebound goals and commitments. International cooperation should be organized around the principle of subsidiarity since, the more concrete and locally-owned a goal, the more viable it becomes as a target for collective advocacy and accountability, and the more likely specific 'owners' of the goal will ensure its enactment. Stronger regional and global monitoring mechanisms can be created to ensure that actors are held accountable for these commitments and goals using evidence-based reviews of each actor's progress.

At the global level, the education sector and relevant global bodies have had difficulty prioritizing across thematic and sub-sectoral issues, often leading to a plethora of performative declarations, thinly spread activities and failure to achieve some of our most cherished and longstanding educational goals. Global institutions should not try to do everything. Their job is to strengthen the capacity of others to act. To do so they should concentrate on enhancing global and regional capacity for generating consensus-based commitments, ensuring accountability for these commitments. Global actors are also effective when they act as brokers of knowledge and evidence – ensuring participation of diverse actors in knowledge generation and utilization. They can also play an important role as the funders of last resort for acute educational challenges, particularly those in lower income countries and emergency contexts.

In shaping common educational futures, global institutions can play a unique role in orienting our attention to longer term challenges. For example, more research and debate should be focused on education's role in responding to the changing world of work and automation; on how to best address cross border externalities from migration and climate change; and on how to govern educational services that are increasingly digitized and provided transnationally.

> Global institutions can play a unique role in orienting our attention to longer term challenges.

A common agenda must be built together through broad processes of participation and joint decision-making. It must address the tension between long-term thinking to govern for the future, and the urgency of intervening in the present to rectify educational inequalities and exclusions inherited from the past.

Cooperation in knowledge generation and the use of evidence

Research and evidence are essential global goods in education. Together, they help governments and their partners problem-solve and innovate to accelerate educational transformation. They are also fundamental to strengthening international accountability for global, regional, and national commitments.

There has been much criticism of the misuse of disembodied data, league tables and other forms of 'governance by numbers' in the work of major international organizations from the OECD to the UN agencies. These criticisms are pertinent, yet we need shared statistical data to govern education systems equitably and ensure the common good. As demonstrated in the health and climate sectors, and by recent transnational advocacy in education, efforts to monitor and evaluate progress can contribute to greater global accountability for meeting our shared goals, and engaging different types of educational stakeholders.

To date, global actors have failed to pool and coordinate investments to maximize the availability and utility of international evidence and data. In contrast to global health, where major multilateral organizations pool resources to ensure the production of good quality monitoring data, there is no partnership arrangement among UN agencies to support joint standard-setting, statistical and related capacity-building roles. Effective aggregation and dissemination of evidence, mapping gaps in evidence and research, and strengthening capacity require new levels of coordination and financing from global actors.

Support to strengthen the capacity to generate and use knowledge, data and evidence must also be better financed and coordinated. At times, international efforts in knowledge and research appear to be unilateral conversations. This is unacceptable. International cooperation must open more space for countries from the Global South to define new and innovative research paradigms suited to their unique circumstances. In health, recent efforts to this end have focused on creating coordination platforms with the express goal of enhancing national and local capacity and supporting countries to learn from one another. New models for investing in South-South cooperation in educational problem-solving are essential. As highlighted in Chapter 8, this requires special attention be paid to the diverse epistemologies and ways of knowing that enrich thinking and support a wider diversity of innovative solutions.

Financing for international research, evidence and data is a major challenge in education. While about 25% of global ODA for health is spent on such global goods (about USD 7 billion); estimates placed funding for common knowledge, evidence, and data goods at less than 3% of ODA (or $200 million) in 2015. New options to improve global financing for research, knowledge and evidence should be considered, for example, through the establishment of a predictable pooled fund for educational knowledge and evidence generation under a group of UN agencies.

Financing education where it is threatened

While it is necessary to fundamentally rethink international cooperation in education and move away from the logic of dependency on aid, we must also reassess the role and focus of new relationships with international aid in education.

Aid supplies an ever-shrinking share of national needs, and as such will have declining influence and relevance on the global stage. It has reinforced the power imbalances derived from colonialism and has done too little to strengthen the sustainability of educational systems. At the same time, a pool of financing is needed that can support low and lower middle income countries – especially those in Africa where most youth will live in coming decades. Today only 47% of aid goes towards K-12 education in low and lower middle income countries. We also need to ensure that global funding is earmarked to support the educational needs of displaced populations and involuntary migrants, whose numbers will grow as the climate crisis deepens. As demonstrated by the COVID-19 pandemic, we will continue to need a reserve of international financing for emergency response and educational reconstruction after crises and emergencies.

To get from here to 2050, we will need to improve our current multilateral channels so that they can raise new resources to fill gaps, while strengthening national resource mobilization and national capacity. Greater harmonization of aid and coordination among donors around country-owned education plans and national systems remains as relevant today as it was when international donors approved the Paris Declaration on Aid Effectiveness in 2005.

Multilateral channels offer better opportunities for enhancing aid effectiveness and are more likely to direct aid to countries and populations that are most in need. But they too will need to improve their work, which remains projectized; unnecessarily ties borrowers and grant recipients to the knowledge and prescriptions they generate; and has a weak track record of supporting national capacity. In global public health, for example, recent proposals to remedy these failures include the separation of technical from financial support across agencies, and joint accountability mechanisms across multilateral organizations.

The role of UNESCO

UNESCO has faced many challenges over the past 25 years. While it has retained the formal responsibility for coordinating global dialogue and standard setting in education, and for ensuring achievement of SDG4 for education, it has struggled to meet these obligations effectively, and has faced severe criticism. It is sobering to note that despite the breadth of its mandate in education, science and culture, UNESCO's entire budget is smaller than that of many European universities. UNESCO's total education sector budget is a fraction of that mobilized by the World Bank for knowledge and capacity-building activities in education.

To play an effective role in our vision for sustainable educational futures, UNESCO will need to rethink its approach to educational development. Building on the principle of subsidiarity, it should see itself first as a partner whose job it is to strengthen regional and national institutions and processes. Secondly it is an evidence broker and an advocate for strengthened data and accountability to citizens at all levels of educational systems. While maintaining its unique role in fostering global dialogue for a new social contract for education, UNESCO must focus the bulk of its financial and human resources on regions where the right to education is most threatened – and particularly on Africa, where the vast majority of the world's youth will live and learn by 2050.

UNESCO will need a clearer sense of its comparative advantage within the complex ecosystem of global and regional actors involved in educational norm setting, financing and knowledge mobilization. It should work with UN partners to find innovative solutions to ensure the right to education of involuntary migrants and displaced populations whose numbers are expected to multiply over the course of our uncertain century. It should utilize its global presence to advocate for enhanced and more equitable access to digital information as a human right. UNESCO must also support the engagement of citizens and civil society in educational governance so that education is responsive to their needs. It must continue to act as the United Nation's beacon on the role played by education in building our shared futures, including by strengthening education for peace, prosperity, and sustainability.

UNESCO has a unique capacity to convene and mobilize people and institutions around the world to shape our shared educational futures. Herein lies its great strength. And it is precisely this strength that is needed to build a new, internationally agreed social contract for education and, more importantly, a new deal for implementing it.

Principles for dialogue and action

This chapter raises a call for renewed international collaboration to respond to the future needs, challenges, and possibilities of education. As we look to 2050 there are four key priorities related to international cooperation for the futures of education:

- **The Commission calls on all educational stakeholders to work together at global and regional levels to generate shared purposes and common solutions to educational challenges.** Creating the new social contract needed to support just and equitable educational futures for all humanity is especially pertinent for those whose right to education is most threatened by global challenges. Participation must include diverse non-state actors and partnerships, move away from top-down towards multi-centric action, and embrace new forms of regional cooperation, especially South-South and triangular cooperation.

- **International cooperation should operate from a principle of subsidiarity, supporting and building capacity in local, national, and regional efforts to address challenges.** Enhanced accountability towards meeting educational commitments and coordinated advocacy for educational improvements will be needed to reinforce new educational commitments, norms and standards.

- **A focus on international development financing for low and lower middle income countries remains important.** This applies particularly to countries with sharply constrained economies and young populations, especially in Africa. We also need financing that targets populations whose right to education is disrupted by crises and emergencies.

- **Common investments in evidence, data, and knowledge are also an essential part of effective international cooperation.** Here our efforts should also be guided by the principle of subsidiarity, emphasizing the need to scaffold local, national and regional capacity to generate and use knowledge. More than ever we need to strengthen mutual learning and exchange of knowledge across societies and borders – both in core areas such as ending educational inequality and poverty and improving public services, and to meet the longer term challenges brought by automation and digitization, migration and environmental sustainability. Pooled platforms and new sources of financing are needed to ensure both dimensions in global knowledge and data for educational progress.

This agenda for global solidarity and action must be built with tenacity, boldness and coherence, and always with an eye on 2050 and beyond. It implies shared responsibility and improved coordination within the United Nations and strengthening the role of UNESCO. Without this, the proposals formulated in this Report, namely in defining education as a global, public and common good and establishing a new social contract for education, cannot be realized. In one generation, we can transform education systems so that they are truly inclusive, relevant and increase our capacity to meet our global challenges.

Epilogue and continuation
Building futures of education together

We must urgently work together to forge a new social contract for education that can meet the future needs of humanity and the planet. This Report has proposed priorities and made recommendations for the construction of this new contract grounded in two foundational principles: an expanded vision of the right to education throughout life, and the strengthening of education as a public and a common good.

At the core of the Report is the proposal for a new social contract for education – the implicit agreements and principles that enable and inspire social cohesion around education, and that give rise to corresponding educational arrangements. This epilogue is dedicated to summarizing the key priorities and proposals that readers are invited to carry forward with others, to reinterpret, and to reimagine for our shared futures of education.

A new social contract for education is not an abandonment of all that we have collectively learned and experienced about education so far, but neither is it a mere course correction on a path already defined and set. A new social contract has long been in the making – by educators, communities, youth and children, families – who have identified the limitations of existing educational systems with precision and have pioneered new approaches to overcoming them.

> A new social contract has long been in the making – by educators, communities, youth and children, families – who have identified the limitations of existing educational systems with precision and have pioneered new approaches to overcoming them.

But without collective moments of coming together and striving to articulate what we are learning in our ongoing endeavour to remake education, efforts often occur in isolation or with limited adjustments to large institutional machinery. It is by actively engaging in the dialogue and practice to build a new social contract for education that we can renew education to make just, equitable and sustainable futures possible. This Report is an invitation to contextualize and to take these public dialogues forward. It is intended as a catalyst and a provocation for dialogues around the world on what a social contract for education will mean in practice and in particular contexts. This Report is therefore a milestone on a road stretching into the future. It is a living document proposing a framework, principles, and recommendations to be further explored, shared, and enriched by people around the world. The aim is to inspire new avenues for policy development and innovative action to renew and transform education so that it truly prepares all learners to invent a better future. It will have meaning in transforming education only as teachers, students, families, government officials, and other stakeholders of education, in particular communities, engage with the ideas in the report and co-construct what these ideas are to mean in practice in those communities.

The Commission calls on UNESCO to develop and sustain appropriate avenues for deliberation, participation and the sharing of experiences that relate to the many ideas put forward here. The future success of the Report rests on its ability to stimulate a process of ongoing reflection and action. The work of education will always be 'in process' and the recommendations presented here are founded on an assumption that they must continually shift and evolve. We need greater cooperation as we learn to live in greater harmony with each other, with the remarkable lifeforms and systems that distinguish our planet, and with technology that is both quickly opening new spaces and potentials for human thriving, as well as presenting unparalleled risks.

The global consensus around the value of education to make and remake our world is our collective point of departure. This shared conviction is unassailable and fortifies our commitment as we face new challenges, many of them without precedent. For things to be done differently, we now need to think, understand, listen, and imagine differently. We need an open examination of which established ways of thinking about education, knowledge and learning can open new paths to transform the future.

Proposals for building a new social contract

The Report examined five dimensions for changes needed to build a new social contract for education. The key proposals for each of these dimensions were highlighted in Part 2 of this Report, along with guiding principles for carrying them forward. While these are not exhaustive, they are summarized here as an initial framework for action that can be localized and advanced to realize new futures through education.

Pedagogies of solidarity and cooperation

Pedagogy needs to be transformed around the principles of cooperation and solidarity, replacing longstanding modes of exclusion and individualistic competition. Pedagogy must foster empathy and compassion and must build the capacities of individuals to work together to transform themselves and the world. Learning is shaped through relationships between teachers, students, and knowledge that go beyond the limitations of classroom norms and codes of conduct. Learning extends students' relationships with the ethics and care needed to assume responsibility for our shared and common world. Pedagogy is the work of creating transformational encounters that are based in what exists and what can be built.

Looking to 2050 we need to abandon pedagogical modes, lessons, and measurements that prioritize individualistic and competitive definitions of achievement. Instead, we need to prioritize the following guiding principles:

First, interconnectedness, interdependency and solidarity are necessary to pedagogy that is individually and collectively transformative. As teachers learn how to foster pedagogical relationships within and beyond the classroom, schools and education systems must find ways to incorporate these practices at more institutional levels. Experience and dialogue, service and meaningful action, research and reflection, participation in constructive social movements and community life – these are but a few of many promising approaches. Schools and education systems must also break down social and sectoral walls to listen to families and communities, and to extend into other domains of life to support new connections and pedagogical relationships beyond the classroom.

Second, cooperation and collaboration should form the basis of pedagogy as a collective, relational process. Teachers can engage in a wide range of learning strategies – from peer feedback, project-based learning, problem-posing and inquiry-based learning, student laboratories, technical and vocational workshops, to artistic expression and creative collaborations – all to nurture students' abilities to face new challenges in creative and unforeseen ways, individually and collectively. Schools and education systems can explore ways to facilitate a wider range of encounters across age groups, interests, social sectors, languages and stages of learning.

> Pedagogy is the work of creating transformational encounters that are based in what exists and what can be built.

Third, solidarity, compassion and empathy should be ingrained in how we learn. Pedagogies enable students to understand a wider range of experiences than their own. Parents and families can also be welcomed to participate in sharing and valuing diversity and pluralism alongside their children, which is essential to unlearning bias, prejudice and divisiveness across the environments and relationships that students encounter. Schools and teachers can create environments that value empathy and sustain diverse histories, languages and cultures, among them, especially, indigenous communities and a broad range of social movements.

Fourth, all assessment is pedagogical, and must therefore be carefully considered to support wider pedagogical priorities for student growth and learning. Teachers, schools, and education systems can use assessments to prioritize identifying and addressing challenging areas, in order to better support learning individually and collectively. Assessment should not be used punitively or to create categories of 'winners' and 'losers.' Educational policy should not be unduly influenced by rankings that put excessive priority on high-stakes, decontextualized examinations, which in turn are shown to put disproportionate pressure on influencing what occurs in the time and space of schools.

Curriculum and the knowledge commons

A new relationship must be established between education and the knowledge, capabilities, and values that it promotes. Curricula need to be framed in relation to two vital processes that underpin education: the acquisition of knowledge as part of the common heritage of humanity, and the collective creation of new knowledge and new possible futures. Looking to 2050, we need to go beyond traditional views of curricula as simply a grid of school subjects and instead reimagine them through interdisciplinary and intercultural perspectives that enable students to learn from and contribute to humanity's knowledge commons. The following guiding principles should be prioritized:

First, curricula should enhance learners' abilities to access and contribute to the knowledge commons which is the inheritance of all humanity and must be continuously broadened to include diverse ways of knowing and understanding. Curricular design and implementation should move away from the narrow transmission of facts and information, and instead seek to foster in learners the concepts, skills, values and attitudes that will enable them to engage with diverse forms of knowledge acquisition, application, and generation.

> Two vital processes underpin education: the acquisition of knowledge as part of the common heritage of humanity, and the collective creation of new knowledge and new possible futures.

Second, our rapidly changing climate and planetary conditions require curricula that reorient the place of humans in the world. Irreversible planetary changes are already accelerating, and education must foster appreciation for the inherent interconnectedness of environmental, societal and economic well-being. Curricula must draw from diverse forms of knowledge, preparing students and communities to adapt to, mitigate, and reverse climate change in a way that sees humans as inextricably interconnected with a more-than-human world. Curricula should highlight the effects of climate change on their communities, the world and, especially those who are often marginalized, for example the poor, minorities and women and girls. Curricular knowledge can provide a powerful framework for meaningful action and support children and youth to continue leading on climate mitigation and environmental protection efforts that will have profound impacts on their futures.

Third, the rapid spread of misinformation and manipulation must be countered through multiple literacies – digital, scientific, textual, ecological, mathematical – that enable individuals to find their way to knowledge that is true and accurate. Such literacies are essential for meaningful and effective democratic participation based on shared truths. Effective literacies must cultivate understanding not only of facts, information, and data, but also of the processes, like corroboration and sensible sourcing, needed to arrive at sound conclusions, validate findings, and communicate them accurately. Curricula can draw on a wide range of historical, cultural, and methodological approaches to develop in students a love for understanding, accuracy, precision, and a commitment to truth.

Fourth, human rights and democratic participation should inform the foundational principles for curricula and learning that transform people and the world. Human rights must continue to be sacrosanct for all people, and as a collective point of departure that underpins our social contract, they must become foundational to the curricula that shape learning. Curricula should emphasize the inherent rights and dignity of all people, and the imperative to overcome violence and build peaceful societies. Interactions with social movements and grassroots communities can imbue curricula with authentic pathways to question, reveal and confront the power structures that discriminate against groups due to gender, race, indigenous identity, language, sexual orientation, age, disability, or citizenship status.

Teachers and the teaching profession

Teachers have a unique role to play in building a new social contract for education through their profession. They are key convenors, bringing together different elements and environments as they work collaboratively to help grow students' knowledge and capabilities. No technology is yet capable of replacing or obviating the need for good human teachers. Looking to 2050, it is essential that we move away from treating teaching as a solitary practice that relies on a single individual to orchestrate effective learning. Instead, teaching should become a collaborative profession where teamwork ensures meaningful student learning. The following principles should be prioritized:

> No technology is yet capable of replacing good human teachers.

First, collaboration and teamwork should characterize the work of teachers. The wide range of purposes that we have for education go beyond what can be expected from even the most talented of individual teachers. We will need teachers to work in teams with their fellow teachers, with subject specialists, literacy specialists and librarians, special needs educators, guidance counsellors, social workers and others. The need for collaborative work will become even more pressing in years to come, as humanity faces an increasing range of disruptions, and teachers will continue to be at the frontline of helping children, youth, and adults to appropriately navigate their changing world in age-appropriate ways. Just as students' well-being, healthy relationships and mental health must be supported in educational settings, support must also be extended to teachers in the form of liveable wages, career advancement, continued education, professional development, and collaborative learning environments to enable them to carry forward their important work.

Second, producing knowledge, reflection and research should be recognized as integral to teaching. Research and knowledge about the futures of education begins with the work teachers perform, and indeed, many of the elements of a new social contract for education may already exist in the transformative pedagogy many teachers are practicing. Teachers' work as knowledge producers and pedagogical pioneers must be recognized and supported, assisting them to document, share, and discuss relevant research and experience with their fellow educators and schools in formal and informal ways. Universities and higher education can imagine new institutional configurations that enable sustained research and professional relationships with teachers in support of their profession-wide knowledge production.

Third, the professional autonomy of teachers must be upheld and protected. The teaching profession requires a wide range of advanced skills and ongoing professional development. In the coming decades, much support will be needed to strengthen and expand high quality preservice teacher education, particularly in sub-Saharan Africa where the demand for schooling continues to outstrip the supply of qualified teaches due to a booming youth population. Professional development for novice teachers can be further provided through ongoing education, mentorship and collaborative co-teaching. Adequate time must be allotted for lesson preparation and reflection, and they must receive fair and equitable pay. Assuring professional autonomy, social respect and decent wages will incentivize skilled educators to remain in the profession and skilled and motivated individuals to enter it.

Participation in public educational debate, dialogue and education policy should be integrated and recognized as part of the core work of teachers. Too often, decisions about what happens within schools or classrooms are made by those far outside of them, with little dialogue, interaction, or meaningful feedback loops. For the futures of education, this will need to change, and teachers must be welcomed as leaders and vital informants in public debate, policy and dialogue on our futures of education. Teacher engagement in these areas needs to be embedded in shared understandings that this constitutes a core function of what it means to be a teacher; they must be seen as key participants in forging a new social contract for education.

Safeguarding and transforming schools

Schools, with all their potential and promise, deficiencies and limitations, remain among society's most essential educational settings. Schools are a central pillar of larger educational ecosystems, and their vitality is an expression of a society's commitment to education as a public human activity and to its children and youth. Looking to 2050, we can no longer have schools organized according to a uniform model regardless of context. In place of current architectural, procedural and organizational models, we need a massive public effort to redesign the times and places of schools in ways that both safeguard and transform them. The following priorities should guide this essential work:

First, schools should be protected as spaces where students encounter challenges and possibilities not available to them elsewhere. Schools will require environments of cooperation and care in which diverse groups of people learn from and with one another. They can enable teachers and students to interact with new ideas, cultures, and ways of seeing the world in a supportive and caring environment, not only preparing children

> Schools are a central pillar of larger educational ecosystems, and their vitality is an expression of a society's commitment to education as a public human activity and to its children and youth.

and youth for challenges in their future lives, but helping them negotiate the rapidly changing world they live in now.

Second, school architectures, spaces, times, timetables, and student groupings should be reimagined and designed to build the capacities of individuals to work together. The built environment and inclusive design have pedagogical value in their own right and influence what occurs in shared spaces of learning. Cultures of collaboration should also guide the administration and management of schools, as well as relations among schools, to foster robust networks of learning, reflection and innovation.

Third, digital technologies should aim to support what happens within schools; in their current and foreseeable iterations they are inadequate replacements for formal and physical institutions of learning. Leveraging digital tools will be useful and essential to enhance student creativity and communication in the coming decades and navigating digital spaces can open new opportunities for accessing and participating in shared knowledge and human experiences. Efforts to apply AI and digital algorithms in schools must proceed with caution and care to ensure they do not reproduce and exacerbate existing stereotypes and systems of exclusion.

Fourth, schools should model the futures we aspire to by ensuring human rights and becoming exemplars of sustainability and carbon neutrality. Students should be trusted and tasked with helping to green the education sector. Local and indigenous design principles that are responsive to environmental conditions and changes can become sources of learning about adaptation, mitigation, and prevention to build better futures and establish greater symbiosis with the natural world and systems of which we are a part and upon which we depend. We will also need to ensure that education and other policies concerning schools uphold and advance human rights for all who inhabit them and beyond.

Education across different times and spaces

One of our major tasks is to broaden thinking about where and when education takes place, expanding it to more times, spaces and stages of life. We need to understand the full educational potential that exists in life and society, from birth to old age, and connect the multitude of sites and often overlapping cultural, social and technological possibilities which exist to advance education. We can imagine our future societies providing and encouraging learning in a multiplicity of sites beyond formal schools and at planned and spontaneous times. As we look to 2050 there are four principles that can guide the dialogue and action needed to take this recommendation forward.

> We can imagine our future societies providing and encouraging learning in a multiplicity of sites beyond formal schools and at planned and spontaneous times.

First, at all stages of life people should have meaningful quality educational opportunities. Education is both lifelong and life-wide. Adult learning and education must be further developed and supported, going beyond deficit conceptions of 'skilling' and 'reskilling' to embrace the transformative possibilities of education at all stages of life. Any planning for education across life must focus on serving those most marginalized and on settings that are most fragile, helping to equip learners with the knowledge, concepts, attitudes and skills they need to realize opportunities and face present and future disruptions.

Second, healthy educational ecosystems connect natural, built and virtual sites of learning. The biosphere – its lands, waters, life, minerals, atmospheres, systems, and interactions – should be understood as a vital learning space. It is among our first educators. In parallel, digital learning spaces must be further integrated into educational ecosystems and should be made to support the publicness, inclusivity and common good purposes of education. Open access and open-source platforms with strong protections for student and teacher data should be prioritized.

Third, public financing and government capacity for the regulation of education should be strengthened. We should build the capacity of states to set and enforce standards and norms for educational provision that is responsive, equitable and upholds human rights. At local, national, regional and global levels, governments and public institutions should commit to dialogue and action around these principles to support the reimagining of our futures together.

Fourth, the right to education should be broadened; we are no longer well served by framing it simply around formal schooling. Looking to the future, we should promote a right to lifelong and life-wide learning enabled by the right to information, to connectivity, and to culture.

Calls to action

The Report has issued two calls to catalyze and harmonize efforts towards a new social contract for education: a call for a new research agenda for education, and a call for renewed solidarity and cooperation to support education as a public and a common good. Principles guiding the response to these two calls are summarized here to help channel and reinforce our efforts to forge new futures of education while responding to rapidly changing conditions.

A new research agenda for education

The priorities highlighted in this report buttress a coherent and common research agenda. The learning, insights and experiences generated from such a far reaching research agenda will be catalytic to forging a new social contract for education together. As we look to 2050, there are four priorities guiding research and innovation for the futures of education:

First, a worldwide, collective research programme on the futures of education must centre on the right to education for all throughout life, while anticipating future disruptions and

> A worldwide, collective research programme on the futures of education must centre on the right to education for all throughout life.

considering their implications. Research must also go beyond mere measurement and critique to explore the renewal of education along the guiding principles recommended in this Report. This research programme needs to recast its priorities in the light of futures literacy and futures thinking to move us towards a new social contract for education.

Second, knowledge, data and evidence for the futures of education must be inclusive of diverse sources and ways of knowing. Insights from differing perspectives can offer different vantage points of a shared understanding of education, rather than excluding and supplanting one another. Researchers, universities, and research institutions must examine methodological assumptions and approaches that are decolonizing, democratic and facilitate the exercise and promotion of human rights. Schools, teachers, social movements, youth movements and communities are vital sources of knowledge and information and should be recognized as such by researchers. Findings from the learning sciences, neuroscience, digital and big data, and statistical indicators, can yield important insights when considered in relation to a wider range of empirical inputs, including qualitative and practitioner research.

Third, educational innovation must reflect a much wider range of possibilities across diverse contexts, times, and places. Comparisons and experiences can inspire people when reconsidered and recontextualized appropriately to the distinct social and historical realities of a given context. Educational innovation should also seek, at times, to break away from institutional convergence that influences current formal systems. Evaluation and reflection should steer educational policies in an ongoing and integrative manner thereby elevating regular refinement as a theory of change, breaking away from stagnation on the one hand and cycles of endless regime change on the other.

Fourth, research for a new social contract in education must be reconsidered to include more people from diverse stakeholder groups, including those not normally active in discussions about education. The seeds of a new social contract are already alive, particularly among teachers, students, and schools. Special responsibilities rest with research institutions, governments and international organizations to participate in and support a research agenda that catalyzes the co-construction of this contract. UNESCO can play an important role as a clearing house for knowledge, visioning and idea generation about our shared futures of education.

Renewed international solidarity and cooperation

The ambitious vision articulated in this Report cannot be accomplished without solidarity and collaboration at every scale – from the immediate settings of classrooms and schools to broad national, regional, and global commitments and policy frameworks. The Report calls for renewed commitment to global collaboration in support of education as a public and a common good, premised on more just and equitable cooperation among state and non-state actors at local, national and international levels. As we look to 2050, we should adhere to four guiding principles related to international solidarity and cooperation for the futures of education.

First, the Commission calls on all educational stakeholders to work together at global and regional levels to generate shared purposes and common solutions to educational challenges. Efforts must harmonize and reorient themselves around the vision of just and equitable educational futures for all of humanity, premised on the right to education throughout life and the value of education as a public and a common good. Collective action must especially prioritize learners whose right to education is most threatened by global disruptions and change. Over the coming decades, global collaboration must address power imbalances by including diverse non-state actors and partnerships. It should further move away from top-down towards multi-centric action and embrace new forms of regional cooperation, especially South-South and triangular cooperation.

> Collective action must especially prioritize learners whose right to education is most threatened by global disruptions and change.

Second, international cooperation should operate from a principle of subsidiarity, supporting and building capacity in local, national and regional efforts to address challenges. Enhanced accountability at every level will be needed to reinforce new educational commitments, norms and standards. UNESCO will need to rethink its approach to educational development to see itself first as a partner, whose job it is to strengthen regional and national institutions and processes, and second as an evidence broker, knowledge producer and an advocate for strengthened data about education systems and accountability to citizens.

Third, a focus on international development financing for low and lower middle income countries remains important, in particular for those with sharply constrained economies and young populations. International cooperation must urgently focus the bulk of its financial and human resources on regions where the right to education is most threatened – and particularly on sub-Saharan Africa, where the vast majority of the world's youth will live and learn by 2050. These resources should also be directed towards emergency settings which are likely to increase in frequency as climate change accelerates.

Fourth, common investments in evidence, data, and knowledge are also an essential part of effective international cooperation. Over the coming decades, we will need to strengthen mutual learning and exchange of knowledge across societies and borders – both in core areas such as ending educational inequality and poverty and improving public services, and to meet longer term challenges brought by automation and digitization, migration and environmental sustainability. UNESCO is crucial to facilitating this exchange between countries and regions.

Dialogue and participation

There is great reason for hope. Large-scale change and innovation are possible in the design of education systems, the organization of schools and other educational systems, and in curriculum and pedagogical approaches. Collectively we can transform education to help build just, equitable, and sustainable futures drawing on what already exists and building what else is needed. We will change course through millions of individual and collective acts of courage, leadership, resistance, creativity and care. We have deep, rich, and diverse cultural traditions to build upon. Humans have great collective agency, intelligence, and creativity. Promising practices can be innovative or rooted in tradition, as both can unleash new possibilities.

> We will change course through millions of individual and collective acts of courage, leadership, resistance, creativity and care.

The dialogue proposed in this Report must involve the widest participation possible. Education is a decisive factor in citizenship, at the local, national and global levels. It concerns everyone, and everyone can participate in building the futures of education in whatever spheres of influence they are situated within. This report has proposed that there are particular participation roles for teachers, universities, governments, international organizations and youth to further extend this forward-looking dialogue and action:

- **Teachers.** Teachers remain central to the futures of education. In the same way that they have been foundational to the social contract that has been in force since the nineteenth century, they will also be decisive convenors, practitioners and researchers for the construction of a new social contract for education. For this, it is necessary to assure their autonomy and freedom, support their development throughout their professional life and recognize their role in society and their participation in public policies. Teachers will naturally be central protagonists in the construction of processes of dialogue and innovation, bringing together and convening other people and groups.

- **Universities and higher education.** Special calls to universities and higher education institutions have been present in every chapter of this report, just as they are present in all the realities of the new social contract of education. Today, few people question the crucial role that universities, and all higher education institutions, play in the creation and dissemination of knowledge. This is the case in all disciplines, but it is particularly true regarding education. Much of the future of basic education depends on work done by universities, and vice-versa. Much of the future of universities depends on the work done in basic education. Universities are also expected to find new and more impactful ways to educate children and youth, especially young children, and to become more involved in adult education practices. Higher education is, by definition, a locus of an intergenerational and transformative dialogue, and a large part of the futures outlined in this Report depend on them. Without strong, autonomous, credible and innovative higher education, it will be impossible to build the social contract of education envisioned in this Report.

- **Governments.** This Report has stressed the irreplaceable role of governments. However, this does not mean that its proposals are only situated at the level of national educational systems. Instead of following the usual government-centric logic of reports about educational reform, this Report aims to encourage a wider range of stakeholders to participate, with research, knowledge, innovation, analysis and action. It is a question of valuing the action of government at multiple levels, less through a logic of reform, and more from the perspective of becoming promoters of broader participation and catalysts for innovation. Furthermore, governments have unique roles in preserving and consolidating the public character of education by ensuring adequate and sustained public financing of education and building capacity to properly regulate education.

- **International and civil society organizations.** This Report has emphasized the importance of international and civil society organizations, especially through the repeated affirmation of education as a public and a common good. This repetition is intended to signal an important shift in perspective, giving space to new voices in educational cooperation, locally, nationally, regionally, internationally and across sectors. A strong mobilization of international and civil society organizations is expected to take forward the dialogue proposed in this Report, and do so with their unique knowledge, expertise and mobilization capacity. These organizations also hold a special place in ensuring that people who are discriminated against because of their ideas, gender, race or ethnicity, culture, religious beliefs, or sexual identity are heard, visible and supported in their right to education.

- **Youth and children.** Finally, and unquestionably, the dialogue proposed here must involve young people. The future must be reframed for them as one full of possibility rather than a burden. It is not just a question of listening to or consulting them, but of mobilizing and supporting them in the construction of the futures that will be – and are already – theirs. Recent examples of important youth and children's movements, particularly in the fight against climate change, against racial discrimination, against patriarchy and restrictive gender norms, and for the diversity of cultures and indigenous self-determination, show us essential paths for the future. The youth leading these movements did not ask for authorization, but rather responded with urgency and moral clarity to issues that too often overwhelm or paralyze adults. They have a seminal and guiding role to play in building our and their futures. The most important aspect of the continuation of this Report is the ability to enlist young people in the construction of a new social contract for education.

Around the world teachers, communities, organizations, and governments have already embarked on many promising educational initiatives to create the change that is needed. Countless examples show us the many ways that knowledge can be co-created and publicly shared. Other examples illuminate how education can create meaning, empower and emancipate, and the ways that learning can be more effectively organized for the common good. These existing practices need to be nurtured as they chart courses for the creation of futures filled with hope.

The good work unfolding around the world needs to become better known, and the Commission recommends that UNESCO become a catalyst and a clearinghouse of promising practices and innovative implementations of the principles put forth in this report.

Invitation to continue

At core, this Report calls for and aims to facilitate and provoke broad social dialogue about desirable futures and how education can help build them. Its ideas reflect a moment in time, building on the result of a two-year process of dialogue and consultations. The Report's proposals culminate with invitations to continue multiple conversations, collaborations and partnerships into the future. It is those conversations, collaborations, and partnerships that will most matter to the future of education – not the Report itself.

While the Report articulates a vision of the challenges and hopes that should animate efforts to educate for the future, and puts forward ideas about how to do this, it also insists that a new social contract for education is not self-executing. For it to take form and have impact, it must be translated into programmes, resources, systems, and processes, that transform the everyday activities and experiences of students and teachers.

Education engages a large number of individuals and groups in a complex web of relationships. It involves students, teachers, families, education administrators and leaders at multiple levels of government, and touches the public sector as well as civil society, within communities, provinces, nations, regions and globally. The transformation of educational culture is the result of processes of co-construction in which many groups bring forth their interests and understandings to re-examine them in light of new ideas and in conversation with others. Cooperation is essential to translate the principles, proposals, and strategies raised here into new realities. It is such co-construction of ideas about how we teach and learn and towards what end, that ultimately leads to clarity, commitment and support for the resources and activities that can transform educational practices. Practices change when the conditions that can support this change are well understood, accepted and implemented.

Each one of us can improve the communities we live in. The possibility to convene dialogue lies with us all. This is especially true in an era in which the ubiquity of communication technologies gives ordinary people the means to connect and organize to achieve ambitious purposes. Access to technology and to the internet make possible unprecedented collaboration between teachers, educational institutions and communities to realize opportunities and find solutions to challenges.

The COVID-19 pandemic has cast a shadow over the release of this Report and most of its preparation. This global event has awakened recognition for the importance of wide collaboration and co-construction. We have yet to take full measure of the educational harm and loss caused by COVID-19, but we know it is severe, and risks erasing decades of progress. Its consequences have been felt most harshly by the poor and marginalized, in the Global South and where it is compounded with other challenges. Its trail of death and loss, combined with the accelerating and intensifying realities of climate change, remind us most powerfully that we live on this planet connected to others. The invention of vaccines to protect against COVID-19 previewed the scope and speed of what is possible when we come together around knowledge, science and learning to find solutions. This Report hopes that this newfound recognition gives impetus to the call to come together and build new and brighter educational futures.

In this context of urgency, but also of great possibility, the ideas outlined in this Report help us to reimagine our futures together and build a new social contract for education. This Report is an invitation to think and act together in building the futures of education together. It is a starting point, the beginning of a process of dialogue and co-construction. This Report, like education itself, is not finished. On the contrary, its actualization begins now, through the labours of educators around the world and those who work alongside them.

Appendices

Selected references

Independent reports

The following reports were received in response to an open call to organize seminars and workgroups to help identify key challenges and opportunities and provide inputs and recommendations to the International Commission on the Futures of Education. Some 200 other organizations also provided reports to UNESCO's Futures of Education initiative on the basis of focus groups and these partners are listed in the section below on Contributors to the Global Consultation.

Arab Campaign for Education for All. 2020. *Summary report on the Futures of Education in the Arab States: Building the future (2020-2050)*. Ramallah, Arab Campaign for Education for All. http://www.teachercc.org/articles/view/379

Asia South Pacific Association for Basic and Adult Education. 2021. *From the margins to the center: Youth informing the futures of education*. Manila, Asia South Pacific Association for Basic and Adult Education. http://www.aspbae.org/userfiles/2021/Futures_of_Education_Report.pdf.

Barber, P., Bertet, M., Choi, J., Czerwitzki, K., Njobati, F. F., Grau I Callizo, I., Hambrock, H., Herveau, J., Kastner, A., Laabs, J., Manalo, A., Mesa, J., Mutabazi, S., Muthigani, A., Richard, P., Scheunpflug, A., Sendler-Koschel, B., White, M., and Wodon, Q. 2020. *Christian schools and the futures of education: a contribution to UNESCO's Futures of Education Commission by the International Office of Catholic Education and the Global Pedagogical Network – Joining in Reformation*. International Office of Catholic Education and Global Pedagogical Network – Joining in Reformation. http://oiecinternational.com/wp-content/uploads/2020/12/OIEC-GPENR-contribution.pdf

Bridge 47. 2020. *The role of education in addressing future challenges*. Bridge 47. https://www.bridge47.org/sites/default/files/2020-12/bridge47_-_report_to_unesco_foe_international_commission_final.pdf

Éducation, Recherches et Actualités. 2021. *L'Éducation du futur - L'enseignement supérieur : défis et paradoxes*. Beirut et Paris, Université Saint Joseph et Université Gustave Eiffel. https://www.periodicos.ufam.edu.br/index.php/larecherche

Emmaüs International. 2020. *Rapport à l'attention de la commission internationale de l'initiative de l'UNESCO : « Les futurs de l'éducation : apprendre à devenir »*. Montreuil, France, Emmaüs International. https://emmaus-international.org/images/actualites/2020/10/EMMAS_INTERNATIONAL_-_Contribution_Les_futurs_de_lducation__juillet_2020_003.pdf

Garcés, C. E. 2020. *Aportación para la Comisión Internacional*. Madrid.

International Council for Adult Education (ICAE). 2020. *Adult Learning and Education (ALE) – Because the future cannot wait*. International Council for Adult Education. https://en.unesco.org/futuresofeducation/sites/default/files/2020-10/ICAE%20-%20Futures%20of%20ALE%20FINAL.pdf

International Task Force on Teachers for Education 2030. 2021. *The futures of teaching: Background paper prepared for the Futures of Education Initiative*. Paris, UNESCO https://teachertaskforce.org/knowledge-hub/futures-teaching-background-paper-prepared-futures-education-initiative-0

International Union for Conservation of Nature (IUCN) Commission on Education and Communication (CEC). 2021. *Visions and Recommendations for the Futures of Education*. Gland, Switzerland, International Union for Conservation of Nature. https://www.iucn.org/sites/dev/files/content/documents/cec_report_to_unesco_foe_-_6.5.pdf

Mouvement International ATD Quart Monde. 2020. *Contribution du Mouvement International ATD Quart Monde aux Futurs de l'Éducation*. Pierrelaye, France, Mouvement ATD Quart Monde – Agir Tous pour la Dignité. https://nextcloud.atd-quartmonde.org/index.php/s/DzMMci4yqP6dkPA

Red Regional por la Educación Inclusiva de Latinoamérica. 2020. *Los futuros de la educación - Contribuciones de la Red Regional por la Educación Inclusiva de Latinoamérica*. Buenos Aires, Red Regional por la Educación Inclusiva de Latinoamérica. https://rededucacioninclusiva.org/wp-content/uploads/2020/09/Los-futuros-de-la-educaci%C3%B3n-Contribuciones-de-la-Red-Regional-por-la-Educaci%C3%B3n-Inclusiva-de-Latinoam%C3%A9rica.pdf

Schulte, D., Cendon, E. and Makoe, M. 2020. *Re-Visioning the Future of Teaching and Learning in Higher Education: Report on Focus Group Discussions for the UNESCO Futures of Education Initiative*. University of the Future Network. https://unifuture.network/wp-content/uploads/sites/2/2020/08/20200722_UFN_UNESCO-report_fin.pdf

SDG-Education 2030 Steering Committee. 2020. *Contribution to the Futures of Education*. Paris, UNESCO. https://sdg4education2030.org/sites/default/files/2020-07/Futures%20of%20Education%20SDG-Ed2030%20SC%20contribution%20July%202020.pdf

Sefton-Green, J., Erstad, O. and Nelligan, P. 2021. *Educational Futures Across Generations*. Centre for Research for Educational Impact (REDI) at Deakin University and Department of Education at the University of Oslo. https://www.deakin.edu.au/__data/assets/pdf_file/0005/2298551/Educational-Futures-Across-Generations.pdf

Seguy, F. 2021. *Penser l'avenir de l'éducation en contexte de pandémie*. Port-au-Prince, UNESCO. https://unesdoc.unesco.org/ark:/48223/pf0000378392

UNESCO. 2020. *Humanistic Futures of Learning: Perspectives from UNESCO Chairs and UNITWIN Networks*. Paris, UNESCO. https://unesdoc.unesco.org/ark:/48223/pf0000372577/PDF/372577eng.pdf.multi

UNESCO Institute for Lifelong Learning. 2020. *Embracing a culture of lifelong learning: Contribution to the Futures of Education Initiative*. Hamburg, UNESCO Institute for Lifelong Learning. https://unesdoc.unesco.org/ark:/48223/pf0000374112/PDF/374112eng.pdf.multi

UNESCO International Institute for Higher Education in Latin America and the Caribbean (IESALC). 2021. *Thinking Higher and Beyond: Perspectives on the Futures of Higher Education to 2050*. UNESCO International Institute for Higher Education in Latin America and the Caribbean. https://unesdoc.unesco.org/ark:/48223/pf0000377530

UNESCO. 2021. *Caribbean Futures of Education – Final Report*. Kingston, UNESCO. https://en.unesco.org/caribbean-futures-of-education

UNESCO's Collective Consultation of NGOs on Education 2030. 2021. T*he role of Civil Society Organisations in 2050 and beyond*. Paris, UNESCO's Collective Consultation of NGOs on Education 2030. https://en.unesco.org/system/files/the_role_of_csos_in_2050_and_beyond.pdf

Unescocat and Fòrum Futurs de L'educació. 2020. How to Get to the Future of Education: Lessons Learned from the Escola Nova 21 Alliance in Catalonia. Unescocat-Center for UNESCO of Catalonia. https://catesco.org/wp-content/uploads/2020/10/Unescocat-contribution-to-Futures-of-Education.pdf

Wong, S., Kwok, V., Kwong, T. and Lau, R. 2020. Individuality, Accessibility, and Inclusivity: Applied Education and Lifelong Learning in Revolutionising Education for the 21st Century. Our Hong Kong Foundation. https://ourhkfoundation.org.hk/sites/default/files/media/pdf/UNESCO_submission_13102020.pdf

World Council on Intercultural and Global Competence. 2021. Contribution from the World Council on Intercultural and Global Competence to the UNESCO Futures of Education Initiative. https://iccglobal.org/wp-content/uploads/World-Council-Futures-of-Education-Learning-to-Become-Initiative_.pdf

Background papers

The following background papers were commissioned by UNESCO in order to help advance the thinking on key issues laid out by the International Commission on the Futures of Education.

Assié-Lumumba, N. T. 2020. *Gender, knowledge production, and transformative policy in Africa*. Paper commissioned for the UNESCO Futures of Education report. https://unesdoc.unesco.org/ark:/48223/pf0000374154

Buchanan J., Allais S., Anderson M., Calvo R. A., Peter S. and Pietsch T. 2020. *The futures of work: what education can and can't do*. Paper commissioned for the UNESCO Futures of Education report. https://unesdoc.unesco.org/ark:/48223/pf0000374435

Common Worlds Research Collective. 2020. Learning to become with the world: Education for future survival. *Education Research and Foresight Working Paper 28*. Paris, UNESCO

Corson, J. 2020. *Visibly ungoverned: strategies for welcoming diverse forms of knowledge*. Paper commissioned for the UNESCO Futures of Education report. https://unesdoc.unesco.org/ark:/48223/pf0000374085

Couture, J. C., Grøttvik, R. and Sellar, S. 2020. *A profession learning to become: the promise of collaboration between teacher organizations and academia*. Paper commissioned for the UNESCO Futures of Education report. https://unesdoc.unesco.org/ark:/48223/pf0000374156

Damus, O. 2020. *Les futurs de l'éducation au carrefour des épistémologies du Nord et du Sud*. Paper commissioned for the UNESCO Futures of Education report. https://unesdoc.unesco.org/ark:/48223/pf0000374047

Desjardins, R., Torres, C. A. and Wiksten, S. 2020. *Social contract pedagogy: a dialogical and deliberative model for Global Citizenship Education*. Paper commissioned for the UNESCO Futures of Education report. https://unesdoc.unesco.org/ark:/48223/pf0000374879

D'Souza, E. 2020. *Education for future work and economic security in India*. Paper commissioned for the UNESCO Futures of Education report. https://unesdoc.unesco.org/ark:/48223/pf0000374880

Facer, K. 2021. *Futures in education: towards an ethical practice*. Paper commissioned for the UNESCO Futures of Education report. https://unesdoc.unesco.org/ark:/48223/pf0000375792

Facer, K. 2021. It's not (just) about jobs: education for economic wellbeing. *Education Research and Foresight Working Paper 29*. Paris, UNESCO. https://unesdoc.unesco.org/ark:/48223/pf0000376150/PDF/376150eng.pdf.multi

Facer, K. and Selwyn, N. 2021. *Digital technology and the futures of education – towards 'non-stupid' optimism*. Paper commissioned for the UNESCO Futures of Education report. https://unesdoc.unesco.org/ark:/48223/pf0000377071

Gautam, S. and Shyangtan, S. 2020. *From suffering to surviving, surviving to living: education for harmony with nature and humanity*. Paper commissioned for the UNESCO Futures of Education report. https://unesdoc.unesco.org/ark:/48223/pf0000374086

Grigera, J. 2020. *Futures of Work in Latin America: between technological innovation and crisis*. Paper commissioned for the UNESCO Futures of Education report. https://unesdoc.unesco.org/ark:/48223/pf0000374436

Hager, P. and Beckett, D. 2020. *We're all in this together: new principles of co-present group learning*. Paper commissioned for the UNESCO Futures of Education report. https://unesdoc.unesco.org/ark:/48223/pf0000374089

Haste, H. and Chopra, V. 2020. *The futures of education for participation in 2050: educating for managing uncertainty and ambiguity*. Paper commissioned for the UNESCO Futures of Education report. https://unesdoc.unesco.org/ark:/48223/pf0000374441

Hoppers, C. 2020. *Knowledge production, access and governance: a song from the south*. Paper commissioned for the UNESCO Futures of Education report. https://unesdoc.unesco.org/ark:/48223/pf0000374033

Howard, P., Corbett, M., Burke-Saulnier, A. and Young, D. 2020. *Education futures: conservation and change*. Paper commissioned for the UNESCO Futures of Education report. https://unesdoc.unesco.org/ark:/48223/pf0000374087

Inayatullah, S. 2020. Co-creating educational futures: contradictions between the emerging future and the walled past. *Education Research and Foresight Working Paper 27*. Paris, UNESCO. https://unesdoc.unesco.org/ark:/48223/pf0000373581/PDF/373581eng.pdf.multi

Labate, H. 2020. *Knowledge access and distribution: the future(s) of what we used to call 'curriculum'*. Paper commissioned for the UNESCO Futures of Education report. https://unesdoc.unesco.org/ark:/48223/pf0000374153

Lambrechts, W. 2020. *Learning 'for' and 'in' the future: on the role of resilience and empowerment in education*. Paper commissioned for the UNESCO Futures of Education report. https://unesdoc.unesco.org/ark:/48223/pf0000374088

Mengisteab, K. 2020. *Education and participation in African contexts*. Paper commissioned for the UNESCO Futures of Education report. https://unesdoc.unesco.org/ark:/48223/pf0000374155

Moore, S.J. and Nesterova, Y. 2020. *Indigenous knowledges and ways of knowing for a sustainable living*. Paper commissioned for the UNESCO Futures of Education report. https://unesdoc.unesco.org/ark:/48223/pf0000374046

Saeed, T. 2020. *Reimagining education: student movements and the possibility of a Critical Pedagogy and Feminist Praxis*. Paper commissioned for the UNESCO Futures of Education report. https://unesdoc.unesco.org/ark:/48223/pf0000374157

Schweisfurth, M. 2020. *Future pedagogies: reconciling multifaceted realities and shared visions*. Paper commissioned for the UNESCO Futures of Education report. https://unesdoc.unesco.org/ark:/48223/pf0000374077

Smart, A., Sinclair, M., Benavot, A., Bernard, J., Chabbott, C., Russell, S. G. and Williams, J. 2020. *Learning for uncertain futures: The role of textbooks, curriculum, and pedagogy*. Paper commissioned for the UNESCO Futures of Education report. https://unesdoc.unesco.org/ark:/48223/pf0000374078

Sriprakash, A., Nally, D., Myers, K., and Ramos-Pinto, P. 2020. *Learning with the past: racism, education and reparative futures*. Paper commissioned for the UNESCO Futures of Education report. https://unesdoc.unesco.org/ark:/48223/pf0000374045

Stitzlein, S. M. 2020. *Using civic participation and civic reasoning to shape our future and education*. Paper commissioned for the UNESCO Futures of Education report. https://unesdoc.unesco.org/ark:/48223/pf0000374034

Vasavi, A.R. 2020. *Rethinking mass higher education: towards community integrated learning centres.* Paper commissioned for the UNESCO Futures of Education report. https://unesdoc.unesco.org/ark:/48223/pf0000374442

Wagner, D., Castillo, N. and Zahra, F. T. 2020. *Global learning equity and education: looking ahead.* Paper commissioned for the UNESCO Futures of Education report. https://unesdoc.unesco.org/ark:/48223/pf0000375000

Ydesen, C., Acosta, F., Milner, A.L., Ruan, Y., Aderet-German, T., Gomez Caride, E. and Hansen, I. S. 2020. *Inclusion in testing times: implications for citizenship and participation.* Paper commissioned for the UNESCO Futures of Education report. https://unesdoc.unesco.org/ark:/48223/pf0000374084

Alongside this background research, an interactive game was developed for the Futures of Education initiative to think about alternative learning systems and explore their implications with different groups.

Keats, J. and Candy, S. 2020. *Accession: Building an intergenerational library.* Game developed for the Futures of Education initiative.

Global consultation inputs

The following papers were commissioned by UNESCO to analyze and synthesize perspectives and ideas that were received through the focus group, online platforms and surveys and polling channels developed for the initiative.

Jacobs, R. and French, C. 2021. Women, robots and a sustainable generation: Reading artworks envisioning education in 2050 and beyond. Paper commissioned for the UNESCO Futures of Education report. https://unesdoc.unesco.org/search/faad9f2c-4a70-4b7a-8ac7-c3cffecd156c

Melchor, Y. 2021. *Analysis report of the online consultation modality: Your ideas on the futures of education.* Paper commissioned for the UNESCO Futures of Education report. https://unesdoc.unesco.org/ark:/48223/pf0000378271/PDF/378271eng.pdf.multi

TakingITGlobal. 2021. Focus group discussion analysis: Perspectives from the UNESCO Associated School Network's community of students, teachers and parents. Paper commissioned for the UNESCO Futures of Education report. https://unesdoc.unesco.org/ark:/48223/pf0000378054/PDF/378054eng.pdf.multi

UNESCO. 2021. *Education in 2050: Analysis of social media polling campaign for UNESCO's Futures of Education report.* Paris, UNESCO.

Moeller, K., Agaba, S., Hook, T., Jiang, S., Otting, J., Sedighi, M. and Wyss, N. 2021. *Focus group discussions analysis: September 2019 - November 2020.* Paper commissioned for the UNESCO Futures of Education report. https://unesdoc.unesco.org/ark:/48223/pf0000375579/PDF/375579eng.pdf.multi

Publications by the International Commission on the Futures of Education

In the course of developing this report, for the purposes of receiving feedback and suggestions, the Commission published several interim bulletins on its work-in-progress. Additionally, the Commission offered recommendations on the educational disruptions prompted by COVID-19 crisis.

International Commission on the Futures of Education. 2020. *Visioning and Framing the Futures of Education*. UNESCO, Paris. https://unesdoc.unesco.org/ark:/48223/pf0000373208

International Commission on the Futures of Education. 2020. *Protecting and transforming education for shared futures: joint statement by the International Commission on the Futures of Education*. UNESCO, Paris. https://unesdoc.unesco.org/ark:/48223/pf0000373380

International Commission on the Futures of Education. 2020. *Education in a Post-COVID World: Nine ideas for public action*. UNESCO, Paris. https://unesdoc.unesco.org/ark:/48223/pf0000373717

International Commission on the Futures of Education. 2021. *Progress update of the International Commission on the Futures of Education*. UNESCO, Paris. https://unesdoc.unesco.org/ark:/48223/pf0000375746

International Commission on the Futures of Education

Mandate

The mandate of the International Commission on the Futures of Education is to collectively reflect on how education might be re-thought in a world of increasing complexity, uncertainty, and precarity, and to present analysis and recommendations in the form of a flagship report which can serve as an agenda for policy dialogue and action at multiple levels. Looking at the year 2050 and beyond, the report should suggest visions and strategies for both education policy and education practice to adopt. As an integral part of the process of developing the report and engaging with relevant stakeholders from around the globe, the Commission shall consider how best to maximize the ongoing impact of the report beyond its release.

The Commission is to take into consideration recent geopolitical shifts, accelerated environmental degradation and climate change, changing patterns of human mobility, and the exponential pace of scientific and technological innovation. At the same time, the report should envisage and analyse the multiple possible futures of technological, social, economic, and environmental disruption and how education might both affect and be affected by these futures.

The Commission will include in its report a consideration of the longstanding UNESCO commitment to a pluralistic, integrated, and humanistic approach to education and knowledge as public goods. The Commission is invited to challenge and re-evaluate the foundational principles laid out in previous UNESCO global reports on education. In sum, the Commission will focus on examining the role of education, learning and knowledge in light of the tremendous challenges and opportunities of predicted, possible, and preferred futures.

Members

H.E. Sahle-Work Zewde
President, Federal Democratic Republic of Ethiopia
Chair, International Commission on the Futures of Education

Sahle-Work Zewde was elected as the first woman and the fifth President of the Federal Democratic Republic of Ethiopia on 25 October 2018. After joining Ethiopia's Ministry of Foreign Affairs in 1998, she served as Ethiopia's Ambassador to Senegal with accreditation to Cape Verde, the Gambia, Guinea, Guinea-Bissau and Mali; Ambassador to Djibouti and as Permanent Representative (PR) to IGAD; Ambassador to France with accreditation to Morocco and Tunisia and PR to UNESCO; and PR to the AU and Director-General for African Affairs.

President Sahle-Work joined the UN in 2009 and served as Special Representative of the Secretary-General and Head of the UN Integrated Peacebuilding Office in the Central African Republic. In 2011, she was appointed as the first dedicated Director-General of the UN Office at Nairobi at the level of Under-Secretary-General. In June 2018, Secretary-General Antonio Guterres appointed her as his Special Representative to the AU and Head of the UN Office to the AU. She was the first woman to hold these positions at the UN.

António Nóvoa
Professor at the Institute of Education of the University of Lisbon, Portugal
Chair of the research-drafting committee of the International Commission on the Futures of Education

António Nóvoa is Honorary President of the University of Lisbon, after having served as its President between 2006 and 2013. A professor of education, he holds PhDs from the University of Geneva and the University of Paris IV-Sorbonne. He has been granted the title of Doctor Honoris Causa by various universities. He has conducted seminars and delivered lectures in more than 40 countries and is the author of more than 200 academic works. Nóvoa currently serves as the Portuguese Ambassador to UNESCO.

Masanori Aoyagi
Professor Emeritus, University of Tokyo, Japan

Masanori Aoyagi was born in Dalian, China in 1944. As one of the leading researchers on ancient Greek and Roman Art History, Dr. Aoyagi has excavated Mediterranean ruins for over 40 years. Upon graduating in 1967 from the University of Tokyo's Faculty of Letters, he studied Classical Art History and Archaeology at The University of Rome from 1969 to 1972. He holds a PhD in Literature. Positions previously held include Commissioner of the Agency for Cultural Affairs. His current positions include President of Archaeological Institute of Kashihara of Nara Prefecture, and Chairman of the Board of Directors of Tama Art University.

Arjun Appadurai
Emeritus Professor Media, Culture and Communication at New York University and the Max Weber Global Professor at the Bard Graduate Center in New York, USA

Arjun Appadurai is Emeritus Professor Media, Culture and Communication at New York University and the Max Weber Global Professor at the Bard Graduate Center in New York. He is a leading analyst of the cultural dynamics of globalization. His scholarship addresses diversity, migration, violence and cities. His most recent book (with Neta Alexander) is Failure (Polity Press, 2019).

Patrick Awuah
Founder and President, Ashesi University, Ghana

Patrick Awuah is the Founder and President of Ashesi University in Ghana, which aims to propel an African renaissance by educating a new generation of ethical, entrepreneurial leaders. Under Patrick's leadership, Ashesi combines a rigorous multidisciplinary core with high-impact majors in business, computer science, MIS, and engineering. Patrick is a MacArthur Fellow and recipient of the WISE Prize for Education. In 2015, Patrick was named one of the World's 50 Greatest Leaders by Fortune.

Abdel Basset Ben Hassen
President, Arab Institute for Human Rights, Tunisia

Abdelbasset Ben Hassen is the President of the Arab Institute for Human Rights based in Tunisia. With three decades of expertise in the field of human rights education, Ben Hassen has worked in the development and implementation of human rights programs and education reform in the Middle East North Africa region. He has written on human rights, human rights education and culture and was a member of the drafting committee of the United Nations Decade for Human Rights Education.

Cristovam Buarque
Emeritus Professor, University of Brasília, Brazil

Cristovam Buarque obtained his doctoral degree at Sorbonne Université before working at the Inter-American Development Bank in Washington DC for six years. He is emeritus professor and former rector of the University of Brasília. In Brazil he has served as Minister of Education, Governor of the Federal District and Senator of the Republic. Cristovam Buarque is a pioneer in the concept of conditional cash transfers related to education and he has published extensively on the future of basic and higher education both on improving access and on pedagogical innovation.

Elisa Guerra
Teacher and Founder, Colegio Valle de Filadelfia, Mexico

Elisa Guerra is a teacher and the founder of Colegio Valle de Filadelfia in Mexico and Director for Latin America for The Institutes for the Achievement of Human Potential. She was awarded the 2015 "Best Educator in Latin America" prize by the Inter-American Development Bank and Fundación ALAS and has also been a finalist for the Global Teacher Prize. Elisa holds two Master's degrees, from the Instituto Tecnológico y de Estudios Superiores de Monterrey (ITESM) and from Harvard Graduate School of Education. She has authored 26 books and textbooks and is passionate about early learning, global citizenship, and innovative teaching.

Badr Jafar
CEO, Crescent Entreprises, United Arab Emirates

Badr Jafar is CEO of Crescent Enterprises and President of Crescent Petroleum. Badr founded the Pearl Initiative, a non-profit, private sector-led organization committed to promoting a corporate culture of transparency and accountability, in cooperation with the UN Office for Partnerships. Badr serves on the advisory boards of the Sharjah Entrepreneurship Centre and Gaza Sky Geeks. Badr is engaged with a number of higher education institutions, serving as an advisory board member of the Cambridge University Judge Business School, MIT Legatum Centre for Development and Entrepreneurship, American University of Beirut and American University of Sharjah. Badr is the Founding Patron of the Centre for Strategic Philanthropy at the University of Cambridge.

Doh-Yeon Kim
Professor Emeritus of Seoul National University, Former Minister of Education, Science and Technology, Republic of Korea

Doh-Yeon Kim worked as a professor in the Department of Material Engineering at Seoul National University. He then served as the President of the University of Ulsan and POSTECH. Professor Kim also served as the Minister of Education, Science and Technology and the Chairman of the National Science and Technology Committee for the Government of Republic of Korea. His interests lie in the changes that will occur in education and teaching because of advances in information and communication technology.

Justin Yifu Lin
Dean, Professor, Institute of New Structural Economics, Peking University, China

Justin Yifu Lin is Dean of the Institute of New Structural Economics, Dean of Institute of South-South Cooperation and Development, and Professor and Honorary Dean of National School of Development at Peking University. Prior to this he was Senior Vice President and Chief Economist of the World Bank, as well as founding Director of the China Centre for Economic Research at Peking University. He is the author of numerous books on economics and development.

Evgeny Morozov
Writer

Evgeny Morozov is a writer and thinker on the social and political implications of information technology. He is the author of The Net Delusion (2011) and To Save Everything, Click Here (2013). He holds a PhD in History of Science from Harvard University and has been a visiting scholar at Georgetown and Stanford universities. He is also the founder of The Syllabus, a media project that seeks to make serious and academic knowledge more accessible to the general public.

Karen Mundy

Director UNESCO International Institute For Educational Planning (IIEP) & Professor (on leave), University of Toronto – Ontario Institute for Studies in Education, Canada

Karen Mundy is the incoming Director of the UNESCO Institute of Educational Planning, and Professor of Educational Policy and Leadership at the University of Toronto. She is a leading expert on education in the developing world and former Chief Technical Officer at the Global Partnership for Education. She has held positions as Canada Research Chair, Associate Dean of Research and Innovation and President of the Comparative and International Education Society. She is the author of 6 books and dozens of articles, book chapters and policy papers dealing with education reform, policy and civil society.

Fernando M. Reimers

Professor, Harvard Graduate School of Education, USA

Fernando M. Reimers is the Ford Foundation Professor of the Practice of International Education as well as Director of the Global Education Innovation Initiative at the Harvard Graduate School of Education. An expert in the field of global citizenship education, his work focuses on understanding how to educate children and youth so they can thrive in the 21st century. He has written and edited or co-edited 40 academic books and published over 100 articles and book chapters focusing on the relevance of education for a changing world. He has also developed, with his teams of graduate students, several project-based curricula aligned with the UN Sustainable Development Goals which are in use in schools around the world.

Tarcila Rivera Zea

President, CHIRAPAQ Centre for Indigenous Cultures of Peru

Tarcila Rivera Zea is one of the most recognized indigenous activists in Peru and the world. For more than 40 years she has been defending indigenous rights through CHIRAPAQ, the Center for Indigenous Cultures of Peru, an association that promotes the affirmation of cultural identity and the education of indigenous women and young leaders. She is also involved with the Continental Network of Indigenous Women of the Americas (ECMIA) and the International Indigenous Women´s Forum (FIMI).

Serigne Mbaye Thiam

Minister of Water and Sanitation, Senegal

Serigne Mbaye Thiam graduated from the Rouen Business School. In Senegal he has served as member of parliament, general rapporteur of the budget, government spokesperson, Minister of Higher Education and Research and Minister of Education. From May 2018 to September 2021, he was Vice-Chairman of the Board of Directors of the Global Partnership for Education. Currently, Mr Thiam is the Senegalese Minister of Water and Sanitation.

Vaira Vīķe-Freiberga
Former President of Latvia, currently co-chair,
Nizami Ganjavi International Center, Baku, Azerbaijan

Dr. Vaira Vīķe-Freiberga served as the President of Latvia from 1999 to 2007, and as President of the World Leadership Alliance/Club de Madrid from 2013-2019. She has served as Special Envoy on UN reform and on numerous High-level groups for the European Union. She is the author of 17 books and over 200 articles, a member of five Academies and an Honorary Fellow of Wolfson College, Oxford University.

Maha Yahya
Director, Malcolm H. Kerr Carnegie Middle East Center, Lebanon

Maha Yahya is director of the Malcolm H. Kerr Carnegie Middle East Center, where her work focuses broadly on political violence, identity politics, inequality, citizenship, and the refugee crisis. She has two PhDs in the social sciences and humanities from Massachusetts Institute of Technology (MIT) and the Architectural Association (AA) in London. She serves on a number of advisory boards and is a global member of the Trilateral Commission; co-chair of the International Advisory Board for the Asfari Institute for Civil Society and Citizenship at the American University of Beirut; as well as member of the Board of Directors of the Ana Aqra Association.

The Futures of Education initiative

Advisory Board

The Advisory Board was mandated to provide strategic guidance to UNESCO on the Futures of Education initiative as a whole.

Mr Tariq Al Gurg
Chief Executive Officer, Dubai Cares

Ms Alice P. Albright
Chief Executive Officer, Global Partnership for Education (GPE)

Mr Gordon Brown
UN Special Envoy for Global Education

Ms Annette Dixon
Vice President for Human Development, The World Bank Group

Ms Henrietta Fore
Executive Director, UNICEF

Ms Susan Hopgood
President, Education International

Mr Carlos Moedas
Commissioner 2014-2019, European Commission, Research Science and Innovation

Mr Matías Rodríguez Inciarte
President of Santander Universidades and Vice President of Universia

Mr Refat Sabbah
President, Global Campaign for Education

Mr Jeffrey D Sachs
Director, Center for Sustainable Development, Columbia University

Ms Cecilia Scharp
Deputy Director General, Swedish International Development Cooperation Agency

Mr Andreas Schleicher
Director for the Directorate of Education and Skills, OECD

Ms Alette Van Leur
Director, Sectoral Policies Department, International Labour Organization

Ms Hilligje van't Land
Secretary General, International Association of Universities

Ms Yume Yamaguchi
Director, Institute for the Advanced Study of Sustainability, United Nations University

Contributors to the global consultation

Organizations and networks

The following NGOs and civil society organizations, governmental entities, academic institutions and research organizations, private sector, youth and student organizations and networks, as well as UNESCO National Commissions contributed to the global conversation on the futures of education (2019-2021) through focus group discussions, thematic reports, webinars or other activities. An updated list of organizations that have engaged with the Futures of Education initiative is available on the website.

Abhivyakti Media for Development

Academic and Career Development Initiative Cameroon

Accademia delle Arti e delle Nuove Tecnologie di Roma

Adream Foundation

African Library and Information Associations and Institutions (AfLIA)

Agastya International Foundation

Agency for Cultural Diplomacy (ACD)

Allama Iqbal Open University

Amala

American Psychological Association (APA) at the United Nations

Amity University

Arab Campaign for Education for All

Arab Institute for Human Rights

Aristotle University of Thessaloniki

Arizona State University

Ashoka

Asia South Pacific Association for Basic and Adult Education (ASPBAE)

Asociación Montessori Española

Association des Parents Adventistes pour le Développement de l'Education (APADE)

Association for Sustainable Development Alternatives (ASDA)

Association internationale des étudiants en sciences économiques et commerciales (AIESEC)

Association Montessori International of the United States (AMI/USA)

Association Montessori Internationale (AMI), Russia

Association Montessori Internationale (AMI), Sub Saharan Africa

Association Montessori Internationale (AMI), United Kingdom

Association Montessori of Thailand

Association Nigérienne des Educateurs pour le Développement (ANED)

Athabasca University

AzCorp Entertainment

Bangladesh National Commission for UNESCO

Bangladesh Youth Forum

Beijing Normal University

Bilingualism Matters

Bilingualism Matters, Siena Branch, University for Foreigners of Siena

biNu

Board of European Students of Technology

Brainwiz

Bridge 47

Cameroon International Model United Nations

Canadian Commission for UNESCO (CCU)

Canadian Department for Employment and Social Development (ESDC)

Catalyst 2030

Center for Education Development and Skill Acquisition Initiative

Center for Engaged Foresight

Center for Intercultural Dialogue

Centre Catholique International de Coopération avec l'UNESCO (CCIC)

Centre for Comparative and International Research in Education (CIRE)

Centre for Research for Educational Impact (REDI) at Deakin University

Centre for Youth and Development Malawi

Centro de Estudos em Educación Superior, Pontíficia Universidad Católica de Rio Grande do Sul (PUCRS)

Centro de Investigación Científica, Académica y Posgrados, México

Centro de Investigación y Acción Educativa Social - CIASES

Centro Regional de Profesores del Este - Maldonado

Centro Regional de Profesores del Suroeste - Colonia

Chartered College of Teaching

Cinglevue

Civil Society Education Partnerships, Timor Leste

Climate Commission for UK Higher and Further Education

Climate Smart Agriculture Youth Network (CSAYN)

Coalition for Educational Development, Sri Lanka

Collective Consultation of NGOs

Columbia University's Teachers College

Comisión Costarricense de Cooperación con la UNESCO

Comisión Nacional Española de Cooperación con la UNESCO

Comité mondial pour les apprentissages tout au long de la vie

Commission nationale algérienne pour l'éducation, la science et la culture

Commission nationale angolaise pour l'UNESCO

Commission nationale haïtienne de coopération avec l'UNESCO

Commission nationale Lao pour l'UNESCO

Commission nationale libanaise pour l'éducation, la science et la culture (UNESCO)

Commission nationale malgache pour l'UNESCO

Commission nationale rwandaise pour l'UNESCO

Commission nationale suisse pour l'UNESCO

Comparative and International Education Society (CIES)

Comparative Education Society of Asia (CESA)

Consejo de Formación en Educación, Administración Nacional de Educación Pública (ANEP), Uruguay

DAP Graduate School of Public and Development Management

Délégation permanente de la Suisse auprès de l'UNESCO et de la Francophonie

Department of General and Preschool Education, Ministry of Education, Azerbaijan

Developmental Action Without Borders - NABA'A

Dhurakij Pundit University

Diálogo Interamericano

Dream a Dream

DVV International (Germany)

E-Net Philippines

e^2: educational ecosystems

ED Wales

EDUCAFIN Mentoring Program

Education for all Somalia

Education for an Interdependent World

Education International

Éducation, Recherches et Actualités (EDRAC)

Education+

Educational Futures Network (EFN), School of Education, University of Bristol

Educational Resource Development Centre Nepal (ERDCN)

Eidos Global

Emmaus International

Epiphany Labs

Erasmus Student Network

ESD Japan Youth

European Democratic Education Community

European Dental Students' Association (EDSA)

European Parents' Association (EPA)

European Student Network

European Students' Union

European Youth Forum

Expert Advisory Board for Transformative Education of the Austrian Commission for UNESCO

Finnish Development NGOs – Fingo

Finnish National Board of Education

Firenze Fiera

Foundation For Youth Employment Uganda

Franklin University

Fundação Calouste Gulbenkian

Fundación Mustakis

Fundación Santillana

Galileo Teacher Training Program (GTTP)

General Direction of Planning, Ministry of Education of Bolivia

GeoPoll

German Commission for UNESCO

Girls Not Brides AR

Giving Hope to the Hopeless Association (GHTHA)

Global Campaign for Education

Global Changemakers

Global Edtech Impact Alliance

Global Education Policy Network

Global Hands-On Universe (GHOU)

Global Pedagogical Network - Joining in Reformation (GPENreformation)

Global University Network for Innovation (GUNi)

Global Young Greens

Grow Waitaha - Ōtautahi (Christchurch)

Hellenic Association for the Promotion of Rhetoric in Education

HundrED

Indonesian National Commission for UNESCO

Initiative for Article 12 UNCRC (InArt12)

Innovazing Vision

Institute for Research on Population and Social Policies, National Research Council of Italy

Institute of Education, University of Lisbon

Instituto de Formación Docente - Rocha

Instituto Politécnico de Beja & Universidade Lusófona de Humanidades e Tecnologias de Lisboa (ULHT)

International Association of Universities (IAU)

International Centre for Higher Education Innovation under the auspices of UNESCO (UNESCO-ICHEI)

International Centre for UNESCO ASPnet (ICUA), China

International Council for Adult Education (ICAE)

International Council for Open and Distance Education (ICDE)

International Development Education Association Scotland (IDEAS)

International Model United Nations

International Pharmaceutical Students' Federation (IPSF)

International Society for Education through Art (InSEA)

International Youth Council

INTI International University and Colleges

Isa Viswa Prajnana Trust

Istituto Comprensivo Statale "Perna - Alighieri" of Avellino

Istituto Professionale di Stato per i Servizi per l'enogastronomia e l'ospitalità alberghiera "R. Virtuoso" of Salerno

IUCN Commission on Education and Communication

Karanga: The Global Alliance for Social Emotional Learning and Life Skills

Kidskintha

Korean National Commission for UNESCO

L'Association Internationale des Professeurs et maîtres de Conférences des Universités – IAUPL

L'Organisation International pour le droit à l'éducation (OIDEL)

L'Organisation Mondiale pour l'Éducation Préscolaire (OMEP)

Latvian National Commission for UNESCO

Learning through Landscapes

Lebanese University (LU)

Maker's Asylum

Me2Glosses, Thessaloniki branch of Bilingualism Matters

Millennium Project

Ministère de l'éducation nationale, Haiti

Ministère de l'éducation, Lao PDR

Ministère de l'éducation, Rwanda

Ministero dell'Istruzione (Ministry of Education, Italy)

Ministry of Education and Science of Republic of Latvia

Ministry of Education of Quebec

Ministry of Education, Belarus

Ministry of Education, Bhutan

Ministry of Education, Ecuador

Ministry of Education, Research and Religious Affairs, Greece

Ministry of Education, Romania

Ministry of Foreign Affairs, Portugal

Ministry of National Education, Indonesia

Montessori Association of Thailand

Montessori México

Mouvement International ATD Quart Monde

National Campaign for Education, Nepal

National Commission of the Democratic People's Republic of Korea for UNESCO

National Commission of the People's Republic of China for UNESCO

National Institute of Educational Planning and Administration, India

National Youth Council of India

National Youth Council of Malta

National Youth Council of Namibia

Neo-bienêtre

Network for International Policies and Cooperation in Education and Training (NORRAG)

Network of Education Policy Centers

Networking to Integrate SDG Target 4.7 and SEL Skills into Educational Materials (NISSEM)

North American Montessori Teachers Association

Northwestern University

Oceane Group

Office International de l'Enseignement Catholique (OIEC)

Office of the Secretary General's Envoy on Youth (United Nations)

Officina Educazione Futuri initiative

Okayama University

Omuta City Board of Education, Japan

One Family Foundation

Our Hong Kong Foundation

Out of the Books ASBL

People for Education

Permanent Delegation of the Kingdom of Saudi Arabia to UNESCO

Permanent Delegation of Viet Nam to UNESCO

Peruvian National Commission of Cooperation for UNESCO

Peruvian National Commission of Cooperation for UNESCO

Philippine Futures Thinking Society

Philippine Society for Public Administration

Polish National Commission for UNESCO

Portland Education

Portuguese National Commission for UNESCO

Portuguese Network of Communities of Learning (Rede CAP)

Prince's Trust International

ProFuturo

Protection Approaches

Proyecto Sinergias ED

Red Regional por la Educación Inclusiva

Regional Center for Educational Planning (RCEP)

ReSource at Burren College of Art

RET International

Rete Dialogues Nazionale

Réussir l'égalité Femmes-Hommes

Right to Education Initiative

Saint Petersburg State University

Santander Universidades

Scholas Occurrentes

Sciences Po Campus de Poitiers

SDG-Education 2030 Steering Committee

ShapingEDU, Arizona State University

Slovene NGO Platform for Development, Global Education and Humanitarian Aid (SLOGA)

Society for Intercultural Education, Training, and Research (SIETAR)

Southeast Asia ESD Teacher Educators Network (SEA-ESD Network)

Strategy and Innovation for Development Initiative

Study Hall Educational Foundation

Subcommittee on Migrant and Refugee Children of the NGO Committee on Migration

SW Creative Education Hub, Bath Spa University

Swedish Association for Distance Education (SADE)

Swedish Association for Distance Learning Härnösand

Swedish National Commission for UNESCO

Sweducation

Swiss Agency for Development and Cooperation (SDC)

Te Pū Tiaki Mana Taonga | Association of educators beyond the classroom

Teach For Liberia

Thammasat University

The Arab Network for Popular Education/The Ecumenical Project for Popular Education – The Lebanese Coalition for Education for All

The Dialogue

The Edge Foundation

The George Washington University

The Goi Peace Foundation

The Hamdan Foundation

The Innovation Institute, Australia

The International Institute for Higher Education Research & Capacity Building (IIHEd), O.P. Jindal Global University

The International Task Force on Teachers for Education 2030

The Millennium Project

The Ministry of Education of the People's Republic of China

The Montessori Society AMI (UK), United Kingdom

Tybed

UN Association of Norway

UNESCO National Commission of the Philippines

Unescocat, Fòrum Futurs de l'Educació

United Nations Association of the United States of America

United Nations University Institute for the Advanced Study of Sustainability (UNU-IAS)

Universidad Católica de Córdoba

Universidad Nacional de Tres de Febrero

Universidad Tres de Febrero

Université de Cergy

Université Laval

University of Bristol

University of Dundee

University of Edinburgh

University of Latvia

University of Leeds

University of Maryland, College Park

University of Oslo

University of Piraeus

University of Salerno

University of the Future Network

University of Tlemcen

VIA University College

Vietnam Association for Education for All   Vilnius University Students' Representation

Visionary Education

Vote for Schools & Protection Approaches

World Council on Intercultural and Global Competence

World Family Organization (South Africa and Europe region)

World Futures Studies Federation (WFSF)

World Heutagogy Group, London Knowledge Lab

World Youth Assembly

Yale University

York University

Young Diplomats Society (YDS)

Youth Agro-Marine Development Association (YAMDA)

Youth Entrepreneurs Corporation, Democratic Republic of the Congo (YEC-DRC),

Zero Water Day Partnership

Schools

The following schools conducted discussions and focus groups with students, teachers and/or parents within the context of the Futures of Education initiative. Note that many of the schools below are from the UNESCO Associated Schools Network (ASPnet).

Algeria

Collège d'enseignement moyen Ahmed Zazoua Djidjel

École des frères Samet Blida

Ecole privée El Awael Annaba

Ecole privée la Citadelle Savoir Alger

Angola

Alda Lara Polytechnic Secondary Institute

Centre for Professional Education

Gregório Semedo College

Industrial Polytechnic Institute of Kilamba Kiaxi No. 8056 "Nova Vida"

Jacimar College

Lyceum Ngola Kiluanji No. 1145

Lyceum No. 8054 - PUNIV "Nova Vida"

Medium Industrial Institute of Luanda

Medium Technical Institute of Hotel Management and Tourism No. 2009

Middle Economics Institute of Luanda

Middle Institute of Administration and Management nº 8055 "Nova Vida" (IMAG-Nova Vida)

Mutu Ya Kevela Secondary School

Primary School José Martí No. 1136

Primary School No. 1134 - ex 1050

Public School No. 1140 (ex 1058) - 1º de Maio

Public School No. 1222 (ex-1107) - Bairro Azul

Secondary School Juventude em Luta nº 1057 - ex 2033

Training School for Health Technicians of Luanda

Azerbaijan

Baku European Lyceum

Modern Educational Complex

School #220 named after Arastun Mahmudov

School-Lyceum # 6 named after T. Ismayiov

Bangladesh

Abudharr Ghifari College, Dhaka

Adamjee Cantonment College

Azimpur Govt. Girls School & College, Dhaka

Bangladesh International School and College, Mohakhali, Dhaka

Cambrian School & College, Dhaka

Dhaka Commerce College, Dhaka

Dhaka Residential Model College

Engineering University School & College, Dhaka

Govt. Bangla College, Mirpur, Dhaka

Govt. Bhiku Memorial College, Manikganj

Govt. Laboratory High School, Dhaka

Madaripur Govt. College, Madaripur

Munshiganj Govt. Women's College, Munshiganj

Udayan Uchcha Madhyamik Bidyalaya, Dhaka

Belarus

Gymnasium No. 1 named after F.Skorina, Minsk

Minsk Gymnasium #12

State Educational Establishment "Gymnasium No. 33, Minsk"

State Educational Establishment "Grodno City Gymnasium"

State Educational establishment "Secondary School No. 201 Minsk"

State Educational Establishment "Labour Red Banner Order Gymnasium No.50 of the city Minsk"

State Educational Institution "Snov Secondary School"

State Educational Establishment "Minsk Gymnasium 12"

Gymnasium No. 2 Orsha

Canada

University of Toronto Schools

China

Hainan Middle School

Ledong Huangliu High School of No. 2 High School of East China Normal University

Qingdao No.2 High School

Shanghai High School

Shanghai Song Qingling School

The Experimental High School Attached to Beijing Normal University

The High School Affiliated to Renmin University of China

Colombia

Corporación Educativa Minuto de Dios

Costa Rica

Colegio Ambientalista de Pejibaye

Colegio de Cedros

Colegio de Santa Ana

Colegio Humanístico Costarricense - Campus Nicoya

Colegio Yurusti

CTP de Orosi/Instituto de Alajuela

CTP de Turrubares

CTP Don Bosco

Escuela Carmen Lyra

Escuela Carolina Dent Alvarado

Escuela Central de Tres Ríos

Escuela de Palomo

Escuela Infantil NP San José

Escuela INVU Las Cañas

Escuela José Cubero Muñoz

Escuela José Ricardo Orlich Zamora

Escuela Juan Flores Umaña

Escuela La Fuente

Escuela La Gran Samaria

Escuela Líder Daytonia Talamanca

Escuela Líder Sector Norte

Escuela Naciones Unidas

Escuela San Francisco

Escuela Thomás Jefferson

Escuela y Colegio Científico CATIE

Golden Valley School

Instituto de Formación de Docentes de Universidad Nacional (UNA)

Liceo de Aserrí

Liceo de Limón - Mario Bourne

Saint Anthony School

Saint Gregory School

Saint Jude School

West College

Denmark

Aalborg Handelsskole

Aalborg Katedralskole

Aarhus Statsgymnasium

Absalons Skole

Alminde-VIUF Fællesskole

Alssundgymnasiet

Askov Efterskole

Asmildkloster Landbrugsskole

Aurehoej Gymnasium

Baaring Boerneunivers

Bagsværd Kostskole Og Gymnasium

Bredagerskolen

Business College Syd

Campus Jelling, UCL

CELF

Christianshavns Gymnasium

Egaa Gymnasium

Egtved Skole

Eltang Skole og Børnehave

Endrupskolen

Espergærde Gymnasium & HF

EUC Nord

EUC Nordvest

EUC Syd

Faxehus Efterskole

Gammel Hellerup Gymnasium

Gefion Gymnasium

Gladsaxe Gymnasium

Haderslev Katedralskole

Han Herred Efterskole

Helsingør skole - Skolen i Bymidten

HF & VUC Fyn

Holluf Pile Skole

IBC Int. Business College

Ingrid Jespersens Gymnasieskole

Jelling Friskole

Jueslsminde Skole

Kold College

Langelands Efterskole

Learnmark

Lillebæltskolen

Lindbjergskolen

Mercantec

Naestved Gymnasium of HF

NEXT

Niels Brock Int. Gymnasium

Nivaa Skole

Noerre Gymnasium

Nykøbing Katedralskole

Odense Katedralskole

Oelsted Skole

Paderup Gymnasium

Pedersborg Skole

Professionshøjskolen UCN

Professionshøjskolen VIA

Randers Social- og Sundhedsudd.

Rantzausminde Skole

Ranum Efterskole

Ranum Skole

Roedkilde Gymnasium

Roskilde Gymnasium

Roskilde Tekniske Skole

Skovbrynet Skole

Sønderskov-Skolen

Sortedamskolen

SOSU Esbjerg

SOSU Nord

SOSU Syd

Store Magleby Skole

Strandskolen

Tech College

Tietgen Business

Toender Handelsskole

Tradium

U/Nord

Vesthimmerlands Gymnasium

Viden Djurs

VUC Storstroem

ZBC

Finland

Alppilan lukio

Björneborgs svenska samskola

Etäkoulu Kulkuri

Haapajärven lukio

Haapajärven yläaste

Helsingin kielilukio

Helsingin yliopiston Viikin normaalikoulu

Iisalmen lyseo

Jyväskylän kristillinen opisto

Jyväskylän Lyseon lukio

Jyväskylän normaaalikoulu

K. J. Ståhlbergin koulu

Kaitaan lukio

Kellon koulu

Kempeleen Kirkonkylän koulu

Kilpisen yhtenäiskoulu

Laanilan lukio

Lapinlahden lukio ja kuvataidelukio

Lyseonpuiston lukio

Mäkelänrinteen lukio

Oriveden lukio

Oulun normaalikoulu

Oulun normaalikoulu (yläkoulu)

Oulun Suomalaisen Yhteiskoulun Lukio

Putaan koulu

Rauman normaalikoulu

Saimaan ammattiopisto Sampo

Suomalais-venäläinen koulu

Tampereen yliopiston normaalikoulu

Tikkalan koulu

Tuusulan lukio

Vaasan lyseon lukio

Germany

Albert-Schweitzer-Schule Hofgeismar

Edith-Stein-Schule Ravensburg & Aulendorf

Freie Waldorfschule Karlsruhe

Gesamtschule Bremen Mitte

Gewerbliche und Hauswirtschaftlich-
Sozialpflegerische Schulen Emmendingen

Heinrich-Hertz-Schule Hamburg

Illtal-Gymnasium Illingen

Limesschule Idstein

Max-Planck-Gymnasium Berlin

Ostendorfer-Gymnasium Neumarkt

Sophie-Scholl-Schule Berlin

Städtische Realschule Heinsberg „Im Klevchen"

Warndt-Gymnasium Völklingen

Greece

1st Junior High School of Serres

1st Senior High School of Ierapetra

2nd Gerakas Senior High School

2nd Junior High School of Geraka

2nd Senior High School of Chania

2nd Senior High School of Serres

2nd Vocational Senior High School of Rethymno

4th Junior High School of Maroussi

4th Senior High School of Serres

5th Junior High School of Agia Paraskevi

American College Pierce

Aristoteleio Junior High School of Serres

Doukas Junior High School

Experimental Junior High School of Rethymno

Experimental Primary School of Serres

Junior High School Athens College

Junior High School of Koimisis, Serres

Junior High School Psychiko College

Music School of Serres

Protypo Junior High School

Protypo Junior High School of Anavryta

Ralleio Junior High School of Piraeus

Senior High School of Pentapoli, Serres

Zagorianakos Junior High School

Guatemala

Cooperativa Agro Industrial Nuevo Amanecer

Haiti

Collège Cotubanama

Collège de Côte-Plage

Indonesia

SMP Labshool Kebayoran

Italy

ITCTS Vittorio Emanuele, Bergamo

Japan

Amagi Junior High School

Amanohara Elementary School

Ginsui Elementary School

Hakko Junior High School

Hayamadai Elementary School

Hayame Elementary School

Hirabaru Elementary School

Kamiuchi Elementary School

Kunugi Junior High School

Kuranaga Elementary School

Matsubara Junior High School

Meiji Elementary School

Miike Elementary School

Minato Elementary School

Miyanohara Junior High School

Nakatomo Elementary School

Omuta Chuo Elementary School

Omuta Special Education School with special care

Shirakawa Elementary School

Tachibana Junior High School

Taisho Elementary School

Takatori Elementary School

Takuho Junior High School

Takuma Junior High School

Tamagawa Elementary School

Tegama Elementary School

Tenryo Elementary School

Yoshino Elementary School

Lao People's Democratic Republic

Collège Sisattanak

Collège Sisavad

École primaire Nahaidiao

École primaire Phonpapao

École primaire Phonphanao

École primaire Phonthan

École primaire Sokpalouang

École secondaire Champasak

École secondaire Phiavat

Lycée Chanthabouly

Lycéee Vientiane-Hochiminh

Vientiane Secondary School

Lebanon

Ahliah School

Al Kawthar Secondary School

Al Manar Modern School - Ras el Metn

Central College Jounieh

Collège de la Sainte Famille Française - Fanar

Collège des Soeurs des Saints Coeurs - Bauchrieh

Collège Notre Dame de Jamhour

Collège Protestant Français Montana - Dik el Mehdi

Collège Saint Grégoire - Beirut

Etablissement Sainte Anne de Besançon - Beirut

Greenfield College Beirut

Hajj Bahaa Eddine Hariri School - Saida

Imam Sadr Foundation-Rehab Al Zahraa School

Institut Moderne du Liban-Collège Père Michel Khalifé - Fanar

International College - Beirut

Les écoles de l'Association islamique
philanthrophique d'Amlieh

Les écoles de l'Ordre Libanais Maronite (OLM)

Makassed Ali Ben Taleb School - Beirut

Our Lady of Annunciation - Rmaich

Rafic Hariri High School Saida

Sagesse High School Ain Saadeh

Madagascar

CEG Ambohimanarina

CEG Antanimena

CEG Nanisana

Collège privé ESSOR

Collège privé La Columba Ambatomainty

Collège privé Le Pétunia

Collège privé Palais des Princes

Ecole privée Pinocchio

EPP Ambatomanoina Lovasoa

EPP Ambohidroa 1

EPP Beravina

Lycée Andrianampoinimerina Sabotsy Namehana

Lycée Horace François Antalaha

Lycée J.J. RABEARIVELO

Lycée Miarinarivo Itasy

Lycée Nanisana

Lycée Naverson Fianarantsoa

Lycée privé La Chanterelle Sabotsy Namehana

Lycée privé Les Petits Chérubins

Lycée Talatamaty

Mexico

Colegio Valle de Filadelfia

Instituto Alpes San Javier

PrepaTec Eugenio Garza Sada

Norway

Steinerskolen i Tønsberg

Pakistan

Karachi Grammar School

Peru

Colegio Peruano Alemán Max Uhle

Institución Educativa Jorge Basadre, Junín

Instituto de Educación Superior Pedagógico Público
Teodoro Peñaloza, Junín

Portugal

Agrupamento de Escolas D. Dinis, Quarteira

Agrupamento de Escolas da Batalha

Agrupamento de Escolas Sé, Lamego

Colégio Diocesano Nossa Senhora da Apresentação,
Calvão

Escola EB/123 Bartolomeu Perestrelo, Funchal,
Madeira

Escola Profissional do Montijo

Escola Secundária Aurélia de Sousa, Porto

Escola Secundária Filipa de Vilhena, Porto

Escola Secundária Jaime Moniz, Funchal, Madeira

Escola Superior de Educação Jean Piaget, Almada

Externato Frei Luís de Sousa, Almada

Instituto Duarte de Lemos, Águeda

Republic of Korea

Chiak Elementary School

Chungnam Foreign Language High School

Chungryol Girls' High School

Daykey High School

Dongil Girls' High School

Hyoyang High School

Incheon International High School

Incheon Yeongjong High School

Jeonbuk Foreign Language High School

Jeonju Shinheung High School

Jeonnam Foreign Language High School

Kyungpook National University Attached
    Elementary School

Masan Girls' High School

Munsan Sueok High School

Namsung Girls' High School

Osong High School

Sejong Global High School

Shin Nam High School

Shinseong Girls' High School

The Attached Elementary School of Gongju National
    University of Education

Wonhwa Girls' High School

Yangcheong High School

Yeongjujeil High School

Rwanda

APADE Kicukiro

Collège Christ Roi de Nyanza

College Christ Roi/Nyanza

Collège de Gisenyi

College de Gisenyi (Inyemeramihigo)

College Saint André

Collège Saint André

Ecole Primaire Saint Joseph

Ecole Primaire Saint Joseph/Kicukiro

Ecole Primaire SOS

Ecole Primaire SOS Kacyiru

Ecole Technique SOS

Ecole Technique SOS Kigali

FAWE Girls School Kigali

FAWE Girls School Kigali

Groupe Scolaire Sainte Bernadette Save

Groupe Scolaire Maie Reine Rwaza

Groupe Scolaire Notre Dame de Lourdes/Byimana

Groupe Scolaire Nyanza/Kicukiro

GS Marie Reine Rwaza

GS Notre Dame de Lourdes Byimana

GS Nyanza/Kicukiro

GS Sainte Bernadette/Save

Lycée de Kigali

Lycée de Kigali

Lycée Notre Dame de Citeaux

Lycée Notre Dame de Cîteaux

Teacher Training College Muhanga

TTC Muhanga

Slovenia

Gimnazija Celje Center, Celje

Gimnazija Nova Gorica, Nova Gorica

Gimnazija Ptuj

IV. OŠ Celje

OŠ 16. december Mojstrana

OŠ Alojza Gradnika Dobovo

OŠ Bratov Polančičev, Maribor

OŠ Cirila Kosmača Piran

OŠ Cvetka Golarja Škofja Loka

OŠ dr. Jožeta Pučnika, Črešnjevec, Slovenska Bistrica

OŠ Dušana Flisa Hoče

OŠ Franceta Bevka Tolmin

OŠ Griže, Griže

OŠ in vrtec Sveta Trojica

OŠ Janka Padežnik Maribor

OŠ Kapela

OŠ Kobilje

OŠ Ledina Ljubljana

OŠ Pesnica

OŠ Poljane, Poljane nad Škofjo Loko

OŠ Selnica ob Dravi

OŠ Sveta Trojica

OŠ Toneta Čufarja Jesenice

Škofja Loka High School

Šolski center Lava, Celje

Šolski center Ptuj, Ekonomska šola

Srednja gradbena šola in gimnazija Maribor

Srednja zdravstvena in kozmetična šola Maribor

Srednja zdravstvena šola Celje

Spain

Colegio Los Abetos

Colegio Público de Hurchillo

Colegio Sagrada Familia (Zaragoza)

Colegio Trabenco

IES Salvador Victoria (Monreal del Campo. Teruel)

United Kingdom

Strathallan School

United States of America

Gunnison Middle School